*Policy Making at the
Margins of Government*

SUNY series in Israeli Studies

Russell Stone, editor

Policy Making at the Margins of Government

The Case of the Israeli Health System

Yair Zalmanovitch

STATE UNIVERSITY OF NEW YORK PRESS

Published by
State University of New York Press, Albany

For information, address State University of New York Press,
90 State Street, Suite 700, Albany, NY 12207

Production by Judith Block
Marketing by Anne Valentine

Library of Congress Cataloging-in-Publication Data

Zalmanovitch, Yair.
    Policy making at the margins of government : the case of the Israeli health system / by
Yair Zalmanovitch.
        p. cm.
    Includes bibliographical references and index.
    ISBN 0 –7914–5185 – 2 (hc : alk. paper)—ISBN 0 –7914–5186 – 0 (pbk. : alk. paper)
    1. Medical policy—Israel. 2. Medical care—Israel. 1. Title.
RA395.I75 Z35 2001
362.1'095694—dc21   2001032206

10 9 8 7 6 5 4 3 2 1

I dedicate this book to my wife, Ofra, my son, Oded, and my daughter, Adi, who bore
with me through the long years of its writing;
to my parents, Avraham and Pnina Zalmanovitch,
who brought me up to strive for excellence;
to my mother-in-law Gilada Dori, and my late father-in-law, Tuvia Dori, who,
when I was a young man courting his daughter,
had more faith in me than I had in myself.

Contents

Part IV The Erosion of the Veto

Tables

Preface

My interest in the politics and policies of Israel's health care system goes back to my days as a master's degree student in the Political Science Department at the University of Haifa. What fascinated me was that Israel's health care services were paid for largely by the government but controlled by a monopolistic non-government body. As a fledging political scientist, I was interested in the question, much debated in those days, of who governs under such circumstances. In the years following, I have delved more deeply into the subject, digging up new information and reevaluating the old and familiar from new perspectives.

Since I started my explorations in the 1980s, health care has become a widely debated, highly controversial subject. Like health systems elsewhere, Israel's has passed through considerable turmoil and a wrenching reform, whose benefits are still uncertain. Israel's unique health care system, featuring almost universal ambulatory and hospital coverage and encompassing practically the entire population, has been transformed into a state-controlled system based on obligatory insurance. The rationale for the change was cost control and better health care, but the motives and dynamic were political.

This book analyzes the political struggle for control of health care policy in Israel over the better part of the 20th century. Starting with the prestate days, the book shows how Israel's largest health care provider, Kupat Holim, affiliated with the General Federation of Labor, was able to exercise a veto over health care policy under both Labor and the Likud, and then how it gradually lost its veto as the newly founded state became stronger and more firmly established.

This book should be of interest to scholars and practitioners in public policy and public health in Israel and beyond, to students of comparative institutions, and to historians of Israel and other states in the making.

Many people have helped me in the research and writing of this book. I am pleased to thank them with all my heart. Let me start with my friends Nissim Shrem and Israel Savion, who used their indispensable political connections on my behalf. They opened doors to the policy makers and bureaucrats whose experiences and observations revealed the dynamics of the struggle that the book traces. They helped me to obtain many of the official reports and other primary sources that went into my analyses. Without this help from my friends, getting my research under way and pursuing it to its finish would been immeasurably more difficult.

My colleagues in academia, who were also my best teachers, provided me with invaluable assistance in formulating and honing my thoughts. Dr. Andre Eshet, a loyal friend and colleague, took an ongoing interest in the study. He referred me to articles, shared his vast knowledge of Israeli politics—especially of the General Federation of Labor and the Labor Party—with me, stimulated my thinking, and read my first draft word by word and commented extensively. Professor Gabriel Ben Dor, who read one of my early drafts, saved me from the mistake of attending solely to the margins and ignoring the state. To him I owe the inspiration for the concept of the political veto that I develop in the book. Professor Ira Sharkansky, under whose supervision I wrote my doctoral dissertation and with whom I now coteach and research, was the first to draw my attention to the power of the margins in Israel. The dozens of conversations we held helped me to develop my ideas: to reject those that did not stand up to his exacting scrutiny and to sharpen and clarify those that did. I am deeply grateful to him for the many hours he spent with me and my concerns at the expense of his own research and writing.

The book has benefited, too, from the comments and questions of my students at the University of Haifa, who, for years, served me as a captive audience as I struggled to make sense of the data I was gathering. I only hope that they did not suffer too much from the confusion to which they were subjected before my thoughts finally took shape.

I am similarly indebted to my professional colleagues outside of Israel, who served as sounding boards for the main ideas of the book, on which I spoke at international conferences. The book is far better for the doubts they raised and the criticisms they rendered.

It is also better for the criticisms of the two anonymous reviewers appointed by SUNY Press. At first, I was frankly piqued by what I saw as their faultfinding. In the end, however, their complaints led me to refine the theoretical framework for my findings and to sharpen the conclusions of the book.

To the University of Haifa, which I consider my second home, I owe another type of gratitude. The political science department kept me on its faculty for years as I worked on the book, in both its original and extensively revised versions, without any promise of publication. I welcome this opportunity to thank the department publicly for the unstinting faith and patience it invested in me and for the generous material resources with which it backed up its belief. I also thank the university's Research Authority, and the various deans who headed it, for providing me with generous financial assistance to help cover the costs of researching and writing the book.

Finally, I wish to extend special thanks to my editor, Dr. Toby Mostysser, without whose work it is doubtful that my research would ever have seen the light of day. Toby is much more than a language editor with a penchant for rendering the most detailed information and complex ideas in readable prose. She is a critical reader and thinker, as discerning and sharp minded as any of my professional colleagues, with an eagle eye for fuzzy thinking and unsupported assertions. In many respects, the writing of this book was a joint endeavor on which we worked together for several years. During the hours and days that we sat over the text, she made me spell out every argument and justify every claim. She helped me both to analyze and to synthesize my data. On more than one occasion, her insistent probing led me to modify my perceptions. Our work together was difficult, but worthwhile, and thus my great appreciation.

With all the invaluable assistance I received, I must emphasize that the full responsibility for the contents and conclusions of this book, including any errors, oversights, and misjudgments that emerge, is mine and mine alone. I also want to apologize in advance to any person whose assistance I have overlooked and whose name has been unjustly omitted from these acknowledgments.

CHAPTER I

Policy Making from the Margin

Governments throughout the Western world have long delegated governmental functions to nongovernmental bodies (Asher, 1987; Barker, 1982; Cambell, 1986; Hall & Reed, 1998; Rehfuss, 1989; Savas, 1987). These functions may include such diverse tasks as garbage collection, firefighting, ambulance, transportation, and water and sewage services; maintenance of government buildings; the design and provision of health and other human services, or any other task that is deemed necessary by the state or demanded by its citizens but that the government prefers not to do directly (Powell, 1987; Sharkansky, 1980, 1983). The list may go on ad infinitum.

Almost equally endless are the forms that the nongovernmental bodies may take. They may be private or nonprofit contractors; special or statutory authorities created by national, state, or local governments; semiautonomous agencies established by government departments; state-owned companies or public–private ventures (Aharoni, 1986; Etzioni, 1973; Friedman & Garner, 1970; Smith, 1975). In Great Britain and much of Europe, a large variety of bodies are subsumed under the term *quango,* or quasi-governmental organization (Hood, 1983). Rhodes (1996) speaks of integrated self-organizing "networks" consisting of any permutation of government and private and voluntary organizations, which join to exchange resources and maximize their influence over output. These bodies vary widely in size, structure, financing, and relation to the state— in how much control the government has over their operations and in the mechanisms of that control. There is no saying that organizations called by the same name will share similar characteristics.

In their multiplicity of forms, these bodies constitute what Sharkansky (1979) calls the "margins" of the modern state. They perform government functions, receive state funding, and take actions and make decisions that may impact deeply on the lives of the state's citizens. At the same time, unlike government departments, they are not part of the formal government structure or subject to its constraints or chain of command. Their budgets are not part of the state budget and do not require legislative authorization. Their workforce is not subject to the regulations generally imposed on civil servants or to rigid civil service pay scales.

Their relative autonomy and freedom of action are a source of their vaunted efficiency, flexibility, and responsiveness to community needs. Bodies on the margin can hire personnel, design procedures, and create regulations without reference to the preferences or inclinations of established departments. Politicians can use them to circumvent government budget and manpower limitations or the restrictions or foot-dragging of government agencies. Such bodies can be used to roll back the welfare state and reduce the direct role of government while ensuring the provision of desired human and other services. In the 1980s and 1990s, they proliferated to an unprecedented degree, becoming an increasingly prominent part of the public scene.

Along with their benefits, they are also a source of a host of concerns. Even where they are required to report to government departments, which is not always the case, bodies on the margin are notoriously difficult to audit and their activities and output difficult to monitor by state agencies strapped for resources and short on institutional capability. Complaints abound about waste, mismanagement and fraud, while government reliance on their services gives them leverage that they can exploit to further their own organizational or financial interests (Sharkansky, 1979; Smith & Lipsky, 1994). Warnings have been raised both about the inevitable confusion and lack of coordination of disparate or competing entities (Rhodes, 1994) and the monopolistic growth of some of the bodies coddled by government protection or privilege (Kettl, 1993). The balance of their benefits and drawbacks has not yet been tallied.

A major concern is the role such bodies play in making public policy in their domains. Not all scholars are worried. Nadel (1975) recognizes that nongovernmental groups that perform government functions may make public policy without accountability to the people affected by that policy, but argues that this is essentially government policy because the government delegated the function. Salamon (1995, p. 41), arguing for closer cooperation between government and the nonprofit sector, conceives of the federal government as "managing" the services and of the nonprofits as operating them with a substantial degree of discretion. Essentially, he welcomes the fact that "third-party government" calls into question the hierarchical conception of the modern state. Smith and Lipsky (1994) see the nonprofit contractors who provide government services in the United States as "delivering" government policy to the citizens. Although they recognize the existence of conflicts over policy, they argue, not very happily, that their control over the government purse strings and their power to regulate ultimately give government officials the last word.

Others are less sanguine. Sharkansky (1979), comparing the margins in Australia, Israel, and the United States, claims that bodies on the margin remove public activities from the rule of elections and government. In the United States, Milward (Milward, 1994; Milward, Provan, & Else, 1993) contends that the privatization of government services has "hollowed" the state and warns that public policy becomes cloudy as authority and who is funding what become mixed in a nonprofit that delivers services for government and for its own purposes. He asks whether individuals who are neither agents of the state nor publicly accountable should be making the vital decisions they do with respect to people's lives.

In Great Britain, Rhodes (1994, 1996) argues that the integrated self-organizing networks that deliver the bulk of public services in that country are a form of private government, much of whose work is invisible to the parliamentary and public eye. Warning that they resist government steering and regulation, develop their own policies, and mold their environments, he calls them a danger to democratic accountability and sees them as "set fair to become the prime example of governing without Government" (1996, p. 666).

The question of whether the shifting of policy making to the margins is desirable is befuddled by the question of whether it actually occurs. To this question, we currently find no clear answers. Although there seems to be a growing consensus that the proliferation of the margin is shrinking the state and changing our definitions of it, as Milward (1994, p. 76) points out, the evidence that bodies on the margin operate in the policy-making realm is largely anecdotal. Milward (1994, p. 73) offers evidence that coalitions of providers have become reasonably powerful political actors influencing the level and nature of government funding of nonprofits. We also find evidence that contractors may exercise control over who gets which government-funded services and under what conditions (Milward, Provan, & Else, 1993). But, for the most part, theory and speculation dominate scholarly discussion of the policy-making powers of bodies on the margins. Little if any hard data exists either confirming or refuting their policy-making powers. Nor, assuming that at least some of them do exercise a policy-making role, is there much knowledge of how they have come to do so.

This book examines policy making from the margin in Israel, a country whose margin, until the 1990s, was particularly large and sturdy (Aharoni, 1991; Sharkansky, 1979). It uses as its prism Israel's quasi-public, nonprofit health system, in which both health care and health insurance were provided by four autonomous sick funds, legally defined as nonprofit voluntary organizations and financed jointly by the subscribers, employers, and government.

Other prisms may have been used: A wide array of goods are (or have been) provided by bodies on the margins in Israel, including power generation, transportation, water provision, and the exploitation of minerals; manufacturing; construction; banking; wholesaling and retailing; agricultural production, distribution, and export (Sharkansky, 1979, p. 70); certain educational programs and facilities, and other social services. Any of these may have provided ample material for study.

But health care is of particular interest. It touches on virtually all our lives, and its production, provision, and financing are major conundrums throughout the Western world. Questions of access and equity, costs, and priorities plague modern welfare states as their aging citizens demand ever more and increasingly expensive medical care. Closer to our concern, for many decades the roles and responsibilities of government versus other sectors in health care have been a problematic and contentious issue both in Israel and elsewhere. In many communities in the United States, even though health and human services are funded by public agencies, the distribution of these funds is controlled and monitored by nongovernmental third parties (Milward, Else, & Raskob, 1991; Milward, Provan, & Else, 1993). The questions of who should finance health care, who should provide it, and how it should be provided are at the heart not only of health care debate but of the core–margin dilemma.

Within Israel the prism of health care is of interest because for the better part of the country's history this service was clearly dominated by a single sick fund: Kupat Holim. For decades, the relationship between the Sick Fund and the government of Israel was a contentious public issue, with repeated, unsuccessful—though possibly not genuine—attempts at reforming it to bring it under government control. At the time the study was launched, this Sick Fund was engaged in a tooth-and-nail struggle with the government to retain not only its ascendancy in the provision of health care, but also its autonomy and its self-declared role as a health policy maker.

Kupat Holim

The Hebrew term *kupat holim* is properly translated *sick fund*. But when Israelis say "I belong to Kupat Holim," they do not mean just any sick fund, they mean the Sick Fund that, for the better part of Israel's history, belonged to the General Federation of Labor, or Histadrut, as it is called in Hebrew. The three other sick funds operating in Israel today must be identified by name: Maccabi, Leumit (National), and Me'uhedet (United). "I belong to Maccabi," "I'm in Leumit," "I'm a member of Me'uhedet," people say, leaving out the *kupat holim*. Only the Sick Fund previously of the General Federation of Labor is called Kupat Holim without further qualification. Which sick fund is perfectly understood. The ready abbreviation and absence of any need for an identifying tag are testimony to Kupat Holim's almost total identification in the public mind with the very concept of a sick fund. Occasionally, Israelis refer to it as *Clalit*, an appellation added in the mid-1960s. *Clalit* is Hebrew for *general*. The word links Kupat Holim with its former parent organization, the General Federation of Labor, but more than that, it is yet another affirmation of the wide sweep and inclusive embrace of Israel's oldest and still by far largest supplier of health services.

Even today, when Kupat Holim is on the wane, its scope is truly wide and encompassing. It owns and operates eight general hospitals, three geriatric hospitals, and three psychiatric hospitals, with a total of nearly 6,000 hospital beds; 11 convalescent homes with another 3,000 beds; and a countrywide network of some 1,300 outpatient clinics of various kinds. These are large numbers in a country of Israel's size. The beds in its general hospitals constitute 30.6% of the total number of general hospital beds in Israel. The beds in its general, geriatric, and psychiatric hospitals constitute 20% of all the country's hospital beds of all kinds. The rest of the beds are owned by the government or by Jewish, Moslem, or Christian religious and charitable organizations. It has seven nursing schools and several hundred well-baby clinics, and it supports and runs a school of medicine at the University of the Negev in Beer Sheva and a school of dentistry affiliated with the University of Tel Aviv. It has its own x-ray and imaging facilities, medical and research laboratories, and pharmacies, as well as a network of convalescent homes and recreational hotels. It employs a veritable army of doctors, nurses, clerks, administrators, technicians, teachers, researchers, social workers, and engineers, and the list can go on (Arian, 1981, pp. 43–56; Arian, 1985, pp. 209–10; Chinitz, 1994; Medding, 1990; Ministry of Health, Budget Proposal for 1990, p. 50; Report of the Histadrut 16th National Convention, 1990, p. 195; Steinberg & Bick, 1992; Vilan, 1980; Zalmanovitch, 1981, 1991).

None of the other sick funds comes near it in the facilities they own and run, the services they provide, or the ambitions they harbor. None of the others has built or owns its own hospitals or supports the academic institutions and research that Kupat Holim does. Kupat Holim's outpatient clinics liberally dot not only Israel's major cities and larger towns but also its less populated, more remote, and sometimes poorer Arab villages and Jewish settlements, moshavim, kibbutzim, and development towns where until the 1990s the other sick funds were reluctant to go. Moreover, it has taken under its wide wing a widely disproportionate number of poor, elderly, sick, and new immigrant members, most of whom the other sick funds, more intent on solvency, had pointedly excluded or avoided before the 1995 National Health Insurance Law required them to accept all applicants.

For almost four decades, up until the late 1980s, Kupat Holim insured approximately 80% of all those with health insurance in Israel. It employed some 40% of Israel's health services work force. Its budget constituted some 40% of the total national expenditure on health (Histadrut, Executive Committee, 1987; Report of the Histadrut 16th National Convention, 1990, p. 195).

What makes Kupat Holim a body on the margin rather than simply an independent provider of health services is that in Israel the providing of health care has always been considered the responsibility of the government. Kupat Holim was perceived, by admirers and detractors alike, as performing a function that the government owed its citizens and was obliged to help fund and otherwise ensure they received. To a large extent, Israel's governments relied on Kupat Holim to deliver health care and provided a considerable portion of its budget.

Yet Kupat Holim has never been part of Israel's core government and has always had its own separate legal identity. Like the other sick funds, it is a voluntary, nonprofit organization, a designation that gives it the right to provide medical services and gives it various tax deductions. Unlike them, however, it is also a limited liability company, which gives it the right to hold and manage its extensive assets and shields its executives from the personal consequences in the event of the sick fund's bankruptcy.

Up until 1995, when the country's health system was reformed, Kupat Holim had its own electorate, made up mainly of representatives of the various political parties that formed the Histadrut; a legislature, or National Council; an Executive Committee, which ran its day-to-day affairs; and its own judiciary and comptroller. It operated with much autonomy within the Histadrut and with complete autonomy with regard to the Israeli government. Its legal status and independent structure of authority placed it beyond direct government control.

Founded before the state of Israel, Kupat Holim regarded the Ministry of Health, the core body created after the state, as an intruder on its domain. As a core body, the ministry was the country's official health policy maker responsible for the health of the entire population and accorded the legal authority to allocate the health budget and regulate the health system. But for most of Israel's history as a state, Kupat Holim and the Ministry of Health struggled with one another for control of health policy.

This book follows that struggle to answer two questions: The first, aimed at examining the empirical evidence of the policy-making power of a body on the margin, is: Who controlled health policy in Israel: Kupat Holim or the Ministry of Health? The second, derived from the expectation that the evidence would point to the sick fund, is: How did Kupat Holim acquire, maintain, and exercise its control? This question probes both the actions that a body on the margin may take to secure a veto and the conditions and circumstances under which it may be able to exercise control over policy in its domain and those under which it cannot.

Veto Power: Control of the Tools of Policy Making

The first step in the study was to determine empirically whether Kupat Holim in fact had the power to control health policy in Israel.

The answer to this question was sought in the government's use and implementation of the instruments of policy making. The literature identifies a wide range of policy-making tools. The study focuses on the three key families: allocation, regulation, and restructuring. Generally, these are the instruments that governments have at their disposal to effect their aims and policies.

Allocation involves the channeling of tax money and benefits. *Regulation* refers to the use of rules, ordinances, standards, criteria, fees, permits, licenses, and other means to impose limitations on or to grant authority. *Restructuring* means changing the lines of authority, balance of power, and division of responsibility in a system. Each of these tools can be utilized in myriad ways. Allocation can be contingent on performance or automatic, evenhanded or preferential, tight or generous. Regulation can be formal or informal, detailed or vague, abundant or sparse, and enforced or not. Restructuring, the most fundamental and potentially the most conflictual of the tools, can compel radical changes in deep-rooted patterns of behavior or anchor those patterns in the law of the land. Other permutations can be enumerated.

As Peters and van Nispen (1998, p. 2) point out, examining policy instruments may reveal a great deal about the choices that governments make when they set policy. Policy instruments are not always employed to optimize the association between goals and means or because their characteristics best satisfy the requirements of a particular job. They can be designed to reward or penalize, promote or block a target group's aims, or to improve the position of some actors and weaken that of others (Bressers, 1998, p. 96; Linder & Peters, 1998; van Nispen & Ringeling, 1998, p. 209). Conversely, examining the implementation of the instruments may reveal a good deal about the ability of the government to carry out its policies with respect to the target body.

The investigation of the utilization and implementation of these policy instrument families was conducted along several lines. It looked at what was done with each instrument: How much money and other benefits were allocated and to whom: Kupat Holim or the Ministry of Health? How many and what ordinances were passed to regulate the health system? What restructuring efforts were made? It looked at means: Was allocation contingent or noncontingent on performance? Were the regulations formal or informal? How and by whom were the restructuring efforts orchestrated? Were the various tools employed unilaterally by the core or bilaterally in conjunction with Kupat Holim? And it looked at outcomes: Who most benefited from the molding of these policy tools: Kupat Holim or the Ministry of Health? Whom did they empower and whom did they restrict? Whose interests did they further? To what extent were the policies the tools were aimed to promote implemented? The assumption was that the body that benefits from the tools of policy is the body that controls them and that makes policy (Krasner, 1978; Nordlinger, 1981; Peters & van Nispen, 1998).

The investigation was carried out over the course of Israel's history. A historical perspective was adopted because power relations evolve and change in time. As Skocpol (1994, p. 10) and others point out, historical analysis is highly relevant to understanding the limits and possibilities of social policy making. A historical study was required to reveal not only whether Kupat Holim exercised policy-making power, but also how much, what kind, when, and under what circumstances and conditions.

Two assumptions underlie the empirical investigation. The first was that a powerful body on the margin can appropriate the tools of policy and thereby exercise a decisive role in the policy-making process in the area of its domain. The second was that this ability would vary with the body's relationship with the party in government. The expectation was that Kupat Holim would be able to exercise policy-making power under Israel's socialist leaning Labor governments, to which it was linked politically and with which it shared interests and ideological affinities, and would not be able to do so under the capitalist-leaning Likud, which was hostile to it on both ideological and political grounds.

The findings of the initial analysis confirm that Kupat Holim exercised policy-making power in its domain. But they also show a more complex pattern of control than predicted. They reveal a progression over four periods in which Kupat Holim exercised different kinds of veto power under Labor and the Likud, and then ironically lost its veto when Labor, its traditional patron, was in office.

The first period covers the prestate and early statehood years, in the course of which the core government gave Kupat Holim informal, de facto control of health policy. The second period covers 1970–1977, when the Ministry of Health formally took Kupat Holim into the policy-formation process, for the purpose, paradoxically, of wresting for itself a role in making health policy. In both these periods, Labor was at the helm of government and Kupat Holim was able to protect its interests from within government circles by exercising policy-making power in the formation stage of the policy-making process.

The third period spans 1977–1984, when the Likud was in government and unilaterally set out to take the tools of policy back from Kupat Holim in order to establish core control over the health system. Banished from the policy-making table and unable to make health policy in the formation stage, Kupat Holim fought successfully to protect its interests by obstructing the implementation of the Likud's policies after they were formulated. It exercised policy-making power from outside government circles in the policy-implementation stage.

The fourth period was 1984–1995, during which Kupat Holim's policy-making power was gradually eroded and finally revoked with the passage in 1994 of the National Health Insurance Law, which restructured the health system.

The findings show that up until the fourth period, under two radically different governments, Kupat Holim was consistently able to impose its preferences and to exercise control over the tools of policy. The literature does not have any term for this long-term, unbroken imposition of policy in a broad area by a body on the margin. The literature on bodies on the margin speaks of their impact on various aspects of policy that affect their clients and the government. The literature on lobbies and other parapolitical groups speaks of *involvement, pressure,* and *influence* (Baumgartner & Jones, 1991; Baumgartner, 1993; Kingdon, 1984; Schlozman & Tierney, 1986; Wootton, 1985; Yishai, 1991).

To articulate the kind of policy-making power that Kupat Holim exercised in Israel's health system, I chose the concept of *veto*. As used in this study, *veto power* is the power to prevent or obstruct policy that threatens the vital interests of the margin organization (Kornhauser, 1962). It refers to an organization's ability to stall, block, check, prevent, or stop an intended course of action or to reverse an action in process, not occasionally, but consistently over a long period of time. It is a strong term whose connotations—if we can judge them by the thesaurus—include potency, authority, command, and prerogative. I have chosen it intentionally for these connotations, which imply greater force, consistency, and legitimacy than the terms *involvement, pressure,* and *influence.*

It is meant to conceptualize the consistent, long-term power to mold government policy and to say no to policies that threatened it that Kupat Holim exercised under both Labor and the Likud. It is meant to distinguish Kupat Holim's imposition of policy from the influence exerted by lobbies, interest groups, and other traditional nongovernmental organizations in a relatively narrow area of life on behalf of a particular segment of the population. In contrast to such groups, Kupat Holim was not only involved in the policy-making process, as the corporatistic and pluralistic models suggest, and did not merely influence and pressure governments, as lobbies and interest groups do, but actually imposed public policy. It regarded itself as a legitimate actor in the making of public policy and went so far as to contend with Israel's governments both for the resources and the right to do so.

Although the concept of veto is familiar enough, little in the literature sheds light on the type of veto power that Kupat Holim exercised. Most of the literature refers to formal, constitutional or parliamentary vetoes built into the structure of a government (Sartori, 1997, p. 161–63; Spitzer, 1988). The veto at issue here is political rather than structural or formal. It is fluid, dynamic, and changeable. It is acquired—and potentially, although with difficulty, lost—in the give-and-take of the political game.

In the first two periods, Kupat Holim was given a *preventive veto* by the ruling Labor Party, first informally, then formally, much in the way that certain countries have granted vetoes over policy to potentially troublesome segments of their populations in exchange for the latter's help or cooperation (Lijphart, 1977). In the third period, it wrenched from the Likud an *obstructive veto,* similar to the veto obtained by Riesman's (1968) "veto groups"—rival interest groups that use their power to stall, obstruct, block, or otherwise prevent the passage and implementation of laws and policies that they perceive as counter to their interests (Galbraith, 1956, 1985). The two types of veto were not entirely exclusive. Under Labor, Kupat Holim occasionally obstructed policies it could not prevent. Under the Likud, it prevented the passage of restructuring legislation. Nonetheless, under each government, one type of veto was dominant.

Process Tracing Through Four Cases

The four periods identified in the exploration of the tools of policy serve as the basis for four case studies tracing the acquisition, formalization, transformation, and loss of Kupat Holim's policy-making power. Each case provides evidence of the veto (or lack thereof) in the period under discussion while trying to account for the veto's development and variations at each point of time. To this end I asked the following questions:

- How did Kupat Holim acquire its policy-making powers in the early years of the state?
- What led to the formalization of those powers in the early 1970s?
- Why did Kupat Holim adopt an obstructive veto when the Likud came to power?
- What enabled Kupat Holim to exercise such a veto?
- What led to the erosion and abolition of its veto power in the mid-1990s?

In key ways the approach is consistent with Alexander George's (1979) structured, focused comparison method and Guy Peters's (1998) case process method, both of which suggest how a single historical case may be analyzed to enable the formation or examination of a midrange theory. George maintains that a "controlled comparison" in which data collection and analysis are focused selectively on certain aspects of the historical case and structured, or guided, by general questions that can contribute to the identification of causal patterns. Building on George, Peters similarly points out that a single case can be examined over time as a means of observing the play of variables under different conditions to gain a better understanding of cause and effect. According to Peters, a historical case can be divided into time periods demarcated by changes in dependent and independent variables. The observation of their changes, he argues, enables one to understand better the conditions and circumstances under which certain relations hold true. In the cases here, the variations in Kupat Holim's veto power serve as the dependent variable, whereas factors related to the veto in each period are analogous to independent variables.

I use the term *analogous to* judiciously because the factors that were examined cannot properly be termed *variables*. These cases diverge from the George and Peters models in an important way. George and Peters stress the importance of beginning the inquiry with a theory and a predefined set of variables derived from it. When I began my study, however, the workings of both Kupat Holim and the Ministry of Health were unknown territory, and too little was known about the capacity of bodies on the margin to impose policy to formulate any convincing hypothesis or to chose among the existent approaches to political science inquiry. To do so would have been to put on blinders to factors that were not predicted in advance and would have prematurely constricted the investigation.

This problem is familiar to historical institutionalists, who point out that in most historical analyses, conclusions are derived from the historical data that are gathered and come more naturally at the end than the beginning of the analysis (Immergut, 1998; Peters, 1999; Rothstein, 1996, 1998; Steinmo, Thelen, & Longstreth, 1992). In fact, George (1979) himself had hinted at this order in his somewhat self-contradictory assertion that his structured, focused comparison offered "an inductive approach to theory development" (p. 48). In the present study, too, theory is the product rather than the precursor of the analysis, as are the "variables" that stem from theory.

In the way of historical institutionalism, the analysis proceeded rather loosely by looking at the various players in the struggle, their assets and liabilities, interests and ideologies; their complicated and shifting actions and interactions; and the changing historical, cultural, institutional, and political contexts in which their actions and interactions took place.

The chief players were Kupat Holim and the Ministry of Health, along with the people who ran them under Israel's two main governments. But they also included others. Until the 1990s, Kupat Holim was connected with the Histadrut and the Labor Party (in its various forms) in a closely knit subsystem: Kupat Holim was part of the Histadrut, the Histadrut was governed by the Labor Party, and Histadrut functionaries held many key positions in the Labor Party machine. Getting to the bottom of Kupat Holim's veto thus also meant understanding relevant aspects of the Histadrut and the Labor Party, Kupat Holim's relations with them, and their relations with the core. In particular, it meant exploring the intricate workings and development of Mapai, the largest, best-organized, and most influential of the prestate Labor parties and the party that controlled the governing coalition in the first three or so decades of statehood. As for the core, the relevant actors also included the Ministry of Finance and Ministry of Labor and Welfare, through which the core government also made health policy; as well as Israel's prime ministers, its Knesset, and key coalition partners in its various governments.

At the end of each case, interim conclusions could be drawn regarding the features and bases of the particular type of veto power that was revealed; and, after the first case, comparisons could be made to the preceding ones. But it was only with the completion of the research for the last case, tracing the demise of the veto, that the process as a whole could be understood and that the roles, interplay, and relative importance of the many factors involved in the veto could be fully appreciated and highlighted retrospectively at the end of each case study. Only then did it become clear that Kupat Holim's veto was dependent on the Sick Fund's utility to the Labor–Histadrut subsystem and on the subsystem's readiness and ability to support the veto.

Data Collection and Presentation

The vast bulk of the data gathered for this book come from archival sources and personal interviews. I scoured the archives of Kupat Holim, the Histadrut, the Labor and Likud parties, the Knesset, the Ministry of Health and the Ministry of Finance, as well as several newspaper archives, private archives, and Israel's national archive. These contained both published and unpublished documents whose contents were barely known at the time. In addition, I conducted 30 unstructured personal interviews with key figures and bureaucrats in the Ministry of Health, Ministry of Finance, Histadrut, and Kupat Holim, and with politicians involved with the health system. These interviews were essential to fill the enormous gaps in public information on the making and implementation of health policy in Israel because the inner workings of both Kupat Holim and of the various government ministries involved in health policy were virtual blanks, as were the relations among them.

The data were both difficult to obtain and difficult to analyze. At the time of this study, Israel had neither a freedom of information act nor a culture of information provision. Both Kupat Holim and the relevant government ministries consistently avoided publishing information that might have bearing on their power struggle. Key people on both sides of the struggle were reluctant to reveal facts and figures, claiming confidentiality. Basic information became "intelligence" which neither Kupat Holim nor government sources were ready to reveal to one another, let alone to a researcher. Interviews were scheduled reluctantly and far in advance, and then repeatedly canceled and rescheduled.

When information finally was extracted, each side had its own set of data, consistent with its own interests and perspective. To take only one of many examples, when I tried to find out how many members Kupat Holim had, I received different figures from Kupat Holim, the Ministry of Health, the Ministry of Finance, and the Central Bureau of Statistics. No one in any of the agencies involved would provide computer printouts of their raw data. The very idea of providing such data was unthinkable to all concerned. In the end, I was fortunately able to obtain primary data on some matters. On matters where these were discrepant, the data from each of the various sources are given and the reasons for the inconsistencies analyzed. Where this was impossible, the data were discarded.

The problem of obtaining reliable and meaningful data has plagued not only me, but also others who tried to study public health in Israel. The authors of a 1983 study comparing various proposals for national health insurance stress that "the lack of information poses a grave problem when dealing with the organization and economy of the health service" (Ellenzwieg, De-Fries, Halevi, & Chernichovsky, 1983, p. 4). The writers of a 1988 report on health funding complain about the difficulty of obtaining a clear numerical picture and note that "the sick funds, which are all government funded, refuse to detail their expenditure—against every rule of public fairness" (Arieli, 1988, p. 54). Even the state comptroller met with difficulties of information gathering. The 1986 annual report observes that "from the documentation made available to the state comptroller's office, it is impossible to ascertain the way in which cash flow charts are prepared in Kupat Holim" (*State Comptroller Report, 1987, p. 362*).

The lack of relevant data, the disinclination to publish up-to-date information, the atmosphere of secrecy and distrust, and the presentation of skewed contradictory data by both Kupat Holim and the relevant government agencies made the research a Sisyphian enterprise.

The Case of Israel

Israel's margin is distinctive in that it has its roots in the country's prestate era. Under the British Mandate, a large range of quasi- governmental functions were performed for the Jewish population by indigenous Jewish political movements, parties, and institutions that worked separately and together to meld a new Jewish society and to pave the way for the Jewish state to which they and the people they represented aspired. These functions included defense, agricultural and industrial development, and the provision of social services, such as education and culture, employment and welfare, and health care. Among the dominant institutions in these respects were the Histadrut and the Jewish

Agency, both of which were active in various sectors of the economy and provided a range of social services. With the formal establishment of the state in 1948, the Jewish Agency and the Histadrut, along with the many bodies they had created, adopted, or associated themselves with to perform their quasi-governmental functions, continued to operate on the margins.

Israel's margin is thus the product not only of government delegation, but also of the activities of the Histadrut and the Jewish Agency. It consists of a bewildering array of collectivist enterprises, social services, and companies and their subsidiaries. For the sake of simplicity, it can be divided into three main sectors: (1) public companies owed by the government, alone or in conjunction with the Histadrut, Jewish Agency, or private entrepreneurs from Israel or the Diaspora; (2) bodies owned or associated with the Histadrut; and (3) bodies owned or associated with the Jewish Agency (Aharoni, 1991; Elazar & Dortort, 1985; Friedberg, 1985; Rosenthal, 1988; Sharkansky, 1979). The fact that Kupat Holim was part of and owed its primary allegiance to a nongovernmental body constituted yet another barrier to core government control.

Like many Histadrut enterprises, Kupat Holim was an ideologically based organization which passed into the state with its prestate resources and roles intact, and formed part of the Mapai-led subsystem that dominated both the prestate Jewish community and the first three decades of statehood. It had become accustomed to making health policy in the prestate era and, like its parent organization, demanded and for a time received from Israel's core governments the right and resources to continue to act in that capacity.

In these respects, Kupat Holim is very different from the bodies on the margin in Western Europe and North America. There the margin was formed through the voluntary devolution of the core, driven in part by economics and in part by the desire to retreat from the large, cumbersome administrative state of the welfare era. Kupat Holim preceded the core and acquired much of its power in the early years of the state when the core was undeveloped and weak.

The development and demise of Kupat Holim's veto power occurred in tandem with Israel's state formation and institutionalization. In his analysis of the formation of Western European states, Tilly (1975) points out that the concentration of power in the core is accompanied by concerted, determined, and sometimes violent resistance by other semiautonomous authorities and requires, among other things, that the government bring them under control, whether by accommodating, subordinating, or eliminating them.

Kupat Holim can be seen as a force of resistance, which was empowered by Israel's first governments, but which subsequent governments tried to bring under control: Labor in the 1970s by accommodating it, the Likud through subordinating it, and, finally, both by so clipping its wings as to eliminate it as a political force. The struggle over the instruments of policy making documented in the cases can be seen as a struggle over stateness—that is, over the degree to which these instruments are wielded in conjunction with a body on the margin or autonomously by well-coordinated agencies of the core government without significant participation by nongovernmental organizations (Tilly, 1975, p. 32). The government's eventual restructuring of the health system, and of Kupat Holim with it, can be seen the achievement of stateness in the area of health.

The process was the opposite of that currently occurring in the West, where the deliberate downsizing of government by transferring activities to the margins is shrinking the core and raising concern about the "hollowing" of the state, to use Milward's (1994) term. This study traces the efforts of successive Israeli governments to strengthen the core by shrinking the body on the margin.

The question thus arises of what the case of Kupat Holim can teach about the relationship between margin and core in the making of public policy. The answer lies in the fact, shown in this study, that Kupat Holim did shift policy making in its domain from the state to itself. The study reveals an inverse relation between Kupat Holim's veto power and the level of institutionalization and stateness of Israel's core government. It thus validates the apprehension that a powerful margin is a threat to the core.

Discussion of the question of whether and under what circumstances and conditions bodies on the margin can make public policy must thus begin with in-depth investigation of specific bodies. In the 1980s and 1990s a fair number of books and papers were published on nonprofit contracting in the United States and Europe, but these focused on general issues rather than on a single organization. Much the same can be said for the books and papers published on government-subsidized privatized industries, quangos, regulated utilities, and so forth. The need for specific study emerges from the fact that bodies on the margin vary greatly, both in themselves and in the ability of the government to control them. They vary with the history, institutions, and political culture of the country they are in (Greve, Flinders, & van Thiel, 1999; Sharkansky, 1979), as well as with differences in their own leadership and organizational cultures.

This study is a detailed investigation of the development of such a body from its birth through its transformation nearly a century later. On the microlevel, it opens the black box of health policy making in Israel, looking in depth at Israel's health care system and tracing the twists and turns of its development, institutionalization, and reform. On the macrolevel, it offers an indepth analysis of how a body on the margin may attain, anchor, fight for, and lose control of the tools of policy. It provides hitherto unavailable empirical evidence of the policy-making power of a body on the margin and tackles the question of how and under what conditions and circumstances it can exercise such power. Moreover, by shedding light on the impact Kupat Holim had on the design and implementation of health policy in Israel, it contributes to the debate on government by proxy. Even though Israel may well be a special case, the findings of the study can serve as a hitherto unavailable point of departure for comparison to other countries where large, nongovernmental organizations provide essential services to large sectors of the population.

The Shape of the Book

The four cases trace the struggle between Kupat Holim and the Ministry of Health for control of health policy. They follow two interrelated trajectories: that of the acquisition and loss of Kupat Holim's veto and that of Israel's development as a nation and a state.

The cases combine political science analysis with large doses of historical narrative and description. The latter is needed to convey the flavor of the battles that were fought, the times they were fought in, and the people who fought them so as to provide what Ashford (1992) calls the social and historical context. It is needed to enable the broad readership unfamiliar with Israel's development and the workings of its political system to understand the motives driving the struggle and how its government institutions and health care system became enmeshed and unmeshed. And it is needed because almost nothing has been written about Israel's health system, so it was impossible to rely on previous work and necessary to provide detailed evidence for even the most basic claims. The analytical work, stressing the changing nature of Kupat Holim's veto in each period and the changing conditions and circumstances under which Kupat Holim was and was not able to exercise it, is reserved for the end of each case.

The first case traces the roots of Kupat Holim's informal preventive veto in the legacy of the prestate period, the needs of the new state to build an infrastructure and absorb immigrants, and the Sick Fund's utility to Mapai, the party in power. It suggests that the underdeveloped nature of the core, with a weak administrative structure and a nearly total absence of an effective opposition, permitted Mapai, a dominant party, to transfer resources of the state to the Sick Fund to consolidate its own power.

The second case shows the core's unsuccessful efforts some two decades into statehood, when most of the infrastructure had been laid and the immigrants absorbed and Mapai's hold on the polity was weakening, to play a greater role in health policy making by increasing the level of institutionalization of the Ministry of Health while accommodating Kupat Holim through the formal delineation—and hence circumscription—of its policy-making role.

The third case begins with the end of the long Labor dominance, which had supported Kupat Holim's preventive veto. It shows the efforts of the new Likud government to centralize control of health policy in the core by reappropriating the tools of policy making from Kupat Holim and subordinating it to the Ministry of Health—and Kupat Holim thwarting those efforts by obstructing the implementation of the policies designed to promote them.

The fourth case deals with the restructuring of the Israeli health care system. It shows the revocation of Kupat Holim's veto in a period when Israel was ruled by a succession of national unity governments though the serendipitous cooperation of the two major parties. It shows how the Kupat Holim lost its veto when it became a burden to its partners in the subsystem and when they, in turn, became unable and unwilling to continue to support it.

Following the four cases, the book ends with a chapter discussing the development of stateness in health in Israel and considering the relative merits of health care controlled by a powerful body on the margin, which resists the state, and a government-controlled health care system. It looks at the quality of health care achieved by these two models: the first politicized, the second depoliticized, with an eye to contributing to the current debate on how to best handle the increasing demands for health care and its burgeoning costs.

Part I

THE INFORMAL PREVENTIVE VETO

CHAPTER 2

Kupat Holim in Prestate Days:
1911–1947

Kupat Holim has the peculiar, and possibly singular, attribute of being a health service that developed before the state itself. It was founded during the *yishuv*, a term that literally means "settlement" but that refers to the prestate Jewish population and social organization. Its origin is generally traced back to December 1911, when the second convention of the Federation of Agricultural Laborers of Judea met in the town of Petah Tikva to establish the Sick Fund for Agricultural Laborers (Slutzky, 1973, p. 228). In the coming years, other sick funds were established in other parts of the country.

From the beginning Kupat Holim was an ideologically based sectarian organization that was an integral part of the *yishuv*'s budding Labor movement. It was founded as a self-help organization to provide medical services to laborers whose wages could not cover the fees of the private physicians (about a week's wages per visit) that were available to the wealthier landowners and city dwellers. Its creation was an answer to the pressing practical needs of the early Zionist pioneers as well as an expression of both the socialist convictions that they had brought with them from Eastern Europe (Eliav, 1976; Nederland, 1983) and of the deeply rooted Jewish tradition of mutual responsibility developed under the difficult conditions of the centuries of Jewish Diaspora (Dowty, 1988).

The rules and regulations of the Judea Kupat Holim, numbering 150 laborers at its founding, reflect this interweave of practical considerations and ideological fervor (Kupat Holim, 1912–1913, p. 4). On the practical end, Kupat Holim provided doctor's care, medicine, a place to sleep, and, when necessary, a hospital bed, in exchange for a membership fee and monthly dues. In this way, it set out to provide the tiny settlement with a modicum of medical care at affordable prices, functioning as both an insurance agency that distributed the risk and a direct supplier of services. All subsequent sick funds in Israel have served these dual functions.

On the ideological side, membership was restricted to laborers and wage-earning craftsman, reflecting the idealization of manual labor and the proletariat by the country's Zionist settlers. The merchant and shopkeeper, the academic and professional, and the self-employed were all excluded. Monthly membership dues were set in accordance with wages, in keeping with the Marxist principle to each according to his need, from each according to his ability. The provision that new immigrants were to be given two months of free membership, providing they worked as laborers, reflected the same principle while serving as an attraction to join.

The Sick Fund was underpinned by the philosophy of communal interdependence and responsibility so dear to the early settlers. In the ideological climate of the time, health was considered an essential public service that the community as a whole had to provide. From very early on, medicine in Israel was public medicine and with incursions has remained public medicine to this day.

Two other features of the Judea Kupat Holim require mention: The early statements envision an apolitical fund and a self-paying one. With remarkable speed, both these ideals came to be honored more in the breach than in the observance. Within two years, the addition of new members and expanded need for medical care made financing its services solely with membership dues impossible for the fund (Rubinstein, 1976, pp. 223–24). Thus, almost from its conception Kupat Holim sought and obtained money and other resources from virtually any and every body that could be rallied to the cause. At about the same time, its initially apolitical sick funds aligned themselves with two rival Labor oriented parties, the Achdut HaAvodah (Unity of Labor) and the Poel Ha Tza'ir (Young Laborers), whose names they assumed (Horowitz & Lissak, 1978, pp. 69 –72). Abandoning the ideals of economic and political independence was a necessary concession to reality and the first step in Kupat Holim's rapid institutionalization and assumption of hegemony in health care.

Kupat Holim, the Histadrut, and the Labor Party

The institutionalization and hegemony of Kupat Holim can be traced back to 1920, when the sick funds of the rival Labor parties united under the auspices of the newly created Histadrut. This move proved to be of momentous consequence.

Explaining the development of Kupat Holim is difficult without going into the labyrinthine intricacies of the Histadrut; the various Labor parties that founded, governed, and used it as a power base; and the prestate Jewish "national institutions" which helped to sustain it as a partner in the joint enterprise of state building. This is not a history book, however, and in the interests of simplicity, the following account focuses on the points that help to explain how its patronage by the Histadrut and, through it, the Labor parties helped to make Kupat Holim the major health services provider in the prestate period. (Arian, 1985; Horowitz & Lissak, 1978; Medding, 1972, 1990; Zalmanovitch, 1981, 1990).

The full name of Histadrut, The General Federation of Labor, is misleading. Created by the socialist parties and laborers' groups of the day to meet a broad range of needs, the Histadrut from its conception was far more than a federation of trade unions. In addition to its trade union role of representing workers in their negotiations with employers, it took upon itself the multifarious tasks of providing employment and social services in an underdeveloped spot of land, short on capital and natural resources and populated by successive groups of largely penniless Jewish immigrants. It thus took under its wing many of the country's collectivist enterprises. It affiliated with the collectivist agricultural settlements, the kibbutzim and moshavim, established factories, laid down roads, and built houses, becoming in the process a major employer in its own right. Moreover, in addition to health, it oversaw or supplied a whole range of social services, including education, culture, and sports, and financial services, such as banking and insurance (Arian, 1985, p. 33). These various functions, so incongruous if one thinks of the Histadrut simply as a trade federation, make consummate sense in the context of the Histadrut as it was initially conceived: as a comprehensive organization involved in building a workers' society and meeting all of the needs of the workers therein.

The various Labor parties played a crucial role in the development of both the Histadrut and Kupat Holim. Throughout the prestate period (and roughly the first three decades of statehood), Labor was the dominant political power in the country, putting the parties to the right in deep shadow (Horowitz & Lissak, 1978, p. 76). For all the variety of separate parties, it had the largest membership, the most cohesive structure, and the greatest continuity of form and leadership. In the 1920s the Histadrut was stronger and more prestigious than any of the Labor parties that constituted it. In the 1930s the two largest of those parties united to form Mapai (Party of the Workers of the Land of Israel), which became the first Labor party to win an absolute majority in the Histadrut and dominated it for many years.

As the largest party in the country, it also held the central positions in the "national institutions" that ran the *yishuv*'s internal affairs where the Mandate authorities left a vacuum, conducted the *yishuv*'s foreign relations, and raised and allocated the capital mobilized from the Jewish Diaspora to build and maintain the prestate infrastructure and services. The relevant national institutions here are the Jewish Agency and the National Committee. In the 1930s the

National Committee took charge of the current affairs of the *yishuv,* including health matters. The Jewish Agency served as a liaison between the *yishuv* bodies and the British government authorities and as a conduit for funds raised from the Jewish Diaspora for Jewish institutions in Eretz Israel (the Land of Israel; Arian, 1985, pp. 31–32). Mapai and members of the smaller Labor parties served in key positions in the Histadrut and in the executives of these bodies as well. To take the most prominent example, the head of Mapai, David Ben Gurion, also became general secretary of the Histadrut and the chairman of the Jewish Agency, posts that he held simultaneously. The pattern extended to lower positions as well. It meant that from the 1930s onward, the Labor political elite held the key to both decision making and to the allocation of resources in the *yishuv.* Moreover, its power was further bolstered by what was called the "key principle," whereby both the positions in these institutions and the resources received were divided among the various political groups in proportion to their size. Needless to say, Mapai consistently received the heftiest chunk. It naturally channeled funds and other resources to its own institutions, among them Kupat Holim.

At the least Kupat Holim's affiliation with Labor and the Histadrut meant that it was part of two broad, interrelated organizations that affected many areas of many people's lives and that it could avail itself of their energy and status. It also meant that it benefited from their fervent sense of mission. Beyond getting votes and amassing power, the various Labor parties comprising the Histadrut were infused with nothing short of a missionary drive to build a new Jewish society—a socialistically inclined society of Jewish laborers—in the Land of Israel.

The United States was settled largely by groups of individuals, each intent on pursuing his or her own interests in a land of seemingly boundless opportunity and loosely held together by their common inhabitation of their new home. Israel was settled by Jews, bound by a common history and religion, returning to their common homeland, and, after the Balfour Declaration of 1917, intent on creating a state in which they could express their shared identity. The settlement of Israel was not the endeavor of individuals, but largely the collective endeavor of persons who, for all their differences, belonged to a single people and whose religion, moreover, taught that each is responsible for the other. In the early part of the 20th century, this long ingrained religious sense of mutual responsibility was translated among many poor Jews of Eastern Europe into ardent socialism. A good portion of the immigrants who arrived in Palestine between the end of the 19th century and the early 1930s were not simply Zionists, but specifically socialist Zionists whose vision of a Jewish society meant a collectivist society. This conviction very much suited the arduous conditions of the land to which they came. It is doubtful that through merely individual effort they would have succeeded in drying the swamps of the Hula Valley, farming the desert, protecting themselves from hostile Arabs, and providing themselves with the goods of culture and civilization that their European background had taught them to expect. Their conviction was reflected in the ideology of the Labor movement and in the monumental organizational efforts that the various Labor parties undertook. Building a socialist society, as they saw it, required creating and maintaining collectivist organizations. Kupat Holim was one of many such Labor movement organizations, which the various Labor parties promoted not only to enlarge their own power base—although that motive became increasingly important as the years went by—but as an expression of their state-building efforts.

The backing and resources of the Histadrut and the Labor parties enabled Kupat Holim to build its massive infrastructure, to expand its membership to nearly monopoly proportions, and to dwarf the other sick funds founded during the prestate period. Shortly after the Histadrut took it under its auspices, Kupat Holim set about building hospitals and clinics. Its first hospital, begun in 1923, was opened in Afula in 1929. The second hospital, Beilinson Hospital, was founded in Petah Tikva in the early 1930s (Zalmanovitch, 1991, p. 31).

Up through the mid-1930s, Kupat Holim's affiliation with the Histadrut kept its membership down. Kupat Holim was permitted to accept into its ranks only persons who were members of the Histadrut. On the several occasions when its leadership asked to open the doors to non-Histadrut members, so as to access a larger pool of dues, it was turned down on the grounds that ideological considerations had to precede financial ones (Zalmanovitch, 1990). Then in 1936 the Histadrut made membership in Kupat Holim compulsory for all its trade union members and imposed a single levy for the two (Histadrut, Central Tax Bureau, 1962).

Although the Histadrut and Kupat Holim would disagree about the exact proportion of the levy that went to each body, the single tax did more than any other device to enlarge Kupat Holim's rolls. In those days of high immigration, getting a job without membership in the Histadrut, which as a powerful trade federation *cum* large-scale employer, controlled much of the labor market, was extremely difficult if not impossible. The Jewish population at the time contained a disproportionate number of young and impoverished immigrants who were more interested in jobs than health care. The sequence thus became: to get a job, you had to join the Histadrut, and when you joined the Histadrut, you joined Kupat Holim. The fact that membership in the trade union meant automatic membership in Kupat Holim thus brought to the Sick Fund a sizable proportion of the *yishuv*'s workforce, many of whom would probably never have joined on their own.

Its affiliation with the Histadrut and the Labor parties enabled Kupat

Holim to push the four other sick funds formed in the prestate period to the sidelines. Its rivals were the Popular Sick Fund established by the Hadassah Medical Federation in 1931, Kupat Holim Leumit (the National Sick Fund) established in 1933 by the Revisionist Party, Kupat Holim of the General Zionists established in 1936 by the Independent Liberal Party, and the Maccabi Sick Fund, founded in 1941 by immigrant German doctors who wanted to work in an apolitical sick fund concentrated in the big cities (Halevi, 1979, pp. 6–11). Like Kupat Holim, these sick funds were all created by social or political organizations that regarded them as a force that could attract members and add to their prestige. But because these patrons were small and lacked the means and the muscle of Labor and the Histadrut, none of their sick funds attained anything near the proportions of Kupat Holim.

Autonomy and Assistance from the Core

Kupat Holim's hegemony was also furthered by the pattern of relations it formed with the major actors in the *yishuv's* health arena: the British Mandate government, the Hadassah Medical Federation, and key Jewish national institutions.

Under the British Mandate, the *yishuv* had two levels of government. One was Mandate government, which had legal authority but no legitimacy with the public. The other consisted of the various bodies that comprised the de facto Jewish prestate governing institutions, which had popular but not legal legitimacy and certain de facto but no formal enforcement powers.

The Mandate government's Department of Health devoted the better part of its energy to the Arab population, relegating the health services in the Jewish community to benign neglect (Makover, 1988, pp. 166–67). Its Department of Health rented beds in Mandate hospitals to the various health funds, but gave Jewish medical institutions only the most minimal financial support. In 1933 Mandate government aid came to 1.6% of Kupat Holim's budget; in 1943 and 1944 to less than 1% (Kanivsky, 1944–45, p. 6). Pressed by Kupat Holim for greater participation in its budget, assistance for its hospitals, and tax exemptions, the Mandate government suggested efficiency measures such as closing hospitals and clinics.

At the same time, the Mandate government's Department of Health refrained from imposing its authority on the various health service providers, Kupat Holim included. In 1930 it rejected a proposed health insurance plan designed by the Histadrut to institute compulsory health insurance and to obtain Mandate government funding for the sick funds (Kupat Holim, 1930, p. 19). The rejection of the proposal may have temporarily checked Kupat Holim's expansionist aspirations, but did nothing to check its autonomy.

From the Hadassah Medical Federation, Kupat Holim attained assistance it did not get from the Mandate authorities, without the restrictions or regulation that government assistance generally entails. The Hadassah Medical Federation was established in the *yishuv* at the beginning of the 20th century by Henrietta Szold, an American Jew who brought a Zionist vision unencumbered by socialist ideology and sought to provide medical care for the entire population (Dash, 1979). In the 1920s and 1930s, before Kupat Holim's hospital infrastructure was laid down, it erected well-baby stations and founded hospitals in all the major towns in the *yishuv* (Halevi, 1979). In the mid-1930s, when the Jewish community was well organized and could run its own medical facilities, it gave its hospitals in Tel Aviv, Jaffa, Safed, Haifa, Tiberius, and Jerusalem to the leaders of the *yishuv* to use for the good of the community (Rubinstein, 1976, pp. 223–24) while continuing to help manage and finance them (Hadassah Medical Organization, 1939, pp. 13–21).

Throughout the entire period, the Hadassah Medical Federation contributed generously to Kupat Holim's coffers. In 1923, for example, Hadassah's contribution to Kupat Holim amounted to 12% of the Sick Fund's income (Histadrut, 1923, p. 12). Moreover, like the Mandate authorities, it rented beds in its hospitals to Kupat Holim, which did not have enough hospital beds of its own to meet the needs of its growing membership. The availability of these beds enabled Kupat Holim to provide its members with hospitalization outside its own facilities, a practice that it still maintains and that allowed it to increase its membership beyond the capacity of its infrastructure.

The same pattern of assistance without regulation developed in Kupat Holim's relations with the prestate Jewish national institutions. The relevant Jewish Agency department assisted the Jewish community in matters of health until January 5, 1931, and then transferred the job to the National Committee, which in turn established a health committee, among whose functions was coordinating the activities of the various sick funds to solicit funding from the Mandate government (Atias, 1963, p. 36; Havad Haleumi, 1942, pp. 36–37). But without powers of enforcement, the National Committee could rally only voluntary compliance: the Mandate government kept its purse strings tightly shut, and the sick funds rarely coordinated their activities.

Controlled by the Labor parties and run by many of the same people who ran the Histadrut, the National Committee served mainly as a channel for funding, legitimacy, and status for the various sick funds. The outcome was that the sick funds were largely self-regulating and had a wide scope for initiative and action independent of the prestate's quasi-governmental institutions. They came to view such institutions much as they viewed the Hadassah Medical Federation: as a source of assistance but not as a source of authority. This perception would last into Israel's statehood.

The Prestate Legacy

By the time of the declaration of the state in 1948, Kupat Holim had amassed a wealth of tangible and intangible resources, which made it a potent and even formidable organization. It was the largest and most powerful of the various sick funds, covering 84.8% of the insured population. The Leumit Sick Fund, the next largest, insured only 8.6% of the population, and the Maccabi Sick Fund, the third largest, a meager 1.8% (Halevi, 1979, p. 12). Kupat Holim had 373 clinics dispersed throughout Israel, about 90% of the country's total. It surpassed all the other health bodies in the scope of its infrastructure, the dispersion of its facilities, and the range of its services. It was the only sick fund with its own hospitals: three of them by 1941. Its affiliation with the Histadrut and the Labor parties afforded it status and legitimacy as well as access to money and preferential treatment by the national institutions.

Kupat Holim also had a good deal of credit and prestige to its name. It was founded and developed in a period of urgent need with few to meet it. Kupat Holim nurses and doctors provided health care in a land rife with cholera and malaria, plagued by primitive sanitary conditions and short not only of medical facilities and personnel but also of the transportation and infrastructure to make them available to the scattered population. Kupat Holim staff, who shared the hardships of the rest of the population, who went to the effort of reaching distant settlements, who provided care to poor laborers and penniless immigrants, were rewarded with deep warmth, affection, and gratitude that extended to Kupat Holim itself (Becker, 1982). In the isolated farming communities of the prestate Galilee region, the Kupat Holim doctors and nurses who arrived on their weekly or monthly visits were symbols of Jewish self-help and nation building. The goodwill that Kupat Holim accrued in the prestate period would serve it for several decades as a major bargaining chip in its power struggle with the Israeli government.

The sheer size and scope of Kupat Holim and its ability to organize itself meant that, more than any other health services provider, Kupat Holim was identified both with medical care and with the ideals that, at the time and for many years after, drove the better part of the country's leadership and population. With the possible exception of the Hadassah facilities, the other sick funds were seen as small, partisan organizations. Kupat Holim was certainly partisan, but the fact that its partisanship coincided with that of the *yishuv's* power elite and the majority of its population brought it as close to establishment as a prestate organization could be. Indeed, working for Kupat Holim brought better pay, better conditions, and more job security than the state to come would be able to match for many years.

At the same time, a pattern of relations developed that was beneficial to

Kupat Holim and persisted into the state. The pattern was characterized by the anomalous combination of Kupat Holim dependency and autonomy. From its earliest days, Kupat Holim had become accustomed to having a good part of its operations financed by external sources, whether the Mandate authorities (although their contribution was minuscule), the Hadassah Medical Federation, or the Jewish national institutions. Kupat Holim also became dependent on government facilities for about half its hospital beds (Ellenzwieg et al., 1983, p. 35). On the other hand, the prestate Jewish authorities needed Kupat Holim patients to rent their hospital beds, while the national institutions benefited from the aura that Kupat Holim had secured for itself and from the power of the Labor parties and the Histadrut that backed it. These needs undermined whatever power or will the prestate Jewish authorities might have had to regulate Kupat Holim and assured it considerable autonomy and freedom to make its own decisions.

CHAPTER 3

The Formative Stage: 1947–1949

Throughout most of the prestate period the mutual dependencies and shared ideologies of Kupat Holim and the leadership of the *yishuv*'s quasi-governmental national institutions issued in cooperation between the two. They cooperated not only in providing services, but also in the entire endeavor of state building. Mapai had acquired what Horowitz and Lissak call authority without sovereignty (1978, pp. 64–68, 186) through its ability to mobilize and allocate the better part of the resources available to the *yishuv* from the Jewish communities abroad, whereas the legal power to coerce remained in the hands of the British Mandate authorities. As long as the sovereign state was an idea rather than a reality, delineating the authorities of Mapai or any other Jewish agency was not necessary.

This changed in the transition to statehood between mid-1947 and the end of January 1949, when Israel held its first national elections. As the British Mandate drew to an end, the government-to-be, with Ben Gurion as its recognized head, sought to define its spheres of authority, while the institutions of the *yishuv* sought to preserve their powers in the upcoming state.

As Ben Gurion saw it, the movement to statehood meant that the prestate voluntary bodies would have to cede their authority of the sovereign government:

> The transition from the period of the *yishuv* . . . , in which the Haganah,[1] the Zionist Federation, the General Federation of Labor, and other organizations were all built on voluntary membership, personal agreement, and free will, to the period of the state . . . places all the residents of Israel into a framework of imposition and obligation, in which all are subordinate to the rule of the state, which imposes on them its laws and regulations. . . . Voluntary affiliation becomes obligatory affiliation. . . . (Ben Gurion, 1964, pp. 145–47)

The Kupat Holim–Histadrut–Mapai constellation was not prepared to make the concession to "obligatory affiliation."

Thus began the struggle for stateness (Tilly, 1975) in health care in Israel in these formative years on the seam of statehood. This first phase of the struggle took place in two arenas: the committee room and the crucible of war. In both victory went to the forces against stateness.

The Committee Room

In preparation for the upcoming state, the Histadrut, Mapai, the Jewish Agency, and the National Committee established committees to delineate the spheres of government control in a wide range of areas in the public sphere (Horowitz & Lissak, 1978, pp. 186–200). In the field of health the question was the extent to which the provision and control of health care would remain in the hands of the sick funds and the political organizations within which they operated or be transferred to the national government. All sorts of proposals were made along the continuum, with the exception of private health care, which had ceased to be a factor in the early part of the century. The issue was the relative power and responsibility of the government to-be and of the voluntary agencies (Zalmanovitch, 1990, pp. 144–48).

In terms of the concern of this book, the question was, who will be the core and who will be the margin? Up until then, the sick funds and the political bodies that controlled them were virtually the core bodies with the resources and autonomy to make policy. The approach of statehood put Kupat Holim's core position in jeopardy.

To ward off the danger, the Histadrut committee established in January 1948 to discuss the role of the trade federation in the new state offered a set of proposals whose thrust was not only to secure its position, but also to enhance it. Published in June of that year, the proposals called for obligatory national health insurance and public health for all to be delivered by the prestate medical institutions with the expenditures funded jointly by the local authorities and the state (Kanivsky, 1944–1945, pp. 28–30, 1948; Manor, 1965, p. 95). The Histadrut seems to have contemplated using the government to-be to swell its membership roster and to provide it with a steady, guaranteed source of income. Although 80% of the *yishuv's* insured population belonged to Kupat Holim at the time, only 40% of the Jewish population had medical insurance (Halevi, 1979). Given the acceptance of the key principle in the *yishuv*, the assumption may well have been that the new, compulsory insurees would be divided among the various health funds in accord with the proportion of the population that they already ensured with Kupat Holim thus receiving the largest share.

The Mapai committee was divided on the issue. Ben Gurion and the majority of the members urged the immediate, unconditional transfer of the labor exchange, social security, and Kupat Holim from the Histadrut to the state (Tevet, 1980). These functions, they claimed, should be available equally to all the citizens of the state, independent of party affiliation (Milstein, 1972, p. 431). Although Ben Gurion had been head of the Histadrut between 1921 and 1935, with statehood at hand he was determined to lead not a faction but the entire country. The minority on the committee maintained that Kupat Holim should remain part of the Histadrut. Loyal to their socialist ideology, they believed that the Histadrut was the best body to promote the interests of the working class. Moreover, they well appreciated Mapai's indebtedness to the Histadrut for much of its electoral and financial base. In the end, it was decided that Kupat Holim would be transferred to the state. Only the date of the transfer was put off to some distant future, when the state proved its ability to shoulder the financial and administrative burden involved in running the Sick Fund (Zalmanovitch, 1990, pp. 146–47).

The subcommittee known as Committee C, established jointly by the National Committee and the Jewish Agency, supported the postponement. This committee convened shortly after the official declaration of statehood on May 15, when Israel was attacked by five Arab armies, including the crack British-trained Jordan legion and hordes of Palestinian irregulars. Guided by the desire to keep the system intact in its current form during the war, Committee C recommended postponing dealing with the organization, financing, and regulation of health care until after the state was properly functioning. The only significant change they recommended was transferring the Mandate health facilities to government agencies (Hareuveni, 1974, p. 12; Zalmanovitch, 1990, pp. 144–46).

In short, none of the committees that dealt with the future of health care during this formative period saw the need for immediate action to move health care from the voluntary bodies of the *yishuv* to the obligatory framework of a sovereign state. Then, when the Provisional Government, with Ben Gurion at its head, was established after the declaration of statehood, it transferred the responsibility for health care and the Mandate medical installations from the National Committee not to an independent ministry, but to the newly formed Ministry of Absorption and the Interior, where health care was secondary.

The Test of Sovereignty in the Crucible of War

Without a formal delineation of responsibility for health care, events took over. Ironically, although the delineation was deliberately postponed because of the war, it was during the war itself that the foundation was laid for the "rules of engagement" that would come to characterize the relationship between Kupat Holim and successive Israeli governments.

The War of Independence technically started after the United Nations vote on November 29, 1947, recognizing Israel as a sovereign state, but it had been brewing for some time with fighting already begun in the summer of 1947, when armed Arab bands began to attack remote Jewish settlements in the Galilee and Negev. Kupat Holim, whose resources were adequate during peacetime, could not pay for the equipment and manpower to care for the many wounded in these communities. To prepare for the expected intensification of health care needs during warfare, the heads of the Haganah (the major prestate underground movement engaged in the struggle against the British Mandate and in defending the Jewish population against Arab attack) and Ben Gurion decided to establish a Military Medical Service (Bondi, 1981; Zartal, 1975).

Ben Gurion asked Moshe Sorocca, Kupat Holim's administrative head, to organize and run the service and promised him that once the state was formally reorganized, he would be appointed director general of the state's Ministry of Health. Sorocca refused. Of all the people, civilians and soldiers alike, to whom Ben Gurion turned in this period, Sorocca was the only one to refuse his request (Zartal, 1975, pp. 102–5). Sorocca at the time was recognized as the most powerful administrator in the entire medical system. He was a domineering personality, fanatically committed to Kupat Holim and the socialist values it embodied. His convictions were such that he compelled the hospital physicians who worked for the Sick Fund to live in sick fund housing, where he forbade them such capitalist decadences as listening to classical music, hanging pictures on their walls, and sending their children to private schools. Sorocca's biographer, Idit Zartal, points out that this refusal represented his unwillingness to subordinate Kupat Holim to the informal authority of the governing bodies on the eve of statehood.

The service was established and run by a number of physicians who had left Kupat Holim disaffected with Sorocca's dictatorial rule and rigid ideology (Bondi, 1981; Zartal, 1975). With the escalation of the fighting, the service used the authority of conscription that Ben Gurion had given it to issue draft orders to Kupat Holim nurses and doctors. Kupat Holim complained of the burden and protested the drafting of its personnel without prior consultation. It claimed its job was to provide medical services to civilians, the families of fighters and the communities on the borders, and that it needed its doctors for that cause (Zartal, 1975, p. 103).

In March 1948 Kupat Holim finally signed an agreement with the Military Medical Service to treat the members of the armed forces and their families in its clinics and transfer to the Military Medical Service equipment from its warehouses in exchange for a fee for every soldier in the army (Bondi, 1981, pp. 115–16). Even so, Kupat Holim continued to chafe at the service's power to conscript its doctors. It complained that the Military Medical Service drafted its doctors unnecessarily and was intentionally undermining its authority, and it did not always stick to the agreement (Zartal, 1975, p. 103).

The enormity of Kupat Holim's recalcitrance cannot be understated. Of all of Israel's all too many wars, the War of Independence was the most difficult and the most crucial. A full 1% of Palestine's Jewish population was killed in that war, fought by grossly underarmed, hastily trained Jewish soldiers. If the war had not been won by the Jews, the Jewish state sanctioned by the United Nations would have been snuffed out at birth. It was under these dire circumstances that Kupat Holim forcefully demonstrated that its commitment to itself was greater than its commitment to the upcoming state for which it itself had struggled.

Sorocca viewed the Military Medical Service and Provisional Government as "wild rivals" (Zartal, 1975, p. 108) and a life threat to the organization he had spent years building. The following statement is taken from a letter he wrote to his superior, the chief medical administrator of Kupat Holim in the fall of 1948.[2] "In fact, Kupat Holim is fighting for its very existence. There are already claims that now we have a state and there is no longer any need for public medical services paralleling government provided services" (Zartal, 1975, p. 109).

The heads of Kupat Holim, accustomed to their independence and freedom from regulation, had difficulty accepting the existence of a government authority with the right to give orders and demand compliance. Drafting its personnel constituted a threat to the autonomy of Kupat Holim and to its power to employ its personnel as it saw fit. A further threat occurred when the Military Medical Service converted the military hospitals vacated by the British army and other hospitals in the country into military hospitals, staffed with the help of specially recruited new immigrant physicians. Within a year, it had established 16 military hospitals with 3,000 beds, as well as a network of clinics and supply bases on the front (Bondi, 1981, p. 118). This was a threat to Kupat Holim's hegemony, because it meant that the government could provide services that until that time had been almost the sole province of Kupat Holim.

Traditional political theory holds that government policy is characterized by legitimacy, universality, and enforcement (Anderson, 1975; Dye, 1978, p. 20; Fesler & Kettl, 1991). *Legitimacy* means that public policy is made by government, anchored in law, and so preferred over policy made by anyone else. *Universality* means that only public policy can encompass the entire population of a country or any other designated area. *Enforcement* means that only government has the right to enforce its regulations beyond a specific membership group in the population as a whole. Kupat Holim accepted neither the legitimacy, universality, nor authority of the new government. Its compliance with the military orders was grudging, incomplete, and conditioned on negotiated accords that it was an equal partner in formulating (Bondi, 1975, pp. 115–16).

In effect, Ben Gurion failed the test of sovereignty where Kupat Holim was concerned. His inability to impose policy during the war and Kupat Holim's show of muscle created a polarity, in which Kupat Holim and the government both had the power to thwart each other, but neither had the power to control the provision of health services in its entirety and both wanted it.

Kupat Holim Expands

To ensure what he perceived as Kupat Holim's threatened survival, Sorocca set the organization on an energetic program of expansion, even as its finances were inadequate to provide essential medical services to the beleaguered population. Kupat Holim established hosts of new clinics, some of them in old, dilapidated buildings. It added beds and equipment to its hospitals, built a maternity hospital in Kfar Saba, and added buildings to its hospitals, especially Beilinson, its flagship (Vilan, 1980; Zartal, 1975, p. 114).

The expansion on which Sorocca embarked was designed to ensure that Kupat Holim remained the all-encompassing health provider it had become, which was made clear in the same 1948 letter to the chief medical administrator quoted earlier:

> The greatness of Kupat Holim has been its total system of assistance, from the clinic to the hospital, with all its facilities. This is what has characterized our medical services and what has attracted the public. If other public medical services develop alongside us, which take from us sectors [of the population], whether immigrants or civil servants, or if we come to lack excellent medical services and if, God forbid, our medical facilities are too small and of poor quality, then in time our standards will decline and we will be like other institutions, instead of the institution we have been up to now. (Zartal, 1975, p. 107).

The letter shows Sorocca's concern with all and any rivalry to Kupat Holim, whether in the form of the wartime military facilities, the other sick funds, or the government-to-be in the new state. He regarded these "rivals" as grasping competitors for insurees among the civil servants and the immigrant population, which was at this point increasing by leaps and bounds. He feared that the competition would lead to a withdrawal of resources from Kupat Holim and a consequent deterioration of its services, which would topple the Sick Fund from the place on the pinnacle it had hitherto enjoyed.

The program of expansion on which he set the Sick Fund was a clearly thought-out strategy to ensure that Kupat Holim would retain its supremacy in the provision of health services not only during the war but also in the state-to-be. The expansion was not merely a matter of adding clinics, hospitals, and equipment to Kupat Holim's store, but designed to reinforce the organization's all encompassing comprehensiveness: in size; in the type, availability, and quality of its services; and in the inclusiveness of its membership. As Sorocca describes it, the comprehensiveness was meant to ensure Kupat Holim's virtual monopoly in health care and the continuing flow of public resources that its monopoly position would bring it. He already envisioned a large and dependent membership, which would deter any government from impinging on Kupat Holim's autonomy and hegemony in health care.

Years later, Sorocca boasted of the design to a group of Kupat Holim district administrators: "The quarrel between Kupat Holim and the State was determined not at the conference table, not by committees, but in those very days by Kupat Holim's commitment and daring to expand and create facts." The aim of the strategy, he revealed, was to make sure "that the baby got so big it couldn't be swallowed up" (Zartal, 1975, p. 114).

CHAPTER 4

Health as a Political Resource: The First Two Decades of Statehood

With statehood, a fundamental change occurred in Kupat Holim's formal position vis-à-vis the core government: Kupat Holim was formally pushed from the de facto core of the Jewish prestate entity to the margins of the state. In the interests of state building, the core should have taken control of health policy, and Kupat Holim should have receded to second place. Instead, health care became a potent political resource, assiduously cultivated and strenuously exploited by Kupat Holim, the Histadrut, and the ruling Mapai Party, which governed both the country and the Histadrut for the first 20 years of statehood.

This reversal set the stage for the conflict between the new state, eager to extend its authority to areas of life formerly under the control of voluntary bodies, and those bodies and their political patrons (Arian, 1981; Horowitz & Lissak, 1978, pp. 186–212; Medding, 1990, pp. 134–40), who retained a certain disregard for the state as a nonpartisan entity responsible for the well-being of all its citizens regardless of their party affiliation. While Ben Gurion and some other Mapai leaders struggled to demarcate the functions of the state and the party, much of the Mapai machine identified the interests of the party with those of the state—and viewed state resources and state authorities as means to the party's perpetuation rather than as values to be respected and supported (Medding, 1972; Shapiro, 1977). Similarly, Kupat Holim, which entered the state with its prestate resources, powers, and affiliation with the Histadrut all intact, regarded the new government largely as a continuation of the prestate agencies, there to help and promote it, but not to tell it what to do.

This shared disdain informed an elaborate system of exchanges (Blau, 1964; Curry & Wade, 1968; Ilchman & Uphoff, 1969, pp. 3–49; Waldman, 1977; Zalmanovitch, 1981) that developed between Kupat Holim, the Histadrut, and Mapai in the 1950s and 1960s. The system was based on the mutual dependencies already formed between Mapai and Kupat Holim in the prestate period and extended in the early state years to include the government of Israel as well. Through the system of exchanges, Mapai and Kupat Holim shored up each other's power at the expense of the power of the state, resulting in an underdeveloped Ministry of Health and the use of the tools of policy making for the benefit of Kupat Holim.

The Establishment of Exchanges

The system of exchanges developed in the crucible of the new state, which was weak, short on resources, and occupied with the imperatives of nation building after the arduous War of Independence. The newly elected government had an overburdened agenda. It had to create an army that could fend off the hostility of Israel's Arab neighbors, still intent on its destruction. It had to settle vast numbers of immigrants who began pouring into Israel even as the war was raging. Between 1948 and 1951, the country's population more than doubled, from some 650,000 to 1,350,000, with refugees streaming in from Hitler's Europe and the Arabic-speaking countries of Africa and the Middle East. In the first seven months of 1951, 20,000 persons arrived per month (Arian, 1985, pp. 18–19). This immigration was part of the Zionist vision of "ingathering the exiles" of the Jewish Diaspora and essential to establishing the new state's hold on the land and ensuring its survival. To settle the immigrants, many of them impoverished, an entire infrastructure—roads, schools, houses, and entire towns—had to be built from scratch and work had to be found or created. These tasks, all urgent, could not be left to private interests motivated by expectations of profit. They required the leadership of a government motivated by a vision of the public good (Galnoor, 1982).

With these many urgent demands, the government was hard pressed to see to the immigrants' health as well. Nor did it have the means to do so. When the state was established, the government inherited the British Mandate's flimsy health care infrastructure of a few hospitals and public health facilities; it could rely on the Hadassah network of hospitals and clinics; and, in the mid-1950s, the army hospitals were transferred to the state (Halevi, 1979). But, as in the days of the *yishuv*, Kupat Holim was still the major supplier of health services. Whether it wanted it or not, the government needed Kupat Holim.

Many of the immigrants, from Hitler's Europe and underdeveloped parts of the Arab world, arrived with tuberculosis, skin and eye diseases, malnutrition, and other third-world maladies, which made them immediate consumers of health care. Kupat Holim stepped into the breach where the government, with its overloaded agenda, was sore pressed to act. Kupat Holim sent its personnel into the immigrant camps, where the newcomers were housed in tents and tin shacks, and into the new development towns hastily set up in the periphery and border areas. It dispatched doctors and nurses, put up clinics and prenatal and well-baby stations, screened the population for disease, treated the ill, administered vaccinations, and dispensed basic hygiene and sanitation guidelines. It provided these and other vital services without waiting for government directives in the spirit of voluntarism that had imbued its early days.

For Mapai, Kupat Holim was a major political resource. In election after election, Mapai used Kupat Holim's health services to attract voters. Citizens grateful for Kupat Holim's medical services were ready to vote for Mapai out of sheer appreciation. Where more was needed, Mapai was not averse to using muscle. Mapai functionaries, who were active not only in the party but also in Kupat Holim and the Histadrut, crudely linked the new clinics and the new mother and child-care stations, the helpful public health nurses and specialist physicians, to voting for Mapai (Medding, 1972). Israeli folklore has it that before elections, placards transported in Kupat Holim vehicles, erected by Kupat Holim employees, and reading "Health Clinic Will Be Built Here" would suddenly appear in strategic locations.

Kupat Holim also provided Mapai with a source of patronage. Kupat Holim served as a convenient workplace for the multitude of doctors, nurses, pharmacists, lab technicians, and other health professionals who arrived the country in the 1950s and 1960s. It also served as a place to reward party loyalists; of Kupat Holim's 7,800 employees in 1955, 40% were nonmedical personnel.

The basis for the political exchange was Kupat Holim's critical position in the Histadrut, which, as in prestate days, was Mapai's power base. As pointed out in chapter 3, in the mid-1930s membership in Kupat Holim and in the Histadrut were made contingent on one another. Like most of the other prestate features of Kupat Holim, this too stayed intact in the transition to statehood. In prestate days, the joint membership worked largely to the benefit of Kupat Holim, bringing to its ranks persons who joined the Histadrut to obtain employment. After statehood, the new immigrants, mostly refugees, tended to need medical care more than their younger and healthier prestate predecessors, while jobs became more available to non-Histadrut members. The major shift came after the passage of the Social Insurance Law in 1953, which transferred the prestate labor exchanges of the Histadrut and other political organizations to the newly created National Insurance Institute. Although Histadrut membership was still required for employment in the country's many Histadrut enterprises, it was no longer the almost sine qua non for employment as it had been in the days of the *yishuv*. Beginning in the 1950s, Kupat Holim members maintained the ranks of the Histadrut. The growth of Kupat Holim meant the growth of the Histadrut, not only bringing members, but also ensuring Histadrut control of most of the country's workplaces. A stronger Histadrut, in turn, meant a stronger Mapai power base.

The Histadrut, bolstered by Kupat Holim members and membership dues, provided Mapai with both an organized community of potential voters and a major source of funds. The vehicle for this benefit was the Histadrut's Central Tax Bureau, created in the 1930s and controlled by Mapai. This office had numerous functions of inestimable value to a political party intent on holding the reins of power. It recruited and registered members, issued membership cards, compiled the voter register for Histadrut elections, and collected statistical data on all Kupat Holim members (Central Tax Bureau, 1962; Histadrut Comptroller, 1978, 1983). These functions gave the Histadrut and its Mapai masters a significant power apparatus whose operations were independent of the core government.

Moreover, the Central Tax Bureau collected and apportioned the single tax covering both Histadrut and Kupat Holim membership. The tax, allocated in the proportions and for the purposes that suited the trade federation and the party, provided financial resources that Mapai could use for political ends. To take a crude but prevalent example, in election years Kupat Holim and Histadrut staff campaigned for Mapai, transporting voters to the polls in Kupat Holim and Histadrut vehicles and paying for campaign costs with Kupat Holim and Histadrut funds.

More insidiously, Mapai used funds from the single tax for the political socialization of the populace. In the first two decades of statehood, the Histadrut built a wide range of social and cultural facilities, from sports clubs to community centers to camps and youth movements, primarily financed in good part by the single tax. These facilities offered services that neither a private entity nor government provided. Many of them were located in outlying areas where few if any other organized social outlets were available (Arian, 1985, pp. 28–30; Bartal, 1989; Ben Meir, 1978). With their exclusive privileges for Histadrut–Kupat Holim members, they served as examples of what the voters would get in the future if they cast their ballots for Mapai and as places where Mapai activists could come and preach the value of Mapai socialism.

Strengthening the Margins, Weakening the Core

The currency with which Mapai paid Kupat Holim and the Histadrut for the use of their social and economic resources was of government mintage. As the dominant political party during this period, Mapai saw to it that the core health policy making body, the Ministry of Health, remained too underdeveloped to exercise its policy-making functions (Halevi, 1979, 1980) and employed the instruments of policy making (i.e., allocation, regulation, and restructuring) for the benefit of Kupat Holim.

The Ministry of Health

The Ministry of Health was established in 1950, two years after the state and almost 50 years after Kupat Holim. It was administered by physicians who had left Kupat Holim and answered Ben Gurion's call to run the Military Medical Service during the War of Independence. Like Ben Gurion, most of the high-ranking bureaucrats were committed to placing health services under the charge of a nonpartisan government body (Halevi, 1979; Hareuveni, 1974).

Kupat Holim naturally viewed the ministry as a threat to its hegemony. The Mapai machine, for its part, already controlled most of the country's health services through Kupat Holim and was uninterested in having a strong, autonomous Ministry of Health with the ability to make policy. To keep the ministry weak, Kupat Holim consistently entrusted it to one of the smaller, less powerful parties in the Labor coalition. Between 1948 and 1977 a Mapai personality held the Ministry of Health for only a few months. Otherwise, the ministers came from the religious parties (1948–1952, 1961–1966), the General Zionists (1952–1955), and the far-left Mapam Party (1955–1957, 1966–1977; Arian, 1981, p. 51), most of which lacked the political clout to enact ministry policy. Most of the religious party ministers simultaneously held other ministerial portfolios, which meant they could not give the ministry their full attention. Mapai's conduct here contrasted sharply with its practice with regard to ministries that it wanted strong, such as defense and finance, which it kept firmly in its own hands, appointing as their ministers competent, powerful party loyalists.

Contributing to the ministry's weakness as a policy-making body was the fact that at its creation it was assigned to supervise all government health facilities and all former Mandate hospitals and other health facilities. These included most of the general hospitals, psychiatric hospitals, and ambulatory clinics that Hadassah had given to the prestate Jewish authorities, as well as the military installations that the British had left. In the first decade or so of its existence, most of the ministry's time and energy was occupied with transferring the British Mandate health facilities. Even after the transfers were complete, its providing and maintaining health services and managing the large number of employees required to do so reduced the time and energy that Ministry of Health had for policy making (Staff for Establishing the Hospitalization Authority, 1983, 1984).

The real source of its weakness, however, was the way the ministry budget was structured and prepared. Like the budgets of the other ministries, the Ministry of

Health's budget was made under the aegis of the Ministry of Finance, a Mapai stronghold until the mid-1960s and then held by Mapai's heirs, the Alignment and Labor until 1977.

The structure of its budget incorporated the prestate dependency of the Hadassah medical system on Kupat Holim patients to fill—and finance—its hospitals. The Ministry of Health budget consisted (and still consists) of two sums: a net budget provided by the government and what is termed *income-dependent expenditure,* which is derived from the sale of services, mainly hospital and ambulatory services in the government facilities, to the various sick funds and other bodies. In practice most of the services were sold to Kupat Holim to cover the hospitalization of those of its members who could not be accommodated in Kupat Holim beds. As stated, Kupat Holim insured approximately 80% of the population in these years, while the Ministry of Health owned 50% of the country's hospital beds. In short, the ministry's budget was structured so that the ministry had to sell Kupat Holim hospital beds to pay for much of its own operation.

The preparation of its budget was overseen by a subteam from the Ministry of Finance's Budget Division (Arieli, 1986), headed by a person called a *referent.* Referents are essentially delegates of the Ministry of Finance in other government ministries and agencies. In the Ministry of Health, the referent has the last word on the total size of the budget; plays a major role in fixing the rates for the hospital beds and ambulatory services that the ministry sells; and provides the official estimate of the number of government hospital beds that Kupat Holim was likely to purchase (the other sick funds, because of their small size, were an insignificant factor in the overall estimate) in the fiscal year. Together these functions mean that the referent may play an important role in determining how much the ministry receives from the government and how much it has to raise from the sale of beds to Kupat Holim. The referent's involvement in the details of the budget may also give him a strong say about what the ministry may spend its funds on and by implication a major role in the ministry's policies.

The referent's actual power varies from ministry to ministry depending on the balance of his knowledge and determination and the ministry's strength. Through the early 1970s, the Ministry of Health did not have the intraorganizational structures that would place it on a par with delegates from the Ministry of Finance. Its organizational charts in those years reveal that it did not have units to gather and analyze information; to plan, prepare, or manage the health system budget; or even to make the Ministry of Finance aware of its needs. This enabled the Ministry of Finance to dictate the Ministry of Health budget without even prior consultation.[1]

That the Ministry of Finance did dictate without consultation is indicated by examination of the various budget proposals (*budget books,* as they are called) that were sent to the Knesset for approval. These books contain both numerical data and explanations. The explanations relay the purposes for which the funds are allocated and embody the ministry's policy intentions. The explanations may be written by the ministry, the referent, or jointly; if the ministry writes them, the referent may or may not revise them. Until the early 1970s, each year's explanations in the Ministry of Health's budget book closely resembled that of the year before, suggesting that the Ministry of Finance simply copied one year's priorities to the next instead of negotiating policy with the Ministry of Health.[2]

The fact that Kupat Holim was able to meet the health needs of the vast majority of the population enabled Mapai to argue that there was no need for a strong government body to administer or provide health care. While the government is busy with vital matters of defense, immigrant absorption, and creating the infrastructure for a modern state, Mapai argued, Kupat Holim frees it from the burden of health care, and handles it better and more cost effectively than the state would. In the words of Pinchas Sapir, a Mapai strongman who served as director of the Ministry of Finance in the mid-1950, and in the 1960s and 1970s would serve as minister of Finance: "Every lira that I invest in Kupat Holim is worth more to me than the same lira invested in the Ministry of Health. Virtually everything I do through the Ministry of Health is less good and costs me more" (Halevi, 1979, p. 43). The accuracy of the claim is not subject to examination, but it contains the justification for the Labor governments' keeping the Ministry of Health undeveloped and for consistently employing the tools of policy making for the benefit of Kupat Holim.

The Tools of Policy

In the first two decades of statehood, Mapai continued or established procedures and practices that preserved and augmented the policy-making powers Kupat Holim had begun to amass in the prestate period.

Allocation

In the 1950s and 1960s, Kupat Holim received a substantial proportion of Israel's public health funds, both through direct and indirect financing, while effectively controlling much of the budgeting and allocation processes.

Allocation by administrative formula. One of the first acts of the Ministry of Health was to surrender the power of allocation that is essential to institutional autonomy and policy-making ability. It did this through the introduction of allocation for the sick funds by a routine formula that was not contingent on output, efficiency, performance, compliance with Ministry policy, or any other criteria. The procedure was introduced by the Committee for Sick Fund Affairs that was established by the newly created Ministry of Health. This committee set down the principle that "the sick funds must receive financial assistance from public agencies" because they took upon themselves services that in other countries were the responsibility of the government and provided vital medical services to a segment of the population that could not supply them itself (*Report of the Committee on Kupat Holim*, 1950).

The committee decided that government support would be distributed according to an allocation formula that favored Kupat Holim over the other sick funds and ensured it a steady stream of government funding. The formula was based on total income from membership dues, number of insured members, and expenditures on health services, which was supposed to reflect the variety and quality of medical services the fund offered (Halevi, 1979, p. 15; *Report of the Committee on Kupat Holim*, 1950, p. 34). Because Kupat Holim had more members, higher revenues, and more expenditures than the other sick funds, these criteria resulted in the channeling of more than 90% of all government funding for health care to Kupat Holim.

In 1963 the formula was revised after the smaller sick funds complained bitterly that it was inequitable. The new code added two new criteria: the dispersal of services throughout the country and the social-demographic composition of the fund (*State Comptroller Report*, 1969, p. 318). These too favored Kupat Holim, which was the only sick fund with clinics in remote parts of the country and had the most old and impoverished members. Kupat Holim's part in the total support was reduced by a mere 1.5% (Baruch, 1973, p. 28).

Special Supports. In addition to the direct support that it received through the Ministry of Health on the basis of the formula, Kupat Holim also received a large array of special supports, including such things as free land, grants, low cost loans, and special subsidies, which the other sick funds did not receive. It also received funding for its clinics (patients in the other funds were generally treated in the doctor's own premises), the maintenance of wartime emergency services in its eight general hospitals, the construction and maintenance of new hospitals, the coverage of its hospitals' deficits, the provision of care for premature babies, and other items (*State Comptroller Report*, 1969, p. 177). In addition, like the other sick funds, it received full payment for new immigrant and welfare cases; only it had so many more of such cases than the other funds that the reimbursements were significantly more substantial.

The justification for these special supports was that they went to hospital and other essential services that were provided by Kupat Holim but not by the other sick funds and were beyond the government's ability to provide through its own hospitals. Kupat Holim argued that because its insurance fees were not too different from those of the other sick funds, and in some cases lower, it had to be compensated for the extra services. The state comptroller apparently agreed. Its 1969 report justified these supports on the grounds that Kupat Holim supplied unique services and thus had special needs (*State Comptroller Report*, 1969, p. 177).

The single tax. In addition, Mapai propped up the single tax collected by the Histadrut, the source of Kupat Holim's membership dues. Not all the funds collected in this tax went to Kupat Holim. Kupat Holim was only one of many "tax partners" among whom the Histadrut's Central Tax Bureau divided the tax. Others included, for example, the Histadrut pension funds, strike funds, cultural and sport activities, and the Pioneer Women, to name only the major ones. The abundance of tax partners meant that the single tax was thinly distributed, and, moreover, that Kupat Holim's medical services competed for funds with the political services that the Histadrut gave Mapai.

The play of these interests at any given time was reflected the "tax partners key," which indicated the percentage of the revenues that went to each partner. This key was cut by the Histadrut, and the funds disbursed by the Histadrut treasurer. In the 1950s, most of the money went to the Histadrut's social and political activities; only between 40%–43% went to Kupat Holim. By the end of the 1960s, the proportions were reversed, with Kupat Holim receiving approximately 60% and the other tax partners only 40% (Zalmanovitch, 1981, p. 85). This was an improvement, but still less than Kupat Holim needed. The apportionment of the single tax was always a point of contention between Kupat Holim and the Histadrut.

Mapai's need for the Histadrut created a dilemma for it. To attract and keep members in the Histadrut, its power base, Mapai had to make sure that Kupat Holim, on which much of the Histadrut's strength rested, remained attractive. To this end, it had to channel enough money to Kupat Holim to ensure the Sick Fund's continuous expansion and development. On the other hand, Mapai had to channel money to the Histadrut's various social and cultural activities, which served for voter indoctrination.

Its way out of the dilemma was to arrange for the government to cover the shortfall. Mapai made sure that Kupat Holim received the difference from the national treasury, whether directly or through land grants, no-interest loans, hospitalization subsidies, or any number of unknown other means, including the inequitable allocation formula.

The fact that the Histadrut and Kupat Holim could count on unquestioned government support warped their budgeting processes. It enabled the Histadrut to set the single tax unrealistically low to attract members and Kupat Holim to make its budget backwards. First Kupat Holim committed itself to expenditures;

the Histadrut set low membership fees and determined what portion would go to Kupat Holim; and, then, and only then, did Kupat Holim look for the money needed to fund its activities.

Employer participation. Finally, Israel's Mapai-led government also helped to exact employer funding for Kupat Holim, using the government's powers of secondary regulation. The idea of employer participation in health care costs goes back to the early days of Kupat Holim, when the Sick Fund first came under the Histadrut umbrella. At first the contributions were voluntary. Then, after the imposition of the single tax in 1937, they were anchored in the Histadrut's wage agreements with employers and collected by the Histadrut's Central Tax Bureau. The problem was that not all employers agreed to commit themselves in their labor contracts and not all who did agree actually paid.[3] The contributions amounted only to about 5% of Kupat Holim's revenues in the 1920s (Histadrut, 1923, pp. 12–13; Kupat Holim, 1926, p. 28) and an average of 10% in the 1930s and 1940s (Kupat Holim, 1943, p. 31).

After statehood the Histadrut asked for government assistance in extracting payment. It itself was able to obtain a degree of compliance through the labor agreements it made with employers, whether in individual enterprises or whole industries or sectors of the economy. In addition, the minister of labor, empowered by the Collective Agreements Law of 1957, issued "extension orders" which applied these agreements to other sectors, which were not parties to the original accord. Because the Israeli government was the country's largest employer, the extension orders, which applied to government enterprises, meant that the government in effect imposed a hidden health tax on the Israeli public. Employer participation increased dramatically. In the 1950s and 1960s, the employer participation tax,[4] as it may be called, was paid for 70% of the country's employees and accounted for 35% of Kupat Holim's revenues (*Knesset Minutes,* 1972, p. 196; Kupat Holim, 1957, p. 112; Ministry of Health, The Health System in Israel 1948–1968, p. 136). The government justified this allocation policy on the grounds that Kupat Holim was performing a vital national service and therefore could not be expected to carry the entire cost.

Regulation

The Ministry of Health made little use of its formal powers to regulate the health system in the first few decades of statehood: it was too busy putting its newly acquired hospitals in order, it lacked political clout, and its dependency on Kupat Holim patients to fill its hospital beds and thus for a substantial portion of its operating budget compelled it to give considerable weight to Kupat Holim's interests to protect its own.

In Israel ministry regulations often function to implement Knesset legislation. The laws passed by Israel's parliament usually provide general directives for the relevant body to execute, rather than detailed requirements, and authorize the relevant minister to make regulations for their implementation (Bracha, 1986, p. 77). These regulations have the status of secondary legislation, with all the attendant legal weight and sanctions of Knesset-passed laws.

The Ministry of Health made little use of the power to make secondary legislation to regulate the health system or to control the activities of Kupat Holim. Between 1935 and 1977, when Labor was voted out of office, it made only 19 formal health regulations that are still in force today, compared to the 34 that the Likud would make during its period of dominance between 1977 and 1984.[5] Moreover, almost all of these regulations concerned general health matters, such as food and nutrition, diseases, and births and deaths. A very few concerned hospitals, medical care, reporting requirements, or other items that would impinge on Kupat Holim's autonomy.

Important regulation came from outside the ministry and favored Kupat Holim. In the early 1950s, the Jewish Agency, which had taken on itself the responsibility of providing the immigrants with health insurance and in which Mapai people held the majority of posts and virtually all the decision-making positions, signed an agreement with Kupat Holim making this sick fund its insurer. Excluding the other sick funds, the Jewish Agency agreed to pay insurance for each new Kupat Holim member for three months, after which the member would be entitled to a 40% discount for the remainder of the year. The arrangement was soon adopted by the government, which signed an agreement to pay the membership fees of every immigrant for six months (Zalmanovitch, 1981, pp. 62–64). These regulations brought Kupat Holim a great surge in membership. Kupat Holim enrolled the majority of the new arrivals. Many of them, ignorant of Hebrew and unsure of themselves in their new country, probably did not know what they were signing and probably had no idea that the other sick funds even existed. Once registered, they tended to stay.

Another major impediment to its regulatory power was its lack of firm planning or enforcement structures. It was not until 1962 that the ministry established a body to regulate the construction of new hospitals. The Supreme Hospitalization Authority consisted of delegates from the Ministry of Health, Kupat Holim, and Hadassah, and was given a string of regulatory functions, including establishing criteria for and determining what facilities were to be built, expanded, or renovated, where, and at what cost.

It was notably ineffective and could not have been otherwise. It was only an advisory body; the three partners all had parity in making the recommendations and their conflicting interests resulted in paralysis. It met sporadically, and the only outputs I was able to find were two reports to the minister of health: one a detailed report on the hospitalization situation and a master plan for the development of general hospitalization until 1974; the other, updates of that plan for 1978 to 1981 (*State Comptroller Report*, 1972, pp. 259, 262–68; 1976, pp. 341, 344).

Both the Ministry of Health and Kupat Holim circumvented or ignored the authority when it suited them. The Ministry of Health approved a substantial increase in the construction of hospitals without consulting it, among them the Sharon Hospital under the joint ownership of Kupat Holim and the municipality of Petah Tikva (*State Comptroller Report*, 1972, pp. 262–63). It also expanded or constructed seven government-owned hospitals (Zalmanovitch, 1991, p. 99). Kupat Holim expanded two of its large general hospitals, Meir Hospital in Kfar Saba and Sorocca Hospital in Beer Sheba, and started to build Carmel Hospital in Haifa without the authority's involvement. In both cases, the significant construction was undertaken without the authority's participation even though most of the finance for the construction came from public funds.

Restructuring

With the structure of the Israel's health services established during the British Mandate when no sovereign core existed, the new state was confronted with a fait accompli: a network of medical services run largely by the monopolistic Kupat Holim, which had considerable autonomy in running its own affairs while being heavily dependent on the political power structure both for its funding and for ensuring the conditions in which it could operate and grow. This anomalous brew of autonomy and dependence on the part of a large nongovernment body undermines the state's power to control the uses of its resources and to enact and implement its own policy preferences.

Ben Gurion and others in Labor's inner circle continued their struggle, started in the formative years before statehood, to transfer control of the health services from Kupat Holim and the other sick funds to the state. Their efforts were part of their overall position that the sovereign state was responsible for and should take over the tasks and functions previously performed by voluntary bodies. Pinchas Lavon, a close associate of Ben Gurion, enunciated the conception in the latter's name: "Our direction must be to create a state in which the instruments of government are strong and inclusive and encompass all spheres of life. There must be no intermediary between the state and its citizens. . . . The authority to govern must belong only to the state, to the municipalities, and to no one else. . . . There cannot and must not be any quasi-governmental organization" (Milstein, 1972, p. 431).

The view encompassed defense, education, employment, immigration absorption, welfare, and other functions. Within a few years after Israel's assumption of sovereignty, the various prestate paramilitary organizations were melded into the Israeli Defense Forces under national command; the separate school systems run by the various political parties were turned into state secular schools and state religious schools (the schools of the ultraorthodox remained under their own auspices); the National Insurance Institute was created to provide welfare services previously supplied by voluntary bodies, and soon took over the labor exchanges from the political parties that had run them in prestate days (Medding, 1990, pp. 152–156).

Most Mapai functionaries, however, staunchly opposed any restructuring of the country's health system, motivated by the same need for Kupat Holim members and money to sustain the party's Histadrut power base that had issued in the abnegation of the tools of allocation and regulation. Viewing the state as an extension of the party, and the good of the former deriving from the good of the latter, they did not share Ben Gurion's vision of a state that had the right to impose its rules and regulations on the voluntary bodies and quasi-governmental institutions that held sway in prestate days.

By the mid-1950s, Ben Gurion had lost his battle to transfer health services to the state. Additionally, he changed his earlier opinion that the state had to provide health services just as it provided the other major services of a modern society. In 1949 Ben Gurion stated, "There are things that should be done by the powers of the state" and counted among them "health services and the like" (Ben Gurion, 1951–1957, 1, p. 265). By 1956 he seems to have retreated from this position to the view that the job of the state was simply to make sure that all citizens received health care:

Many services can be provided more efficiently by organizations of beneficiaries and consumers, such as, for example, health services. It would be a serious mistake, and a social and public one too, if, for example, the whole health service were to be administered by the official bureaucracy of the state, once the vast majority of the citizens of the state, led by the members of the Histadrut, have by their own efforts organized medical services on the basis of mutual assistance, which have reached a high level. But the state must guarantee general medical insurance for the whole population of the state and that everyone who is not insured in a sick fund will receive medical aid directly from state institutions." (Ben Gurion, 1964, pp. 522–23)

Some years later, Ben Gurion would return to his statist position in health, but to no effect.

Much less far-reaching restructuring initiatives were also thwarted. The drain on the national treasury, the inevitable duplication, the favoritism, and the very operation of a huge, powerful voluntary organization supported by state funds and state authority all evoked strong opposition. Several groups called for health services reform, among them those in the Labor movement who sided with Ben Gurion in his effort to define the state's role more clearly; the professional bureaucrats in the Ministry of Health, who had the formal responsibility for over-seeing Israel's health care without the practical power to do so; and the initially very small but steadily growing non-Labor opposition parties who tried to under-mine the major Labor alliance by attacking its major power base (Halevi, 1979, 1980; Steinberg, 1989; Steinberg & Bick, 1992; Zalmanovitch, 1991, pp. 105–22).

During the first two decades of statehood several initiatives were undertaken to restructure Israel's health care. I use the word *restructure* for lack of a better term to describe what those initiatives actually consisted of. Committees met and legislation was proposed, but virtually nothing happened to change the pre-state structure of authority and roles in health care. Indeed, whether the powers in office who organized the initiatives actually intended to change them is ques-tionable. The story of the initiatives is the story of the struggle between the re-formists and those who wanted nothing better than to reinforce Kupat Holim's powers with the powers of the state.

Red Lines in the 1930s

In one way or another, all the initiatives harkened back to the proposal for com-pulsory health insurance that the Histadrut and Kupat Holim had presented to the Mandate authorities in 1930 (Manor, 1965, p. 47). This proposal already con-tained what would become Kupat Holim's red lines or the cardinal points for which Kupat Holim and its allies would be prepared to fight and beyond which they would brook no change in the period of statehood (Kupat Holim, 1930, p. 19). Together the various provisions of the prestate proposal set out the rights of Kupat Holim and the obligations of the government.

The proposal stipulated that (1) health insurance be made compulsory and that (2) it be supplied by the voluntary sick funds (3) which would have the right to levy dues and to determine which medical services would be provided. At the same time, they stipulated that (4) the government use its legal authority to en-force the compulsory membership and dues payment, and that (5) it pay one third of the costs of the services and (6) legislate compulsory contributions by the country's employers, so that the sick funds' expenditures would be paid for in equal share by the insured, the employers, and the government. In addition, it stipulated that the high commissioner establish a Government Insurance Com-mittee consisting of a chairman, a representative of Kupat Holim, a representa-tive of the employers, and a representative of the insured to supervise the imple-mentation of the law. The committee would have all the authority of the high commissioner's office, but all of its members would have been either Histadrut or Kupat Holim delegates, since the Histadrut was also a major employer and the insured were mostly members of Kupat Holim.

Through these provisions, Kupat Holim hoped to co-opt the government's legal authorities and powers of allocation and regulation to gain and maintain control of the entire health system, with no government impingement on its financial and functional autonomy. Although the British made short shrift of the proposal, Kupat Holim's attempt to use state authority to formalize its own powers while limiting the government's show the structure of the health system that Kupat Holim favored from very early in its development. One may recall that the Histadrut committee that met in 1948 to discuss the position of the trade federation in the new state made similar proposals. In the period of the state, Kupat Holim repeatedly tried to extract the concessions from the Israeli government that it could not extract from the Mandate authorities.

Restructuring Efforts

In the first two decades of statehood, three separate government committees were established to consider reorganizing the health services. They all dealt with the questions of whether universal health insurance, whose desirability was taken for granted, should be voluntary or compulsory, and whether it should be controlled by the state, the sick funds, or some combination thereof. The basic issue was whether the health services would be restructured to give the core the actual powers of allocation and regulation of health care or whether the prestate structure in which these powers were effectively in the hands of Kupat Holim would be retained.

The choice debated by the committees was an either/or one: Private health care was never mentioned. It was out of the reach of much of the population and inconsistent with the prevailing social norms and values, even among the reformers who wanted Kupat Holim's powers trimmed. Nor was pluralism of the voluntary sick funds a genuine option. Although the three committees all referred to the sick funds in the plural rather than to Kupat Holim alone, Kupat Holim's monopolistic powers made real pluralism something of a fig leaf, neither actively promoted nor a genuine possibility (Ellenzwieg et al., 1983). The debate on restructuring became a debate on whether health services would be controlled by the monopoly of the state or the monopoly of the powerful body on the margin.

The First Kanab Committee

The Israeli government made the first formal effort to restructure the health system in November 1948, about six months after the new state was established and the War of Independence not yet over. With health still in the hands of the

Ministry of the Interior and Absorption, the initiative was taken by the new finance minister, Eliezer Kaplan, a Mapai veteran who supported Ben Gurion's view of state responsibility for health and other social services. Kaplan called together an "inter-ministerial committee for the planning of social insurance," in which health care was only one of the various categories of the social insurance to be planned.

The committee, later called the First Kanab Committee, named after its chairman Yitzhak Kanab (Kanivsky), who, along with Sorocca, was one of the leading figures in Kupat Holim (Halevi, 1979, pp. 20 –22). In this appointment, which was much like assigning the cat to guard the cream, the core put the task of structuring the health system into the hands of the body on the margin. Kanab's chairmanship constituted a blurring of the distinction between core and margin and ensured that the committee would not reach any decision that Kupat Holim could construe as even remotely detrimental to itself. Many persons were called upon to testify before the committee. Most of them contended that the responsibility for health care should be moved to the government. Most argued for compulsory national health insurance. Several urged the nationalization of the sick funds. Others supported the creation of a national health service that would replace the sick funds. Kanab, loyal to Kupat Holim, opposed compulsory national health insurance as a waste of state money and energy and argued that health insurance should remain voluntary and in the hands of the sick funds (read, Kupat Holim).

The conflict resulted in a stalemate in which neither side was strong enough to impose its wishes on the other. The report the committee submitted in February 1950 presented the pros and cons for various health insurance schemes without clearly supporting or opposing any of them. The First Kanab Committee thus made no changes whatsoever in the distribution of authority in the health system. Years later, Kanab justified its ineffectuality with the argument that obligatory health insurance was unnecessary because Kupat Holim already provided insurance to most of the population:

> There was already voluntary health insurance in Israel, and 77% of the population already enjoyed such insurance. . . . Two thirds of the population were insured by Kupat Holim of the Histadrut. This permitted putting off the imposition of obligatory health insurance, which was more complex and required greater effort than other obligatory insurance." (Manor, 1965, p. 62)

This explanation ignores the issue of structure and downplays the question of the redistribution of power.

Successive Labor party platforms and Labor government programs were as ambiguous as the First Kanab Committee's recommendations, paying lip service to compulsory health insurance, while being careful to affirm that it would be implemented by the existing sick funds (Baruch, 1973, pp. 40 –44).

The Second Kanab Committee

The creation of the Second Kanab Committee in June 1957 gave Kanab a second chance to reform the health services. Although the Ministry of Health had already been in operation for several years, this committee was convened by Minister of Labor Mordachai Namir, a Mapai veteran who later became mayor of Tel Aviv. This committee was formed to devise ways of integrating health insurance into the functions of the National Insurance Institute established in 1953. But even before the committee started discussion, it was clear that its mandate would not cut into the powers of Kupat Holim. The letter of appointment to the committee members included paragraph 52 of the government's statement of policy principles:

> The government will strive to extend the National Insurance Law to include national health insurance for the entire population; the insurance will be effected through the sick funds. . . . The autonomous administration of the insurees' organizations will be maintained within the national health insurance law.[6]

This paragraph bestowed official recognition on Kupat Holim's prestate idea of government support for both its existence and autonomy. The government would secure Kupat Holim's existence by making health insurance through the sick funds mandatory while protecting Kupat Holim's freedom to do as it pleased. The report submitted to the minister of labor in March 1959 duly recommended that: "In accordance with the government policy principles . . . health insurance be implemented by the insurees' sick funds" (Baruch, 1973, pp. 44–47; Halevi, 1979, p. 23).

This recommendation was accompanied by operational recommendations that seem to have reflected the desire to strengthen the core and that could have impinged on Kupat Holim's autonomy. These included having the state comptroller audit the sick funds' books; having the minister of labor establish a health insurance council to supervise the implementation of all health insurance legislation and to oversee the activities of the sick funds; having the minister of labor, in consultation with the minister of health, formulate standards for licensing the sick funds; having the minister of health establish a national hospitalization authority to coordinate the country's hospital services; and establishing an equalization fund to ensure equal government funding for all the sick funds (Doron, Ninio, & Fishoff, 1969, pp. 335–51).

These recommendations, however, were undermined by others, which gave Kupat Holim a determinant role in the new procedures for both regulation and allocation. The majority of the members of the Health Insurance Council to be established to supervise the sick funds were to be representatives of the sick funds, and the number of representatives per sick fund was to be determined in proportion to the number of the insurees it had. This recommendation would give Kupat Holim substantial weight in the council's regulatory activities. With regard to allocation, no decision was made on whether the government or the sick funds would collect the health insurance fees, effectively leaving collection in the hands of the sick funds. Furthermore, the report recommended the obligatory participation of both employers and the Ministry of Finance in funding health care (Doron, Ninio, & Fishoff, 1969). This mirrored the funding pattern Kupat Holim had proposed to the Mandate government and would have secured for it two firm and obligatory sources of finance.

The recommendations generated a great deal of public debate as well as anxiety in the other sick funds and strong objections by the opposition parties and Israel's Medical Association (Halevi, 1979, pp. 24–31). Nonetheless, the report had little practical impact (Baruch, 1973, p. 46). The Ministry of Health established a health insurance council and a national hospitalization authority, but neither of these bodies had any clout.

The Hushi Committee

In January 1967 yet another committee was established to formulate recommendations on national health insurance: the Hushi Committee, named after its chairman, Aba Hushi, mayor of Haifa and a powerful figure in the Labor machine. In this committee, the Ministry of Health played a role that it had not played in the two Kanab committees. Along with the Ministry of Labor, it chose the Hushi Committee members (Baruch, 1973, p. 47).

Nonetheless, like the two Kanab committees before it, the Hushi Committee was also inherently biased in favor of Kupat Holim. The guidelines under which it worked were much the same as those of the Second Kanab Committee and equally protective of Kupat Holim's vested interests. The Hushi Committee's letter of appointment stated: "Health insurance will be implemented by the sick funds" (Doron, Ninio, & Fishoff, 1969, p. 412). The committee members were charged with making practical recommendations as to how the sick funds would do this. The committee's report was submitted in January 1968.

Like those of the Second Kanab Committee, the Hushi Committee recommendations were careful not to cross any of Kupat Holim's red lines. National health insurance was to be made law, but the law would be implemented by the existing sick funds, meaning that Kupat Holim and the other sick funds would remain autonomous bodies administering and providing the bulk of the country's health services. The insurance premiums would be collected the same way as they had been until then, which meant that the Histadrut would continue to garner the overriding proportion of the moneys, and that persons who were not members of a sick fund would have to join one individually and employees through their trade unions (Doron, Ninio, & Fishoff, 1969, p. 410). The last twist, that wage earners would be enrolled in the sick fund chosen by their labor union, was a patent way of swelling the rolls of Kupat Holim. For it meant that the body that would actually choose the sick fund was the Histadrut, the umbrella organization for all Israel's trade unions. According to Nissim Baruch, a highly respected and knowledgeable Israeli bureaucrat, the recommendations regarding insurance collection and the choice of sick fund were not necessitated by the government's guidelines but "were meant to ensure the approval of the Histadrut . . ." (Baruch, 1973, p. 52).

Reservations were appended to both the Second Kanab Committee's and the Hushi Committee's reports by committee members who objected to the perpetuation of the inequalities among the health funds and the advantages given to Kupat Holim. The reservations in both cases were signed by just under half the committee members. In both cases these were the professional bureaucrats, including the director general of the Ministry of Health, representatives of the Israeli Medical Association, and representatives of the political opposition to Mapai, that is, roughly the same elements who had opposed Kupat Holim's monopoly of health care in the transition to statehood. Both sets of objections called for roughly the same meaningful restructuring: namely, that health insurance be taken out of the hands of Kupat Holim and the Histadrut and administered by the apolitical National Insurance Institute in coordination with the Ministry of Health. The Hushi Committee's counterproposals were more forceful and more detailed; they specifically stated that the insurance premiums should be collected and allocated by the state and that everyone should have freedom of choice in which sick fund to join (Baruch, 1973, pp. 50 –51). But their essence was the same.

The objections were duly noted but not acted on. Mapai firmly held the line on any real restructuring. With all their internal contradictions, the recommendations of all the committees perpetuated Kupat Holim's preferential position, enlisted the powers of the state to bestow formal legitimization on the political-organizational link between Kupat Holim and the Histadrut and on the Histadrut's control of Kupat Holim dues, and reaffirmed the red lines that Kupat Holim and the Histadrut had drawn in the 1930s.

In the first 20 years of statehood the Ministry of Health had not been able to wrest for itself the power to control Kupat Holim, and the failure to restructure the health system left Kupat Holim in charge.

And Kupat Holim Grew

The outcome of the exchanges in which Mapai used the state's money and authority to regulate and legislate for the benefit of Kupat Holim was the realization of Sorocca's vision of a health fund that had grown too big to be thrown out with the bath water. The early 1950s saw the realization of Kupat Holim's pre-state vision of a tripartite network of funding coming from government support, employer participation, and membership dues; the entrenchment of its monopoly; and the proliferation of its assets. Between 1948 and 1955, the years of the greatest immigration, 87% of the new immigrants joined Kupat Holim, bringing its growth rate to around 150% of that of the Jewish population in the country. Kupat Holim membership increased by about 320%, from 304,000 to 1,100,000 persons, whereas the Jewish population grew by 210%. In the same years, its outpatient clinics increased from 370 in 1948 to 885, a growth of 240%; its hospital beds increased by almost 290%, from 753 to 2,140; its convalescent beds from 557 to approximately 1,000, or 280%. Its manpower grew by approximately 399%, from some 2,600 administrative and medical employees to 7,800 (Zalmanovitch, 1981, pp. 65, 71).

The expansion continued through the 1960s. By 1969 Kupat Holim had around two million members, and its health expenditures amounted to IL 350 million, compared to the Ministry of Health's IL 170 million (Zalmanovitch, 1981, p. 86). In the 1950s Kupat Holim had opened up one hospital, Kaplan in Revhovot (1953). In the 1960s, when no new government hospitals were constructed, it built the Sorocca Hospital in Beer Sheba (1960), Meir Hospital in Kfar Saba (1962), Carmel Hospital in Haifa (1967), and Yosephtal Hospital in Eilat (1968); (Kupat Holim, *Managerial Report to the 9th Convention*, 1974).

CHAPTER 5

The Informal Preventive Veto

In the first two decades of statehood, Kupat Holim acquired an informal preventive veto in the formation stage of the policy-making process as evidenced in the employment of the tools of policy. The government's health care allocation not only favored Kupat Holim over the other sick funds but also virtually neutralized the Ministry of Health's ability to use allocation as a tool of policy. The allocation formula through which Kupat Holim received direct budget support and special supplements both mirrored Kupat Holim's needs and cut any link between funding and compliance with government policies. The single tax permitted the Histadrut to set, collect, and apportion health insurance fees without regard for government guidelines, while the Mapai-led government used state funds to pick up the shortfall in Kupat Holim's budget. The Mapai-controlled Ministry of Labor used its powers of secondary regulation to compel increasing numbers of employers to participate in their employees' health insurance, most of which went to Kupat Holim.

Of all these measures, funding through administrative routine was probably the most significant. Administrative routine is generally justified as a way of saving government time and energy, freeing the government from dealing with onerous and conflictual matters, and making it easy to dismiss rival claimants on the grounds of using a rational and objective tool (Sharkansky, 1970, pp. 3–19). These were spurious advantages in comparison to what the government lost in the process. The use of administrative routine guaranteed Kupat Holim a high level of government subsidies, which secured its place at the top of the Israeli health system. It impeded government supervision and control over the resources it allocated to the health system as a whole and to Kupat Holim in particular. It undermined the government's ability to use allocation as a means for enforcing compliance with its policies. Moreover, it augmented rather than reduced the pressures on the government because the other sick funds strongly objected to the use of a formula, which reflected the needs and nature of Kupat

Holim. One of them even brought the matter to court (*State Comptroller Report,* 1979, pp. 318 –19). Finally, in contrast to what is generally expected, it increased expenditures, because it guaranteed Kupat Holim a steady source of government funding without the need either to raise its own revenues or to keep a lid on or justify its expenditures. Because expenditures were calculated into the formula, every time Kupat Holim increased its spending, the government was forced into increasing its aid.[1]

The Ministry of Health made little effort to regulate the health system, to control the activities of Kupat Holim, or to create firm planning or enforcement structures to enable it to do these things. At the same time, the Jewish Agency and government passed discriminatory regulations, which helped Kupat Holim to enroll the better portion of the new immigrants and brought about great upsurge in its membership.

Nor were any serious efforts made to reform the health system. The various committees that were established with the declared aim of restructuring the system all respected the red lines that Kupat Holim and the Histadrut had drawn up in the prestate days: public medicine provided by voluntary sick funds, the linkage of Kupat Holim and Histadrut membership, and the single tax and autonomous decision making that this permitted. Moreover, they all proposed mechanisms for formalizing Kupat Holim's equality of status with the government in the making of health policy.

In short, all three tools of policy were used in a way that promoted Kupat Holim's growth and preserved its autonomy. Through all three the Mapai-led government released Kupat Holim from core control, effectively enabling it to exercise a preventive veto in the formulation of health policy. The veto was informal in that it was granted not by any positive act or formal decision, but passively through the non-act on the part of the Mapai party machine of keeping the Ministry of Health weak, underdeveloped, and financially dependent on Kupat Holim, and through not regulating, not restructuring, and not using allocation as a means of obtaining compliance with core government policy.

In granting the preventive veto, Labor surrendered the core's right to formulate health policy on its own, without Kupat Holim. Why did it do so? And what made it possible?

Historically, the first answer that comes to mind is Israel's prestate legacy. Over the years of the British Mandate, Kupat Holim had garnered for itself a range of physical resources, organizational capacities, political and trade federation connections, and public credit and prestige. It had become both the country's chief health care provider and its chief health policy maker. Its prestate development thus gave it a historical claim to exercise a key role in the making of health policy and the tangible and intangible resources to support its claim.

The prestate period also left a legacy of blurred boundaries between party and government (Sharkansky, 1979). The political parties expanded their activities at the expense of the government and became accustomed to allocating resources through party channels (Horowitz & Lissak, 1978, pp. 15, 186). The prestate period left open the question of whether government-funded public services should be delivered through the party or through the state.

Kupat Holim's informal preventive veto in the first three decades of statehood is unlikely to have occurred without this prestate legacy. Yet in and of itself this legacy was not determinant. Other prestate bodies, including Histadrut bodies, and the functions they performed were nationalized by Israel's new government. If the prestate heritage were the decisive factor, the sick funds might well have been nationalized along with the various party labor exchanges, defense forces, and educational systems.

The main reason that Kupat Holim was permitted to remain a powerful body on the margin and taken into the health policy formation process lies in its utility to the Mapai–Histadrut subsystem that ruled the new state. Through the mechanisms of dual membership and single dues established in the prestate period, Kupat Holim maintained the ranks of the Histadrut and enabled the latter to provide the party with an organized community of potential voters and funds for its electoral propaganda and political socialization of the population. The physical and organizational resources that Kupat Holim had amassed in the prestate period were important to these ends rather than simply as sources of potential pressure, which they were too; so were the credit, prestige, and popularity it had garnered and continued to cultivate.

Equally important, the circumstances of the young state, weak, beleaguered, short on resources, and occupied with the exigencies of nation building, defense, and immigrant absorption, made divesting itself of responsibility for health policy and relegating it to Kupat Holim convenient and acceptable for the government. Mapai's ideological commitment to public health and Kupat Holim's ability to provide it also contributed to the subsystem's readiness to impoverish the core to allow Kupat Holim to exercise a veto in health policy.

Utility, however, was not enough. Mapai also had to have the ability to do what it did. Its ability stemmed from two main sources. One is that for the first 28 years of statehood, Mapai was a cohesive, dominant party. A dominant party is one that rules unchallenged for a long time during which it integrates itself into and comes to control many aspects of the country's economic, social, and political life. In addition, it provides the major symbols and sets the prevailing ideological tone of the country so that its actions come to be considered right and legitimate. By definition, this control blurs the distinction between party, state, and society (Arian, 1985, pp. 95–100; Arian & Barnes, 1974, pp. 592–614; 132; Duverger, 1963, p. 308). Mapai's long dominance gave its party machine access to the resources of the state and the ability to use them as it saw fit. Mapai considered itself the state, identified its interests with those of the state, and acted as though whatever it did was in the interests of the state and its citizens (Medding, 1972). Moreover, as a dominant party, Mapai systematically excluded the opposition from positions of control and the symbols of legitimacy (Arian, 1998, p. 143). There was thus no effective opposition to its allocating funds, privileges, and powers to Kupat Holim in order to serve its own interests or to transferring to Kupat Holim those policy-making powers in which it had no particular interests of its own.

The other source of its ability to allow Kupat Holim a preventive veto was the absence in the young state of a developed administrative structure, a professional corps of public servants, norms of good government, and restraining judicial structures. It is doubtful that Mapai and Kupat Holim would have been able to appropriate the tools of policy making as fully as they did had the Ministry of Health been a preexistent ministry with a good size professional staff and functioning operating structures; had the Ministry of Finance and the Ministry of Labor and Welfare not been politicized bodies under Mapai control; had there been an active state comptroller and supreme court; and had there been norms of good government in place—in short had Israel been a mature state with strong, nonpoliticized institutions.

Thus far, this account of Kupat Holim's informal preventive veto has focused on the historical and environmental factors that enabled it. But no account would be complete without looking at Kupat Holim's leadership and behavior. Although Mapai gave or permitted Kupat Holim's veto, Kupat Holim also fought for control of health policy. Kupat Holim's administrative head, Moshe Sorocca, resisted government authority over the Sick Fund from the very first, in the midst of the bloody War of Independence in the transition to statehood, and then set the organization on a program of expansion explicitly aimed at making the Sick Fund too large and too powerful for the government to subordinate. Kupat Holim's voluntarism in the early years of the state, its provision of health care in the immigrant transit camps, and its readiness to set up ambulatory clinics in poor, sparsely populated and distant parts of the country were driven by more than ideology and public spiritedness. They were calculated measures taken to keep ahead of its rivals, whether the other sick funds or the Ministry of Health, and to make the government ever more dependent on it. Not all organization leaders and not all organizations exhibit such a strong drive to control policy. In Kupat Holim's acquisition of its veto over health policy we see the convergence of the historical realities of the new state and the ambitions of its powerful leader.

Part II

THE FORMAL PREVENTIVE VETO

CHAPTER 6

Accommodation Under Labor: Vision of Supervised Autonomy

By the end of the 1960s Kupat Holim was a well-entrenched organization with a large membership, a huge sprawling infrastructure, and a complex mutual interdependence with the ruling Mapai party, which employed the tools of policy making to ensure Kupat Holim a steady steam of government funding, autonomous operation, and protection from nationalization. Nonetheless, winds of change were blowing.

Cracks were beginning to appear in Mapai's long dominance. In 1965 Ben Gurion, aging but still venerated, broke away and formed the Rafi Party along with Shimon Peres, Moshe Dayan, and other bright young lights who saw no place for themselves in the hierarchical Mapai leadership. The Rafi platform featured the need to improve the quality of government and supported the passage of a national health law to remove the politics from health care. In the 1965 election Rafi won ten Knesset seats (Medding, 1990, p. 239). Although most of the Rafi members soon returned to the Labor fold, and abandoned their vision of good government and health reform, the splitting of ranks weakened Mapai's hold on Israel's voters. To garner votes in 1965, Mapai formed an amalgam with Achdut HaAvoda; and in 1968 it formed the Labor Alignment along with Achdut HaAvoda, the remainders of Rafi, and Mapam, which had previously been a minor coalition partner (Arian, 1985, p. 51).

The dominance of Mapai was also challenged from without. Up through the mid-1960s, Mapai had no effective opposition. Menachem Begin's Herut (Liberty) Party regularly won a small number of Knesset seats, but not enough to pose a challenge. Moreover, it was systematically delegitimized. Herut was political successor to the Irgun, the prestate underground movement that Begin formed. In contrast to the Mapai-led Haganah, the Irgun was ready to use violent means to pressure the British to leave. After statehood, the Labor leadership presented Herut as a fascist party that threatened Israel's young democracy. With its violent roots, it was evidently perceived as such by a good portion of the population. Begin had the ability to arouse strong feelings on sensitive issues related to Jewish honor, but not much clout. Ben Gurion even refused to call him by name, referring to him as the man sitting next to Knesset member Bader (Arian, 1985, pp. 2, 72, 79 –84; Medding, 1990, pp. 61–70, 84–85).

This changed in 1967 when Arab armies amassed troops along Israel's borders in preparation for war, and a National Unity Government was formed to bring the nation together in face of the threat. This government, for the first time in Israel's history, included Begin, now head of the Gahal block (Herut and Liberal parties) as a minister without portfolio. His participation in Eshkol's government legitimized him as a respectable, and ultimately alternative, leader (Arian, 1985, p. 77; Shapiro, 1989).

During roughly the same years, Israel experienced major changes its physical exigencies and initial changes in the priorities and values that stemmed from them. By the mid-1960s, immigrants were no longer coming in overwhelming waves and a basic infrastructure was in place. The stupendous Israeli victory in the 1967 Six-Day War changed Israel from a garrison society to a more secure, self-confident society. Following the war Israel saw a burst of economic activity and a shift in government focus from securing the existence of the state to improving the quality of life (Aronoff, 1989; Eisenstadt, 1985; Horowitz & Lissak, 1989; Mahler 1990; Shimshoni, 1982). Under these circumstances, building health care facilities and offering services was no longer the urgent matter it had been in the 1950s; there was no longer the same justification for massive government support of Kupat Holim and the flaws in the health system became increasingly glaring and enabled those who objected to Kupat Holim's irregularities and partisan nature to get a better hearing.

Mapai itself was changing as the older generation of politicians who had brought the country from the *yishuv* through the early days of statehood aged and left the political arena. The politicians who rose in the party in the 1970s tended to be better educated and less provincial than their predecessors, they were not steeped in European socialism; they placed greater value on order and rational administration; and their outlook was closer to the that professional bureaucrats in the Ministry of Health. By the early 1970s many understood that running a partisan health services system on the Mapai model was no longer possible.

Minister of Health Shem Tov

Against this background Victor Shem Tov became minister of health in June 1970. Shem Tov, like his predecessor, was a member of Mapam. In the 1950s,

Mapam had been a relatively isolated party with a strong Marxist ideology, which had little appeal to the new immigrants who made up an increasing portion of Israel's electorate. A gradual process of moderation brought it into the Labor coalition in the mid-1950s and then into the Labor Alignment, where it had a larger voice in Labor affairs (Arian, 1985, pp. 78–79; Medding, 1990, pp. 82–84).

Shem Tov shared his party's strong socialist leanings and an ingrained partiality to the working-class and labor organizations. Prior to his appointment to this post, he had been a Mapam representative on the Histadrut Vad HaPoel—its legislature—a Knesset member and a member of the influential Knesset finance committee. As an individual, he was highly respected by his fellow Knesset members for his seriousness, commitment, and integrity. He shared much of the Histadrut ideology, valued the spirit of voluntarism with which it had been imbued, appreciated its contribution to the country, and was sympathetic to its needs.

At the same time, unlike the Mapai functionaries, he did not totally identify the country's health services with Kupat Holim. He recognized the need for reform: for reducing duplication and waste and for keeping a tighter hold on the flow of Ministry of Health funds and a closer check on Kupat Holim's building and development.

Shem Tov came into office intent on introducing a rational, system approach to Israel's health care.[1] To do this he had to strengthen the role of the Ministry of Health. Up until that time, Kupat Holim had generally bypassed the Ministry of Health. It received much of its funding directly from the Ministry of Finance, which was also the body that approved its construction. The Ministry of Health had little say in the making of its own budget or in the sums of money that went from its coffers to Kupat Holim. Nor did it know the total amount that Kupat Holim received from other government agencies. It had not initiated any of the government committees that had met to restructure the health system in the past two decades. In the new atmosphere of rationality, Shem Tov determined to change all this, to create a well-run health system in place of the fragmentation and chaos that had hitherto prevailed. As he stated, "I wanted to be minister of health, and not only minister of the Ministry of Health."[2]

The problem was how to make the change without either raising an insurmountable wall of opposition or harming the Sick Fund whose ideals and values he shared. His solution was to enlist Kupat Holim in making the changes he envisioned: to consult with it, to give it a voice in ministry policy making, to accommodate its needs, and to compromise with its demands. He explained his position in a personal interview:

> My colleagues in the Mapam Party and I acted as watchdogs for public health, in which Kupat Holim is all important. Thoughts of putting Kupat Holim in the hands of the

state are a huge mistake. The Histadrut has created health services, which are democratic and equal for all. Their standard is higher and more extensive than any state services. Hence, I welcome any cooperation between Kupat Holim and the Ministry of Health, because my success and the success of the entire health system depend on it. . . . I would go so far as to say that any minister who does not cooperate with a fund that insures 80% of the population and has a health system and tremendous experience would fail miserably at his job.[3]

It was a policy of integration designed, as Shem Tov put it, to "break barriers, make rules and carry out plans with full cooperation."[4] Inherent in his concept was the desire to empower the core without harming the margins.

Shem Tov's approach was supported by the key professional bureaucrats in the Ministry of Health, whose job was to translate his policy to workable practices and to implement it on a daily basis: The bureaucracy's attitude is expressed by the words of Shraga Haber, deputy director-general of the Ministry of Health from 1973 to 1994:

> The Ministry has come round to the realization that we had to establish a harmonious balance of give and take, in which everything is coordinated and nothing is in conflict and all the parts are subject to the whole. We have come to the conclusion that social and economic processes—not only political ones—necessitate coordination and integration to form a whole: a health services system in Israel. Our thoughts about joining and integrating [the workings of Kupat Holim and the Ministry of Health] led to instilling new concepts of system thinking into the Ministry of Health.[5]

Like Shem Tov's, Haber's understanding of integration entailed a quid pro quo in which the Ministry of Health would accord formal recognition to Kupat Holim's rights and roles in exchange for its cooperation. The ministry would relinquish its formal power as a core body to impose its will on Kupat Holim, which it never had in practice, and Kupat Holim would concede some of its treasured autonomy to the ministry. As Haber states:

> The integration required changes in every area where Kupat Holim and the Ministry had contact and, at the same time, a certain restriction of Kupat Holim's autonomy, on the one hand, and of the Ministry's powers of control, on the other. The idea was to bring Kupat Holim from absolute sovereignty over the health system to a supervised autonomy, in which Kupat Holim would have to convince the Ministry of the justice of its demands, as opposed to the previous situation, where the Ministry was completely passive and allocated unlimited resources. We thought this change could be made by persuasion, on the basis of mechanisms of mutual regulation. In fact, we conceded the power to compel and decided that the changes in the rules of the game would be made gradually by those concerned.[6]

The assumption behind this quid pro quo to achieve coordinated action was that fundamentally the Ministry of Health and Kupat Holim shared a common goal: a well-run health system. The concept of *supervised autonomy* was a contradiction in terms. But Haber, and others in the bureaucracy, were convinced that their peers in Kupat Holim shared the same vision of a rational, efficient health system and were eager to play their part:

> It is important to note that Kupat Holim was also willing to move towards integration. Many people in important positions in Kupat Holim nurtured and promoted new organizational and economic thinking rather than sticking to the ideological clichés of prestate days.[7]

Shem Tov's sympathies with Kupat Holim and his recognition of its pivotal role in the health system led him to include it in the Ministry of Health's policy-making process and to abnegate the ministry's formal powers of enforcement. His aim was to give Kupat Holim a nonpolitical way of defending its interests. The assumption was that the surrender of formal core control would foster the development of a well-administered, apolitical health care system.

In the almost seven years that the Ministry of Health pursued the goal of rationalization through integration the political climate increasingly lent credence to the view that it would work. The 1973 Yom Kippur War, which took the army and the country unprepared and resulted in a major loss of lives, sent the country into shock. The entire Mapai establishment was associated with the fiasco. Golda Meir, the last of the Mapai old guard, resigned as prime minister in 1974 amid the general feeling that she and the party had failed the nation in its hour of need.

Yitzhak Rabin, the first Israeli-born prime minister, replaced Golda Meir (Davidson, 1976; Meir, 1975). Unlike his predecessors, Rabin had neither ideological nor political ties to Kupat Holim or the Histadrut. He came to office not from the party ranks but from the Israel Defense Forces and brought with him a new political culture. His attitude toward Kupat Holim and the Histadrut was the same as toward any group with power and influence. He took them into consideration, as he had to do, and recognized that they were vital to the continuation of Labor power, but he felt no moral obligation or special affinity to them (Arian, 1985, pp. 64–65; L. Rabin, 1997; Y. Rabin, 1996). Not being a party functionary, he was sympathetic toward Shem Tov's efforts to rationalize the health system.

Shem Tov's policy, however, had an inherent contradiction. In the 1970s, the Ministry of Health was the weaker entity and Kupat Holim the stronger one. In good measure the policy of integration was chosen for precisely that reason. Shem Tov and the ministry bureaucrats clearly knew that confrontation with Kupat Holim would not bring positive results. On the other hand, one could hardly expect that a stronger body would assist the weaker one to augment its power.

In the last analysis, all that Shem Tov's policy of integration would do was to anchor in formal government policy the informal arrangements whereby the instruments of policy were used for the benefit of the Sick Fund.

CHAPTER 7

Expropriation of the Allocation Process

In the area of allocation Shem Tov set out to endow the Ministry of Health with an institutional structure, which would enable it to play a meaningful part in the preparation of the country's health budget. When he took office, the Ministry of Finance was the real power in the health system. It controlled health allocation through both formal and informal channels. Formally it determined the amount and allocation of the Ministry of Health budget through its referents as described in the previous case. The referents generally drew up the Ministry of Health's budget with no formal input from it and paid little if any attention to its wishes.[1] The power of the referent was such that Ministry of Health personnel were wont to call him "the delegate of the conqueror."[2]

Informally, from the mid-1960s onward, if not earlier, the amount of support that was to go to the sick funds from within the Ministry of Health's budget was determined in casual meetings between the charismatic Pinchas Sapir, one of Israel's most powerful finance ministers (1965–1968, and 1969–1974), and Kupat Holim Chairman Moshe Sorocca. Sapir became Minister of Finance at the height of an illustrious career, which had won him almost unlimited personal credit and a free hand to run the ministry as he saw fit. Bypassing bureaucratic red tape, he ran the Ministry of Finance much like his other affairs, out of a little black book in which he recorded the ministry's public outlays as though they were the family budget. In the Mapai culture from which he came, Kupat Holim was family and the Ministry of Health was not. The family feeling was reinforced by his personal friendship with Sorocca (Yadlin, 1980), whose entrepreneurial bent was similar to his own and with whom he shared a long-standing disdain for the Ministry of Health, which Sorocca saw as a competitor and he as extraneous. The outcome was that Kupat Holim had more of a say in the composition of the Ministry of Health's budget than it itself did.

This state of affairs was the product not only of the Ministry of Health's lack of political clout, but also of its institutional underdevelopment. After more than 20 years in existence, it still lacked the professional manpower and internal structures to present the Ministry of Finance with an itemized statement of its needs and priorities, let alone to fight for them.

Kupat Holim, in contrast, had both the autonomy and institutional mechanisms to make its own budget. Unlike the Ministry of Health, it had no referent to monitor it, and it did not require Knesset approval for its expenditures. Not even the state comptroller audited its books until after the 1977 Likud victory, even though such auditing is considered proper for bodies that receive government subsidies. There was simply no law that would have made an audit possible (Halevi, 1979).

Moreover, unlike the Ministry of Health, Kupat Holim had a large pool of professional manpower and the internal structures to determine its own budget needs and expenditures as it saw fit. It had its own treasurer, who played the major role in the construction of its budget (*Kupat Holim Regulations*, 1983, p. 60; Kupat Holim Managerial Report to the 10th Convention, 1979, p. 3). Its Executive Committee prepared its annual and development budgets, negotiated government subsidies and bank loans, set service fees, and handled its real estate transactions and dealings with contractors. Its legislature, which met several times a year, discussed and approved both its regular annual budget and its development budget, and elected a comptroller to oversee, among other things, how the funds were spent. These structures made Kupat Holim not only master of its own purse but also master of its entire house because they gave it the power to make and enforce its policies.

Division of Planning, Budgeting and Medical Economics

To rectify the imbalance and to give the Ministry of Health greater power in the budgeting process, Shem Tov set out to shore up the ministry's institutional structures. In 1973 he established the ministry's own Division of Planning, Budgeting and Medical Economics (*State Comptroller Report*, 1976, p. 314). According to its head, Shraga Haber, the division was "an attempt to get out of the political familiness and move towards a rational regulation of the system."[3] The division added to the ministry's meager personnel some academically trained health administration, budgeting, and economics staff and placed them in charge of such matters as preparing the Ministry of Health budget, long-range health planning, and regular liaison with the sick funds, especially Kupat Holim.

In addition, Shem Tov demanded that the Ministry of Health take part in the Ministry of Finance's decisions on allocation for the health system.[4] His timing was apt. Sapir left the Ministry of Finance a year after the Division of Planning, Budgeting and Medical Economics was established and was replaced by Yehoshua Rabinowitz, who allowed the Ministry of Health professionals a greater role. In the mid-1970s, Shem Tov's demands were met and Ministry of Health officials began to meet frequently with Ministry of Finance personnel. They were sometimes able to coordinate positions before beginning discussions with Kupat Holim on the level of its subsidies.[5]

Kupat Holim Appropriates the Powers of the Core

The Division of Planning, Budgeting and Medical Economics was established in good measure to recover from Kupat Holim and the Labor-controlled Ministry of Finance some of the allocation powers that are generally due to a core body. This did not happen. The Ministry of Health did not gain a significant role in the budgeting process and, with respect to Kupat Holim, it remained largely a pipeline for the subsidies and other payments on which the Ministry of Finance continued to make the essential decisions.

Direct Funding: Allocation by Administrative Routine

The years under Shem Tov saw the continuation of the allocation of funds through an administrative routine, which mirrored not government preferences but Kupat Holim's needs.

In the early 1970s, the allocation formula underwent yet another revision. Following steady pressure from the smaller sick funds the Ministry of Health established interministerial committees to draft a more equitable allocation formula (Halevi, 1979, p. 16). In keeping with Shem Tov's attempts to rationalize the Ministry of Health's operations and to bring them into the public realm, the committees included Knesset members, making it the first time that the principles for calculating the formula became a matter of public knowledge and justification. This was the first version where the public was informed of the weight of each item in the allocation.

On the surface, the new code was indeed somewhat more equitable than the old ones. Table 7.1 shows that Kupat Holim's share of government support declined slightly from the 1950s and 1960s while the share of the smaller sick funds rose slightly.

Nonetheless, we can also see that Kupat Holim continued to receive not only the lion's share of government funding, but a higher percentage than the number

Table 7.1. Allocation Formula for Government Support (Percentage to Each Sick Fund)[6]

Sick Fund	The Code 1954–1962	The Code 1963–1970	The Code 1970–1977
Kupat Holim	92.55	91.00	85.60
National	4.88	5.60	7.00
Maccabi	0.72	1.00	5.10
Popular } United	1.26	1.26	2.30*
Central } United	0.59	1.14	

*In 1974, the Popular Sick Fund and the Central Sick Fund combined to create the United Sick Fund.

of its membership warranted. The new criteria in the formula worked to Kupat Holim's advantage. The following four criteria were employed in the stated proportions:

1. Progressivity of levies, or the degree to which each fund's levies were based on earnings: 35%
2. Number of persons insured: 30%
3. Expenditures on medical care, which actually covered all the fund's expenditures, including its fixed investments: 25%
4. The public character of the fund, which referred to the extent of the fund's services in Israel's development towns and other financially distressed communities and the degree to which the fund's insurees were represented in its elected institutions: 10%. (*State Comptroller Report,* 1979, p. 318)

The allocations for each sick fund were based on the degree to which it met each of these criteria. How the degree was determined is wrapped in mystery. But the bias can be seen. With the exception of the first criteria, the progressivity of levies, the criteria were not substantially different from those set in the 1950s and 1960s. Two of the criteria, the number of people insured and the expenditures on medical care, are rational and seem fair enough. However, by rewarding Kupat Holim for its size and expenditures, they perpetuated its edge over the other sick funds.

The progressivity of dues and the public character of the fund criteria suggest favoritism. Kupat Holim succeeded in convincing the Ministry of Health that its fee scale was more progressive than that of the other funds, although this was not actually the case. The monthly Kupat Holim–Histadrut dues, set by the Histadrut's Legislature (Histadrut, Central Tax Bureau, 1982, p. 9) were progressive up to a certain income level, but then became regressive because to draw and keep members from the higher income brackets, the Legislature set their dues at a lower proportion of their incomes than those of low-income members.

The fourth criterion concerning public character consists of two parts. One, the provision of services in development towns and financially distressed communities, has a basis in rationality. Income from membership fees in such areas is generally low, while expenditures are relatively high due to their distance from the center of the country and the fact that the general health of the residents in such areas is often poorer than that of the population in more affluent areas. However, the second part of this criterion, the internal "democracy" of the fund, is biased in favor of Kupat Holim, which successfully argued that its internal organization was more "democratic" than that of the other funds. Whether this was really so is questionable. In any case, it is irrelevant from both an economic and a health care point of view.

In a personal interview Oren Tokatley, the Ministry of Finance referent during these years, admitted, "in all of its versions, the subsidies key was as if tailored to Kupat Holim's measure."[7] The truth of this statement can be seen by comparing the percentage of government subsidies in the various sick funds' total revenues, illutrated in Table 7.2, which shows that government subsidies constituted a considerably higher percentage of Kupat Holim's revenues than of those of the United and Maccabi sick funds. The fact that government subsidies comprised an even greater portion of the Leumit Sick Fund's revenues during much of this period does not contradict the point. For one thing, high subsidies were set for Leumit in a concerted effort to save it from collapse.[9] More to the point, the sheer size of Kupat Holim's budget means that every percentage point of government funding represented a far larger sum than for any of the other sick funds.

In addition to subsidies, Kupat Holim enjoyed two other types of direct government support. One was compensation that it received along with the other sick funds to compensate for inflation. This too was determined by the same administrative routine except that the basis for the calculation was not the new 1970 formula, but the 1954 formula, where Kupat Holim's share was 92.55% (*State Comptroller Report*, 1969, pp. 177–79). The second type of support consisted of special allocations for sick funds that had their own hospitalization facilities (Ministry of Health, *Budget Proposal for 1974*, p. 123). In practice, this meant Kupat Holim, the only sick fund that operated independent hospitals (Baruch, 1973, pp. 28–30). The number of beds in each hospital and the size of its deficit determined the support it received (*State Comptroller Report*, 1969, pp. 173–74).

Table 7.2. Percentage of Government Subsidies in the Sick Funds' Total Revenues: 1970–1977[8]

Sick Fund	1970	1971	1972	1973	1974	1975	1976	1977
Kupat Holim	15.10	18.65	19.00	22.30	28.00	29.00	28.00	31.00
Leumit		9.20	22.50	25.00	19.00	22.00	35.00	33.00
Maccabi		0.60	0.50	4.70	3.30	5.00	7.870	12.00
United						9.60	11.00	15.70

Indirect Funding: The Price of a Government Hospital Bed

As may be recalled, Kupat Holim had enough hospital beds to meet the needs of only about one half of its members, whereas the other sick funds had no hospital facilities of their own at all. In 1974 the Ministry of Health's budget book articulated what had been informal government policy until that time: "Since the hospitalization facilities available to the sick funds do not meet all the hospital needs of their members, the sick funds make use of government hospitals to meet these needs. Accordingly, the sick funds benefit from a reduced hospitalization rate" (Ministry of Health, *Budget Proposal for 1974*, p. 123). As Table 7.3 shows, during the first four years of Shem Tov's term in office, the percentage that the sick funds paid of the real cost of the beds was cut almost in half: from a high of 30% in 1966–1967 to a low of 16% in 1972–1974 (*State Comptroller Report*, 1975, p. 244). Put somewhat differently, these figures mean that through its reduced rates, the government paid more than 80% of the hospitalization costs of one half of Kupat Holim's insured members. Not surprisingly, the Ministry of Health incurred a large deficit in the daily maintenance of its hospitals. According to the 1974 State Comptroller's report, government hospitals covered only 26% of their expenses from the sale of their beds (*State Comptroller Report*, 1969, p. 177).

In 1975 the Ministry of Health, pressured by the Ministry of Finance's Budget Division, updated its prices and set the sick funds' rate at 33% of the basic cost (*State Comptroller Report*, 1977, p. 277). Then in April 1976, it eliminated the hospitalization subsidy altogether (Ministry of Health, *Budget Proposal for 1976*, 1975, pp. 56, 79; Ministry of Finance, *State of Israel Budget Principles for 1976*, p. 54). However, lest any harm befall the sick funds, it provided compensation for the increase—set on the basis of the allocation formula (*State Comptroller Report*, 1979, p. 319).

Table 7.3. Costs and Prices* of Beds in Government Hospitals: 1966–1977[10]

Fiscal Year	Real Cost (IL)	Price for Sick Funds (IL)	% of Real Cost
1966	50	15	30
1967	50	15	30
1968	55	15	27
1969	55	15	27
1970	55	15	27
1971	79	15	19
1972	91	15	16
1973	126	30	16
1974	162	26	16
1975	270	90	33
1976	350	350	100
1977	500	500	100

*In Israeli Lirot.

Special Supports

The special supports that Kupat Holim received in the 1950s and 1960s continued. According to the Israeli daily newspaper, *Ha'aretz,* the "huge benefits" given to Kupat Holim between 1972 and 1975 included subsidized loans and outright grants, as well as "exchange rate insurance" to cover the wide-ranging fluctuations in the value of the country's currency, at a nominal premium, and millions of marks and dollars.[11] Asher Yadlin, managing director of Kupat Holim from 1972 to 1976, wrote in his memoirs that Finance Minister Sapir had agreed to convert a linked loan of more than IL100, 000, 000 (equivalent to approximately $65 million at that time) to Kupat Holim to a 17-year unlinked loan to be repaid at 9% interest beginning in the eighth year, until which the interest was to be paid without the capital (Bondi, 1981, pp. 213, 219; Yadlin, 1980, p. 178). Because Yadlin does not tell when the loan was made, calculating the exact loss to the Ministry of Finance is impossible. What must be understood, however, is that in Israel virtually every loan that was made after the mid-1970s was linked to some index of the real currency value to protect the lender from the ravages of the country's extremely high inflation. One can safely say that under the new terms only a fraction of the real value of the loan was ever repaid.

The Single Tax

The years 1970 through 1977 saw the continuation of the single tax system, whereby the dues for the sick fund and the trade federation were collected in the same levy and the apportionment determined independently by the Histadrut. Moreover, the government continued to fund the shortfall between Kupat Holim's expenditures and the funds it received from the single tax and other sources. Neither the minister of health nor the minister of finance could see a way of interfering in the affairs of a voluntary organization.[12] Moreover, funds from the single tax were still going to Labor political activities.

The government foot the bill without asking for an account of either Kupat Holim's income or the fees collected by the Histadrut. Among other things, this enabled the Histadrut to "milk" Kupat Holim. During the period under discussion, every year it siphoned off approximately 40% of the single tax for its organizational needs and then deducted 10% from the 60% allotted to Kupat Holim as a collection fee. The process left Kupat Holim with only 54% of the original single tax. Moreover, because health care costs rose dramatically in the 1970s, the amount transferred to Kupat Holim by the Histadrut came to smaller and smaller proportions of Kupat Holim's overall budget—from almost 31% in 1970 to just over 17% in 1977. Figures based on data provided by the Histadrut's Central Tax Bureau are presented in Table 7.4.

Between 1970 and 1977, the part of the single tax in Kupat Holim's income

Table 7.4. Central Tax Bureau Expenditures and Fees: 1970–1977[13]

Fiscal Year	Percentage of Single Tax Transferred to Kupat Holim	Percentage of SingleTax Transferred to Histadrut	Percentage of Single Tax Transferred in Kupat Holim Income	Number of Employees in Tax Office	Collection Fees
1970	60.53	39.47	30.80	1138	9.90%
1971	60.47	39.53	31.50	1150	9.90%
1972	60.30	39.70	25.60	1186	9.90%
1973	60.18	39.82	24.40	1188	9.90%
1974	60.01	39.99	20.00	1185	9.71%
1975	59.72	40.28	20.00	1057	9.04%
1976	59.84	40.16	21.00	945	8.57%
1977	58.47	41.53	17.00	850	9.10%

fell by 45%. To offset some of this decline, the Histadrut attempted to cut its Central Tax Bureau's manpower and other expenditures, but this permitted only a small reduction in its collection fees. The tax partner key itself was evidently not changed, as is clear from the fact that the amount transferred to Kupat Holim remained stable.

Kupat Holim officials complained bitterly about the exploitation. Asher Yadlin, director general of Kupat Holim at the time, complained that, "The Histadrut has been milking Kupat Holim for all it's worth in order to finance its activities," and raged, "This is fraud. The member thinks he's paying Kupat Holim, but 40% goes to the executive committee and the exorbitant collection fees charged by the Tax Bureau eat away at anything good in their path too." Sorocca, he told, "would fly off the handle after every meeting of the Central Committee. He would run to my office and say angrily: 'parasites,' 'good-for-nothings,' 'a bureaucracy that eats away at health and members' services'" (Yadlin, 1980, p. 120).

The protests had little effect. As Table 7.5 shows, the proportion that membership dues constituted in Kupat Holim's revenues declined steadily during these years. Moreover, membership dues consistently constituted a smaller proportion of Kupat Holim revenues than of those of any of the other sick funds.

The Histadrut kept total control over fee collection policy and apportionment, which enabled it to maintain its own organizational and functional autonomy.

Table 7.5. Percentage of Membership Dues in the Sick Funds' Incomes: 1970–1977[14]

Sick Fund	1970	1971	1972	1973	1974	1975	1976	1977
Kupat Holim	30.80	31.50	25.60	24.40	20.00	20.00	21.00	17.00
Leumit		45.50	34.70	29.40	32.20	30.10	25.20	24.50
Maccabi		60.20	60.10	55.80	47.60	49.00	42.57	36.70
United						46.50	40.50	40.30

The government interfered neither with the level of the membership dues nor with the amount transferred to Histadrut activities. It simply continued to pay the ever-growing bill: Calculations based on Kupat Holim sources show that between 1970 and 1977, government funding rose from 15.5% of Kupat Holim's total revenues to 31%.[15]

The Employer-Participation Tax

As we saw in the previous case, in the first two decades of statehood, the employer participation tax was imposed on increasing numbers of employers through bureaucratic fiat that consistently widened the compass of the Histadrut's collective labor agreements. Nonetheless, the Histadrut continued to clamor for primary legislation to compel all employers to pay (Becker, 1982, p. 166).

The desired bill was introduced by Mapai strongman Minister of Labor Joseph Almogi in the fall of 1972. It aroused vehement objections from the opposition parties on both the right and left, who saw it as an attempt to use government legislation to benefit Kupat Holim. The widely voiced objection was strongly expressed by Uri Avneri of the tiny left wing Olam HaZeh Party:

> State law is being used to extort money from citizens for the sake of the sick funds. . . . Rather than being the major decision makers in the field of health services, as every enlightened person in Israel wants, the State and the Knesset have become secondary factors, while the management of Kupat Holim does as it pleases and uses the state for its own purposes" (*Knesset Minutes,* 1972, Vol. 65, pp. 687–88).

The concern was that the enforcement of the employer participation tax through parliamentary legislation would reverse the proper order of authority between the government and the sick funds by suborning government powers to their interests. A related objection was that the bill did not require the sick funds to give the state any account of their expenditures. A Liberal Party MP tried, unsuccessfully, to insist on a quid pro quo whereby the state would be permitted to supervise the sick funds' expenditures in exchange for imposing the tax (*Knesset Minutes,* 1972, Vol. 65, p. 684). Almogi called the objections "cheap demagogy" and argued that the help was not being given to the sick funds but to the citizens of the country, as is a government's duty.[16]

The bill became law on March 22, 1973. The law required every employer to pay an employer participation tax in addition to the employees' wages and other social benefits, and stipulated the penalties for violation. It also made several other important stipulations.

One was that the tax be collected by the National Insurance Institute, which already collected Israeli's social security. The Histadrut had initially been concerned that the collection of the tax by the National Insurance Institute rather than itself would deprive it of control over the money. But leaving the collection

Table 7.6. Distribution of Employer Participation Tax (Based on the 1974 Census)[18]

Sick Fund	Percentage of Wages	Percentage of Membership	Weighted Average
Kupat Holim	85.92	87.43	86.22
Leumit	3.25	3.17	3.23
Maccabi	8.27	7.21	8.06
United	2.56	2.19	2.49
Total	100.00	100.00	100.00

to the Histadrut was too much even for the Labor alliance. In any case it soon became clear that collecting the tax through the government bureaucracy was highly effective and much to Kupat Holim's benefit.[17]

The other stipulation was that the level of the tax and its allocation among the sick funds would be determined by the minister of labor and welfare (Laws of the State of Israel, *Employer Participation Tax, 1973*, p. 3686). In other words, the law ensured that the tax would be set and disbursed by a minister who was traditionally in the Mapai–Histadrut–Kupat Holim camp. Not surprisingly, the level of the tax rose progressively, from 2.7% of the employee's gross wage in 1973 to 3.4% in 1976 (Baruch, 1973, pp. 34–36).

The allotment of this tax among the sick funds also favored Kupat Holim. At the beginning, the tax was distributed in accord with the total wages of each fund's membership. In 1974 a census of sick fund membership was taken, the wages or income of all the insured in each fund were totaled, and each fund received a proportionate share of the tax. This method of distribution, however, favored the smaller sick funds, whose membership tended to be wealthier than Kupat Holim's. As a result, Kupat Holim pushed for a distribution based on the number of members, arguing that its large membership required it to provide more services than the other sick funds and that this factor, not only income, should be included in the calculations, especially because its members generally earned less than members of the other funds. The final distribution was the weighted average of income and membership. As Table 7.6 shows, this increased Kupat Holim's share of the tax.

The new law benefited Kupat Holim greatly, giving it, along with the other

Table 7.7. Income From Employer Participation Tax: 1970–1977 (Percentage of Revenues Budget)[19]

Sick Fund	1970	1971	1972	1973	1974	1975	1976	1977
Kupat Holim	28.70	29.50	28.90	30.50	34.00	39.00	45.00	41.00
Leumit		17.00	22.00	24.00	29.00	23.00	19.00	25.00
Maccabi		27.40	28.60	32.70	37.80	38.00	44.07	43.90
United						23.10	28.50	32.00

sick funds, a stable source of revenue, which was legislated and collected by the state, but not subject to state supervision after its transfer. By the end of Labor's term of office, the employer participation tax constituted more than 40% of Kupat Holim's revenues and a hefty proportion of the revenues of the other sick funds as well, as Table 7.7 demonstrates.

The proportion of the employer participation tax in the funds' revenues increased slightly to moderately in 1973 and 1974, after the National Insurance Institute took over the collection, and dramatically from 1975 onward, when the law was adjusted. Even if in certain years government participation constituted a larger part of the budgets of other sick funds than of Kupat Holim's, the difference was huge in absolute terms.

These financing arrangements were overwhelmingly favorable to Kupat Holim. Total government support for Kupat Holim is impossible to assess accurately because it was provided in such a variety of ways. However, as is shown at the end of chapter 9, there are numerous indications that during Shem Tov's term in office Kupat Holim not only continued to enjoy the lion's share of government support for health care but also that Kupat Holim's needs determined the way in which public health funds were spent.

CHAPTER 8

Regulating Through Parity in Joint Regulatory Bodies and Through Informal Agreements

In the area of regulation, Minister of Health Shem Tov's aim was to integrate the health services provided by the Ministry of Health and Kupat Holim to reduce overlap and improve the delivery of health care. On the bureaucratic level, this translated into efforts to rationalize Kupat Holim's operations and to induce it to act as part of the larger health system rather than as a totally independent body.[1] Guided by the philosophy of integration, in which Kupat Holim was seen as an equal partner in the health system,[2] the Ministry of Health sought to bring about these changes not through unilateral rules and regulations but through mutual accommodation and coordination and set out to create the joint mechanisms that were needed to do so.

Three committees serve to illustrate the mechanisms: the Supreme Hospitalization Authority, the Supreme Coordination Committee, and the Project Approval Committee. In all of these committees, Kupat Holim and the Ministry of Health were equal partners. Kupat Holim's parity meant that the power to regulate was shared equally by the government ministry and the body on the margins.

The Supreme Hospitalization Authority

The Supreme Hospitalization Authority, established in 1962, was discussed in the previous case, and its ineffectiveness amply documented. During Shem Tov's term in office, Kupat Holim acted largely on its own volition with the apparent blessing of the Ministry of Health. For example, we may take the case of what became Carmel Hospital in Haifa. The authority had originally decided that a hospital should be built in or near the town of Acco, about twelve miles north of Haifa, to meet the hospitalization needs of the population in the northwest of the country. Kupat Holim built it in Haifa, even though there were already two large government hospitals there, and one mid-size government hospital in the nearby town of Naharia. It built in Haifa for political reasons: to have a hospital of its own near the government-owned hospitals.[3] Yet it continued to receive the funds it needed for its development directly from the Ministry of Finance and the Ministry of Health without any Authority input.[4] Shem Tov justified the relocation on the grounds that it was

> the result of a long term macro point of view, which takes into account the population growth of Haifa. . . . As there were already two government owned hospitals in operation there and another hospital would be needed, it was necessary to build a Kupat Holim hospital so as to maintain the pluralism of the health system.[5]

Although Shem Tov recognized that "the Authority acts with the authority of the Ministry of Health and is the supreme agency which allows or rejects the building of hospitals,"[6] his reasoning here is suspiciously close to that of Kupat Holim and effectively undermined the authority's ability to regulate the health system.

The authority stopped meeting in June 1973 when Shem Tov shifted his efforts to pushing through the National Health Insurance Bill of 1973. In 1975 a joint Ministry of Health–Ministry of Finance committee decided to freeze construction of all new hospitals because there was no longer any way of funding them,[7] and the authority thus died a natural death.

The Supreme Coordination Committee

The Supreme Coordination Committee was, as its name states, the major body set up to coordinate the activities of the Ministry of Health and Kupat Holim. Unlike the Supreme Hospitalization Authority, this body was not an inheritance of an earlier era, but established by Shem Tov as part of his integration policy. Shem Tov referred to it as the "Yalta of the health system," a place where representatives of all the bodies involved in the health system met.[8] According to Shem Tov, the committee "examined bills, budgets and sometimes development plans with Kupat Holim." Its purpose was to discuss proposals and try to reach agreement through complete cooperation.[9]

The meetings, held with fair regularity, were attended by the minister of health and his bureaucrats, the minister of finance and senior members of his staff, and the chairman of Kupat Holim and members of its professional staff. The plan was that after the two ministers and the chairman of Kupat Holim reached agreement on policy in the plenary sessions, the director general of the Ministry of Health and the chairman of Kupat Holim would work out the steps needed to implement its decisions.[10]

In its actual operations, however, the committee was far from the Yalta that Shem Tov envisioned. To this joint forum, the Ministry of Health and Kupat Holim generally brought separate issues in keeping with their distinct interests. Rarely did they come with joint proposals.[11] The meeting minutes show that the Ministry of Health generally raised systemic issues, while Kupat Holim raised financial ones. For example, the Ministry of Health submitted proposals for a permanent arrangement for emergency hospitalization in all hospitals, the inclusion of Kupat Holim hospitals in a duty roster, and hospitalization of mentally ill Kupat Holim patients in government hospitals.[12] Kupat Holim initiated discussions on levies and fees, budgetary provisions for the maintenance of its hospitals, and rates and regulations for its purchase of services in the government hospitals.[13]

At all points Kupat Holim assiduously warded off what it regarded as Ministry of Health infringements on what had been sovereign areas until then. In 1971, for example, the Ministry of Health initiated discussions on the opening of Kupat Holim hospitals to the entire population, not just to Kupat Holim members, and on integrating the services of the ambulatory clinics with those of the hospitals to provide continuity of treatment. Kupat Holim saw these proposals as impinging on its autonomy and was also concerned that opening its hospitals to the overall public would cut into its advantage over the other sick funds, which did not have their own hospitals. It took two full years of intense negotiations and guarantees of substantial monetary compensation to cover the extra costs of hospitalizing non–Kupat Holim members before Kupat Holim finally agreed to remove the entrance restrictions to its hospitals, whose construction and operation, it must be stressed, were heavily subsidized by the public purse.[14] Although Kupat Holim did not totally thwart the Ministry of Health's efforts to systematize health care, it certainly delayed the process and extracted a high price.

A similar pattern was evident with regard to the National Health Insurance Bill that Shem Tov repeatedly brought before the forum between 1973 and 1976. The Ministry of Health, the Ministry of Finance, and Kupat Holim each appointed a representative to prepare its position, and several joint committees were established to discuss the details. There were many differences of opinion. The essential differences concerned the provisions to open Kupat Holim membership to nonmembers of the Histadrut and to replace the single tax with separate fees for Kupat Holim and trade union membership. On Histadrut orders,

Kupat Holim refused to discuss either issue in the joint forum, claiming that it did not have the authority to do so because membership and fees were the sole province of the Histadrut.[15]

Yet another illustration concerns the cancellation of the Ministry of Health subsidies for the rental of government hospital beds to the sick funds. In April 1976 the Ministry of Finance and the Ministry of Health proposed canceling the hospitalization subsidy. According to Oren Tokatley, the Ministry of Finance referent at the time, the purpose of this was to "put a realistic price on services, so that the buyers [Kupat Holim] will take into account their true economic value." As matters stood, the low hospitalization fees encouraged Kupat Holim to send patients who needed only ambulatory care to government hospitals. According to Tokatley, the patients enjoyed the better service, the clinic doctors benefited from a reduced workload, and Kupat Holim profited because the highly subsidized government hospital beds cost it less than its own ambulatory care.[16] The Ministry of Health, the loser in the arrangement, wanted to cut the subsidies. Under pressure from the Ministry of Finance, Kupat Holim agreed to the cut, but the cut backfired.[17] With the higher prices for government hospital beds, Kupat Holim created a self-regulatory regionalization plan to meet its members' hospitalization needs in its own facilities (Doron & Ron, 1978, pp. 7–20). The plan cut the number of days each patient spent in hospital and added beds to wards, thereby maximizing use of its own general hospital beds. Whereas until then about 45% of Kupat Holim patients were treated in Kupat Holim hospitals, in 1977–1978, 54% were (Ministry of Health, *Budget Proposal for 1977, Budget Proposal for 1978*).

Kupat Holim's new policy sharply reduced Ministry of Health revenues, bringing strong pressure to cut government hospital staffs and facilities and exposing it to the wrath of the hospital administrators who found themselves with a high percentage of empty beds. The outcome, as seen in the previous chapter, was that to return its patients to government hospitals, the ministry compensated for the rise in hospitalization fees by higher allocations through the formula, which came out of the ministry's own budget. In short, the Ministry of Health's efforts to regulate through the Supreme Coordination Committee backfired, costing it more than it saved.

The Supreme Coordination Committee also dealt with the crucial issue of Kupat Holim's development and the allocation of developmental funds. I will say more about this shortly, in the discussion of the Project Approval Committee. What is of interest here is the agreement reached by the members of the Supreme Coordination Committee in January 1973 on the procedures and extent of government support for Kupat Holim's development budget.[18] The agreement stipulated that one third of the project would be financed by a low-interest loan not linked to inflation; one third would consist of a grant, and the remaining third would be paid by Kupat Holim with the help of exchange rate insurance whereby the government covered the costs of inflation. In other words, most of the financing came from government coffers. In February 1975 the agreement was broadened to include new medical equipment, which the government would finance in accord with the same procedure as applied to its support for development.[19]

The Project Approval Committee

The Project Approval Committee was established by the Supreme Coordination Committee to deal with the myriad technical details involved in the building and renovation of health facilities. The committee consisted of professionals with technical expertise in areas ranging from engineering to financing.[20] It was supposed to have the last word on what and where to build and at what cost.

Up until that time, there were no orderly procedures for building and development. What to build or buy, where, how much, at what cost, and financed by whom—none of these matters was handled in a planned or systematic manner. Building initiatives came mainly from the chairman of Kupat Holim, Sorocca, who reached agreements concerning allocations for building new facilities with the Minister of Finance, Pinchas Sapir, on the telephone, or through written notes,[21] without, it seems, ever consulting with the Supreme Hospitalization Committee. According to the director of Kupat Holim's building division:

> Development was usually approved verbally or in notes. . . . In this way, Sorocca Hospital [in Beer Sheba] and Carmel Hospital [in Haifa] were built. In fact, there was no working procedure in Kupat Holim itself or in the Ministry of Health and certainly not between the two.[22]

I was shown, but not permitted to copy, one such note on file in Kupat Holim's building division. It read, "Dear Pinchas, The matter is one hospital in Beer Sheba." The answer, scribbled on the same piece of paper, was, "Approved." The approval brought with it the land and financing required for the project. No questions were asked about need or rationale.

Up until 1972 the Ministry of Health had no say in how the development funds that went to Kupat Holim were spent. The Ministry of Finance funded each of Kupat Holim's development projects separately, without the input of the Ministry of Health, without any overall plan, and without any attempt to make the provision of funds dependent on Kupat Holim's implementing its own purposes. In effect, there were no principles on the basis of which to determine how much money to transfer to Kupat Holim or for what ends. Nor were there any mechanisms to coordinate Kupat Holim's developmental activities with those of the Ministry of Health.[23]

One outcome of this state of affairs was significantly greater investment in Kupat Holim than in government facilities in the first two decades of statehood. When Shem Tov assumed office, he found a large "property gap" between the Ministry of Health and Kupat Holim. "The Ministry's institutions were housed in shacks and looked like transit camps, whereas Kupat Holim built strong concrete buildings which stood out proudly," he stated angrily.[24]

Various bureaucrats in the Ministry of Health and Kupat Holim termed the procedure by which developmental decisions were made and funds allocated a "politico-familial" one, where the kind of informality that inheres in families characterized the relationship between the government ministry and the body on the margin. In his efforts to rationalize the health system, Shem Tov set out to replace this relationship with a more structured and accountable one. In 1975 he reached an agreement with the minister of finance and the chairman of Kupat Holim whereby

> Kupat Holim's eligibility for government [financial] participation in approved projects will be determined in general discussions, and its development plans will require approval by a committee comprising the Ministry of Health, the Ministry of Finance and Kupat Holim. Its eligibility will be subject to the approval of the program, including the location of the project, its overall cost (regularly updated for inflation), and its rate of implementation. . . . Development plans will be approved on the basis of agreed upon criteria set by the Ministry of Health for the entire system.[25]

This agreement, for the first time in Israel's history, conditioned the allocation of government funds for building, expansion, and the general development of the medical system on clearly stated requirements for approval. Furthermore, it brought the Ministry of Health, which until that time had merely been the vehicle that transferred development funds, into the approval process.

The Project Approval Committee was established to implement the agreement. The idea was to create a joint steering committee that would introduce planned development of the health system based on rational considerations (such as the needs of the population) rather than on the pressures and vested interests that had governed its development in the past. Its functions included establishing standards and criteria to provide equal medical services to all parts of the country and setting priorities for undertaking new projects in view of the population's increasing health needs and the government's decreasing resources.[26]

Like the work of the Supreme Hospitalization Authority and the Supreme Coordination Committee, the work of the Project Approval Committee was also based on the principal of parity, which gave each of the members an equal say in every decision.[27] The other sick funds were represented by the Ministry of Health, whereas Kupat Holim had full rights in every decision, including those regarding the other funds.[28] According to the director of the Ministry of Health's Division of Planning, Budgeting and Medical Economics, the framework enabled

> making the rules in matters of development on the basis of an equal partnership and a good overall relationship. The parity was a trade-off meant to remove the politicking from the process, while the existence of the committee entailed the development of a rational regulatory system.[29]

The trade-off was a formal one. By providing a procedure that required Kupat Holim to justify its requests for support and to persuade the Ministry of Health and Ministry of Finance to authorize its development activities, the Project Approval Committee secured for the Ministry of Health some of the regulatory powers that were rightly its due as a government agency. But the formal parity that Kupat Holim received compensated it for the loss of the informal autonomy in development it had enjoyed until then. Moreover, it gave Kupat Holim a formal say in any building projects that the ministry might have wanted to undertake.

Despite some functional advances, Kupat Holim's status in matters relating to its development remained unchanged. In what may be considered a clever sleight of hand, Kupat Holim submitted for committee approval long-term projects, extending from five to ten years, with an overall price tag but without annual specifications of the expenditures. As a result discussions focused on principles, divorced from the current year's budget, and projects were approved without any provision for monitoring their progress or costs. On many occasions, projects were approved in handwriting by one of the committee members on the same booklet in which Kupat Holim submitted the proposal.[30]

The techniques, procedures, standards, and various tests for the evaluation of development proposals were determined only in the course of the discussions themselves. Often, especially where ambulatory care was concerned, the standards adopted were those of Kupat Holim. Moreover, until 1980, the committee did not have a computer, whereas Kupat Holim's Development and Construction Division had a computerized information network.[31] The outcome, according to the Ministry of Finance referent to the committee, was that:

> In the last few years [until 1978], Kupat Holim initiated and completed a series of projects without the Ministry's prior knowledge or approval, or informing it only afterwards. In spite of the seemingly rigid structure of the Project [Approval] Committee, Kupat Holim in fact does as it pleases. Results show that in the final analysis, everything it wanted, it got.[32]

In short, Shem Tov's attempts to regulate Kupat Holim's building and renovation met with little success. None of the joint committees established to regulate Kupat Holim was effective in doing so. The Supreme Hospitalization Committee was virtually ignored even by the Ministry of Health that established it. The Supreme Coordination Committee and the Project Approval Committee, in which Shem Tov placed his hopes, were effectively manipulated by Kupat Holim.

The result verged on chaos. State audits conducted between 1977 and 1979 for the preceding period show that the Ministry of Health's books did not provide an adequate idea of the sums transferred to Kupat Holim for building and renovation; that Kupat Holim's development expenditure was far in excess of even its own annual budgets; and that Kupat Holim did not even have a long-term development budget, which the government required to monitor the sick fund's expenditures on building and renovation (*State Comptroller Report,* 1979, pp. 147–50, 160). The outcome was that Kupat Holim enjoyed substantial government support for construction and renovation, which it used as it saw fit, without even its own governing bodies knowing the extent of its expenditure.

Regulation by Informal Means

Shem Tov made his predecessors' preference for informal regulation an integral part of his policy of integration. This policy saw voluntary compliance, attained through bargaining and mutual adjustment as the means of winning Kupat Holim's cooperation, and reserved formal legislation as a last resort, to be held over the head of Kupat Holim as a threat should it go too far afield. According to the director of the Division of Planning, Budgeting and Medical Economics during that period: "Formal regulations were available as sanctions in the event that agreed upon directives were not complied with."[33] Among the motives he cites for avoiding formal regulation was "not to force Kupat Holim into a corner of stubborn objection, with no way of backing out."[34] The assumption was that if Kupat Holim were forced into a corner through formal regulations it could not circumvent, it would put up strong resistance—and that it had the muscle to do so.

The degree to which regulations are formalized, that is, written down and accompanied by penalties generally indicates the intention of the regulating body to exert control and make policy. Here that consideration was subordinated to the desire cum need to attain Kupat Holim's cooperation and avoid conflict with it.

In one instance the Ministry of Health did make a determined effort to exercise its regulatory powers, but repeatedly came up against a brick wall. This was in the area of wages. One of the anomalies of the Israeli health system is that although it is virtually all public and supported largely by public funds, Kupat Holim personnel consistently received higher wages and better benefits than Ministry of Health personnel in analogous positions. Such disparity, which would be entirely acceptable in an open market system, was totally unacceptable to the doctors, nurses, paramedics, and others on the Ministry of Health payroll and led to repeated, costly, and disruptive work stoppages, which eventually forced the ministry to act.

In the early 1970s, the government appointed a committee headed by the director general of the Ministry of Health, Baruch Padeh, to devise a single pay scale for all health system workers. Entitled the Comparison Committee, it met with adamant resistance on the part of Kupat Holim employees, who insisted on preserving the differential and embarked on a series of work slowdowns and strikes. As in the past, the Histadrut came to its aid, establishing its own committee to rectify the "distortions" created by the wage raises given Ministry of Health medical employees at the Comparison Committee's recommendation. The Histadrut committee recommended that Kupat Holim employees receive the same increases, which they did.[35] The outcome was a perpetuation of the salary differential, which led to a wage race in which Ministry of Health employees repeatedly went on strike to attain equal wages with Kupat Holim workers, who in turn repeatedly went on strike to maintain their advantage. Adding to the absurdity, the differential was partly financed by the Ministry of Health subsidies to Kupat Holim discussed earlier.

The Implications

Shem Tov's aim in regulation, as in allocation, was to carve out a role for the Ministry of Health, which it had not previously had. As in allocation, his method was to create institutional structures without directly attacking Kupat Holim's interests. The two committees he created, however, the Supreme Coordination Committee to coordinate health policy and the Project Approval Committee to approve health construction projects, were both ineffective, undermined, among other things, by the formal adaptation of the parity principle. This principle formally abolished the fundamental distinction between regulator and regulated—a distinction that had already been violated de facto by the ministry's role in running the government hospitals that it itself regulated. In the joint committees that were set up the Ministry of Health voluntarily relinquished exclusive control over the long-term investment of its moneys and the development of medical facilities, while Kupat Holim was able to proceed with its projects with little if any hindrance or supervision and, moreover, was given a determinant say in approving government construction projects.

Shem Tov continued his predecessors' policy of informal regulation, while the threat of formal regulations, which was supposed to deter Kupat Holim from stepping out of line, did not do so. Kupat Holim consistently outmaneuvered the ministry; every time the wishes of the ministry came up against those of Kupat Holim, the ministry capitulated.[36] Under Shem Tov regulation no more served the Ministry of Health as a policy-making tool than allocation did. Instead of making regulations that created order in the system, the Ministry of Health got trapped into spirals of regulation in which each regulation led to a new one to handle the consequences of the former one.

The major problem was that the Ministry of Health's dependency on Kupat Holim inevitably caused its regulatory efforts to boomerang on itself. For all of Shem Tov's efforts, the Ministry of Health was left with little more than declarations it could not implement and agreements it could not enforce.

CHAPTER 9

Restructuring the Health System

When Shem Tov became minister of health in 1970, no progress had been made in restructuring the health services. The restructuring initiatives had had been controlled by the Mapai-held Ministry of Labor, the Ministry of Health had played only a peripheral role in the discussions, and Kupat Holim's red lines were all firmly in place.

Shem Tov did virtually nothing to change this situation. During his term two national health insurance bills were drafted, both by Minister of Labor Almogi, former secretary general of Mapai and powerful Labor apparatchik who had appointed the Hushi Committee. These bills were not the first efforts at legislation. In November 1966 representatives of two opposition parties—Ben Gurion's Rafi Party (which had split from Mapai) and Gahal Party (forerunner of the Likud)—each presented a private member's health insurance bill to the Knesset. The thrust of both bills was to make health insurance compulsory and place it firmly in the hands of the government. Minister of Health Joseph Barzilai succeeded in having the bills tabled without a vote on the grounds that government policy was that national health insurance should be implemented by the sick funds (Halevi, 1979, pp. 30–31). The two bills Almogi sponsored were consistent with that approach. The aim of both was to provide a stable, legal foundation for Kupat Holim's powers.

The National Health Insurance Bill of 1971

The first bill was drafted shortly after Shem Tov took office, without the involvement of the Ministry of Health, but with the active participation of Kupat Holim (Arian, 1981). Its effect would have been to further empower Kupat Holim at the expense of the Ministry of Health.

The seeds of the bill were planted toward the end of 1968 when Almogi, unwilling to let the Hushi Committee recommendations languish despite the strong opposition they evoked, brought them before a special ministerial committee (Arian, 1981, pp. 43–56). The ministerial committee was driven by much the same controversy that had divided the Hushi Committee. The Independent Liberal Party objected to key recommendations, especially compulsory membership in Kupat Holim through the labor unions and the collection and allocation of the insurance premiums by the sick funds.

The ministerial committee submitted the matters under debate to the government plenum, where Almogi, intent on securing Histadrut control over membership and dues collection, suggested a compromise: that the issue of membership be dropped and fee collection be divided between the Histadrut and the National Insurance Institute. The Histadrut would continue to collect the members' dues, while the National Insurance Institute would collect the employer participation tax, up until then collected by the Histadrut, and allocate it to the various sick funds (Arian, 1981, pp. 43–56; Halevi, 1979, p. 34).[1] The compromise was rather lopsided, in that, as a government agency, the National Insurance Institute was in a better position than the Histadrut to collect fees from recalcitrant employers. On the basis of this compromise, several governmental committees were established in various ministries to draft a bill. But falling foul of the same controversial issues, they drafted repeated proposals and were unable to reach consensus on any of them (Baruch, 1973, p. 55).

When it got wind of the drafts, the Histadrut raised an outcry that it had not been included in formulating them. It was not enough for the Histadrut that Almogi was a Mapai loyalist who pushed its cause with strong personal fervor. The Histadrut was suspicious of any government regulation, however preferential, in which it did not have a full part. Bypassing the government, Aharon Becker, the secretary general of the Histadrut at the time, pressured Mapai to bring Kupat Holim and Histadrut representatives to the drafting table.[2] The pressure proved effective. In April 1970 the secretary general of Mapai convened a special meeting of the party's executive to establish an ad hoc committee "to create a small forum to examine the proposal, together with the Histadrut, Kupat Holim, the Government and the MPs in the Labor Alignment, . . . to reach a unified position to guide all Alignment representatives in all matters of health policy."[3] Kupat Holim and the Histadrut had succeeded in rallying the Labor Party to ensure that no government effort, however benign, to restructure the health system would take place without their being full partners.

The proposal was approved, and the Alignment Committee for Health Policy was created. The committee was headed by Almogi and its members included Mapai MPs and representatives of Kupat Holim, the Histadrut, and the Histadrut's Central Tax Bureau. It was this constellation that prepared the last draft of the National Health Insurance Bill of 1971. The Ministry of Health had no role in drafting the final proposal, and only after the party committee completed its work was the proposal circulated among the relevant government ministries.

The Alignment Committee's proposal was even more favorable to Kupat Holim and the Histadrut than the Hushi Committee recommendations that Almogi had originally brought before the ministerial committee. Like those, it stipulated that the national health insurance be implemented by the existent sick funds, thereby ensuring their continued existence. But it went further. It made membership in the Histadrut incumbent upon all Kupat Holim insurees, thereby securing the prestate link between membership in the two bodies and ensuring the Histadrut a large pool of members who might have had no other interest in joining the trade confederation. And it kept the collection and allocation of Kupat Holim membership fees in the hands of the Histadrut, thus ensuring the trade federation's financial power and autonomy.

The proposal also had one other stipulation, which had never been made before and which Kupat Holim and the Histadrut were apparently able to push through from their position in the Alignment Committee. This stipulation directly concerned the issue of who would have the legal authority to make health policy. The draft established a National Health Insurance Authority to oversee all coordination, regulation, planning, fee setting, licensing, and budget approval in the health system. Many of these duties are normally performed by a core government body, and, at the time, several of them were officially the province of the Ministry of Health and other relevant ministries. But the authority's 15-member board of directors was to consist of only two representatives from the Ministry of Health and 13 from the various sick funds, allocated in accord with the size of their membership. In other words, the majority of the authority's directorship would consist of Kupat Holim representatives—10 according to Nissim Baruch's calculations (Baruch, 1973, p. 59). The proposal not only failed to give the core a more powerful role in health, but also would have given Kupat Holim the legal authority to make health policy.

The senior bureaucrats in the Ministry of Health rightly regarded the bill as a threat to the ministry's continued existence and demanded reopening discussions with their participation. The director general of the ministry, Dr. Raphael Gzebin, resigned on the grounds that the proposal "contradicts the basic principles required to maintain a health system."[4] In a letter to the chairman of the Knesset Finance Committee, he complained that the Ministry of Health was the last of the government ministries to receive a copy of the proposed bill. In particular, he protested the establishment of the Health Insurance Authority, "to which most of the Ministry of Health's duties would be transferred."[5]

The bill was not put before the Knesset.

The Health Insurance Bill of 1973

Almogi persisted. Determined to formalize Kupat Holim's dominant role in Israel's health care, in 1973 he drafted yet another bill. This too was without Ministry of Health input, although Kupat Holim was involved in the process from the start (Arian, 1981, pp. 43–56). As Almogi tells:

> I prepared the wording of the bill myself. There was not one item that I had not worked on. Gideon Ben-Israel of the Ministry of Labor and Haim Doron of Kupat Holim prepared the final drafts.... Only after the bill was approved by the ministerial legislation committee did I give it to Shem Tov.[6]

The 1973 bill was based on Almogi's 1971 proposal, with only cosmetic modifications in response to criticism by the Ministry of Health and much of the public (Baruch, 1973, pp. 59–60; Halevi, 1979, p. 37). Most of the privileges that the first version would have granted Kupat Holim were retained. Once again, the bill would have made health insurance compulsory and placed it under the auspices of the sick funds. Like its predecessor, it withheld from salaried workers the right to choose their sick fund and gave that right to their trade union—that is, to the Histadrut. Additionally, it kept the collection of members' dues in the hands of the Histadrut's Central Tax Bureau and the appropriate bodies of the smaller sick funds.

The major difference from the 1971 version was in the policy-making powers awarded Kupat Holim. The 1973 proposal made no mention of the National Health Authority, which had aroused so much ire, and, instead, proposed what it called a Health Insurance Council. The difference, however, was insubstantial. The new Health Insurance Council was to have many of the same functions as previously proposed for the National Health Authority: planning and coordination, regulation, setting fees, and establishing procedures. It would also have been controlled by Kupat Holim. Only half the council members were to be sick fund representatives, as opposed to almost all the members in the authority; but the composition of the other half of the committee would ensure Kupat Holim control because it would consist of representatives of the government, the National Insurance Institute employers and employees. The employee representatives meant Histadrut representatives, with whom the Kupat Holim representatives could easily team up to form a secure majority (Knesset, *Proposed Bills,* 1973, p. 1077).

The Health Insurance Bill of 1973 was put before the Knesset for first reading on July 12, 1973, and passed on July 19 by a vote of 28 to 17 with four abstentions. The bill's opponents raised the same objections as had been raised against the previous proposals for universal health insurance. Yoram Aridor of the opposition Liberal–Herut alliance (Gahal), who would become a minister of finance under the Likud, opposed the "annexation of members by Kupat Holim," "the collection of dues by Kupat Holim," and the "appointment of a Health Council" (*Knesset Minutes,* 1973, vol. 68, pp. 3915–18). Yehuda Sh'ari of the Independent Liberal Party, which was pivotal in the coalition, insisted on a single national sick fund and, if that were not possible, at least free choice of sick fund and fee collection by the National Insurance Institute (*Knesset Minutes,* 1973, vol. 68, pp. 3928–30).

After passing the first reading, the bill went on to the Knesset Committee for Public Services for preparation for a second reading. There it died. The committee convened 58 times between 1974 and 1976 to discuss the bill without being able to attain a majority on the crucial matters of sick fund membership and dues collection (Baron, 1978). Evidently, the Labor Alignment was either unwilling or unable to bring the Labor coalition, which had only a small majority in the committee, to back the bill (Baron, 1978). The Independent Liberals continued to demand freedom of choice in sick fund and the transfer of dues collection to the National Insurance Institute, and they threatened to leave the coalition if these points were not incorporated into the bill.[7]

Prime Minister Yitzhak Rabin, voted into office in 1974, tried to bridge the gap. He reported to the party executive that he had reached a compromise with the Histadrut whereby dues would be collected by a "social collection center" under the joint auspices of the government and the sick funds. With regard to freedom of choice, he gave his word that he would personally fight to prevent the Histadrut from expelling from the trade union those who joined another sick fund.[8] Whether such a promise could have been kept is doubtful.

In any case, Rabin's position, which would have weakened the Histadrut by depriving it of the Kupat Holim moneys collected by its Central Tax Bureau, was obviously unacceptable. The Histadrut vehemently denied that it had come to an agreement. In the words of the Histadrut's Secretary General Yerucham Meshel: "The Histadrut will not take orders on its internal affairs from any Knesset health legislation, this or any other, and we will demand that Histadrut members be Kupat Holim members too."[9] A clearer statement of the Histadrut's refusal to accept the legitimate authority of the state when it impinged on its vested interests can hardly be made.

The bill was tabled, brought down by the threat of the Independent Liberals to leave the coalition. Again we see a stalemate in the restructuring effort. The government was unable to attain any compromise, however modest, that threatened to cross the red lines that Kupat Holim and the Histadrut had drawn in the 1930s and cemented in the 1950s and 1960s, and which might have enabled it to present a bill that was acceptable to its coalition partner. The Histadrut was unable to push through the kind of restructuring that would lend the legitimacy of parliamentary legislation to its control of Kupat Holim membership and finances and give it an official role in the making of health policy. The outcome was the maintenance of the status quo. Kupat Holim retained on an informal level all the powers that the bill, had it passed, would have cemented in law.

Minister of Health Shem Tov was in principle highly supportive of national health insurance legislation; he regarded the formal designation of authorities as consistent with his efforts to rationalize the health services. His exclusion from the drafting of the 1973 bill, after he had been in office for more than two years, angered him. But he apparently accepted the political logic of the Ministry of Labor's domination of the restructuring process. "I am willing to admit," he told in a personal interview:

> that Almogi's wish to make his mark on the law and establish for himself a position equal to that of the ministry of health stemmed mainly from the fact that the minister of health was a member of a small party, which was not to have complete control over a law which would have the utmost importance for Mapai.[10]

Nor did he object to Kupat Holim's participation in formulating the bill. On the contrary, he considered Kupat Holim's involvement both natural and necessary. Speaking of why no government health coverage legislation was introduced in Israel until the 1970s, he pointed a finger at the misguided attempts in the 1950s and 1960s to nationalize health insurance to the exclusion of Kupat Holim:

> The attempts made over the last 20 years to pass a health insurance bill failed because the so-called patent holders of nationalism wanted to put a stop to the only form of insurance possible in our situation—insurance through sick funds, at the center of which, naturally, stands Kupat Holim.[11]

Once he received the bill from Almogi after it was ratified by the special ministerial committee for legislation, Shem Tov could do little. Even if he wanted to, which we have no way of knowing, it is unlikely that he would have been able to introduce any changes. All that was left for him was to fight for formal recognition of the Ministry of Health's stake in legislation that directly affected it and was logically its domain. At the ministerial committee for legislation, he rose to his feet and demanded that he, rather than Almogi, be the one to make the speech that opened the Knesset debate on the bill. Almogi tells that he consented only after Prime Minister Golda Meir intervened. According to Almogi, the prime minister told him: "You have plenty of occasions to appear before the Knesset. So let Shem Tov open the debate."[12] It was something like throwing a dog a bone.

Implications: Accommodating the Margin

From the very beginning, all of Labor's efforts at restructuring were based on the principle of accommodation. This principle featured not only the core's willingness to negotiate with the Histadrut and to modify its positions in the hope that the Histadrut and Kupat Holim would yield on some of their demands, but also the core's readiness to limit its decision-making options in accord with Kupat Holim's and the Histadrut's imperatives.

Shem Tov's term as minister of health saw the first legislative efforts to restructure the health system. Both bills that were drafted, however, respected the traditional Kupat Holim–Histadrut red lines: public medicine based on the existing, voluntary, independent sick funds; Histadrut control of membership and fee collection, along with complete autonomy in the dispersion of the funds; and Kupat Holim's equal status with the government in all areas of public health policy. Both bills aimed at anchoring in law the informal powers that Kupat Holim had accumulated over the years.

Although Shem Tov was excluded from both restructuring efforts, he apparently favored them. He was ideologically committed to the working class, believed that the public would be better served by their own voluntary health care organizations than by the state, and, schooled by the failures of the earlier restructuring endeavors, regarded Kupat Holim membership and dues collection as intrusive political issues that would undermine any and all efforts to achieve any coordination and rationalization in the health services. To avoid this politicization, he was ready to accept Kupat Holim's red lines. He blamed the Independent Liberals and the Histadrut for killing the National Health Insurance Bill of 1973 with their "politics": "The Liberals vetoed the freedom of [joint] membership, and the Histadrut, with the help of the Labor Alignment, vetoed the method of dues collection."[13]

Kupat Holim Spends and the Ministry of Health Pays

The continued use of the three tools of policy to benefit Kupat Holim is evident in the pattern of health expenditures while Shem Tov was minister. Between 1970–1971 and 1977–1978 Israel's national expenditure on health[14] rose from 5.4% to 6.9% of its gross national product.[15] The increase was not unique to Israel. As elsewhere, it reflected the aging of the population, the increasing sophistication and cost of medical technology, higher health-sector wages, and increased public demand for health care.

Yet the pattern of expenditure in Israel was quite distinct. It reflected Kupat Holim's needs and control of the policy process. Israel spent around twice as much public money (in relation to its total national expenditure on health) on ambulatory care as Great Britain and Holland and some 60% more than the United States, whereas these countries spent between around 30% and 50% more on hospitals than Israel.[16] The bias in favor of ambulatory care, 90% of which was delivered by Kupat Holim clinics, meant that an unusual proportion of Israel's expenditure on health went to fund Kupat Holim's activities.

Moreover, although about one third to one half of the national expenditure on health was financed by the government during these years,[17] the sick funds (mainly Kupat Holim) spent approximately 35% more on their health services than the Ministry of Health did on the government health services;[18] and between over a fifth to nearly two fifths of the Ministry of Health's net budget went to subsidies for the sick funds, rather than to the ministry's own general hospitals and public health offices.[19]

In contrast to the logic of government by which the body that pays determines the object of the expenditures, while Shem Tov was in office, the ministry paid what Kupat Holim decided to spend. In other words, Israel's health policies were determined not by Ministry of Health declarations or intentions but by Kupat Holim's expenditures.

CHAPTER 10

The Formal Preventive Veto

In the 1970s Kupat Holim was given a formal preventive veto in the formation stage of the policy-making process. This veto was anchored in the official parity that the sick fund was granted on the new regulatory bodies that the Ministry of Health established to coordinate health policy and to approve the construction of hospitals and other health care facilities. This parity gave Kupat Holim a controlling say in which regulations the Ministry of Health could and could not enact.

The inclusion of Kupat Holim in the making of crucial health system decisions was nothing new. In this sense Shem Tov's policy was a continuation of past practices. However, granting parity on the newly created committees was a formal act, which gave explicit public recognition, legality, and legitimacy to the informal veto that Kupat Holim had hitherto exercised. On the one hand, it entailed a conscious and public recognition by the new minister of health of Kupat Holim's powers and its ability to disrupt the system. On the other hand, it was underpinned by his ideological affinity with Kupat Holim and a deep-seated respect for its contribution to health care in Israel and was predicated on the assumed commonality of interests between the government and Kupat Holim in the maintenance and development of public health run by the voluntary sick funds.

It was a self-contradictory policy, which invested Kupat Holim with formal power in order to constrain and limit its de facto power. Parity was an act of accommodation designed to win Kupat Holim's cooperation in strengthening the weak Ministry of Health. It was the price that Shem Tov felt he had to pay to rationalize the health system, firm up the ministry's institutional structures, and increase ministry involvement in the policy-making process. Efforts to this end were also made in allocation, where Shem Tov demanded that the Ministry of Health take part in the Ministry of Finance's decisions on allocation for the health system and created the Division of Planning, Budgeting and Medical Economics to prepare the Ministry of Health budget and conduct long-range health planning—both acts aimed at loosening the exclusive grip of Kupat Holim and the Mapai-controlled Ministry of Finance on the process.

However, in both theory and practice, the formalization of the veto through parity limited the ministry's options in accord with Kupat Holim–Histadrut imperatives. The "supervised autonomy" that Shem Tov envisioned for Kupat Holim was an oxymoronic impossibility. Moreover, the parity principle formally abolished the fundamental distinction, which had already been violated in the previous period, between regulator and regulated.

All the tools of policy continued to be wielded by and for the benefit of Kupat Holim.

In allocation, Shem Tov did not succeed in getting rid of the politico-familial in the way decisions were made and funds allocated. Nor did he take any steps to change the financing arrangements that were initiated in the prestate and early state periods. He did not challenge the principle of allocation by administrative routine; the changes in the formula that his ministry made resulted in an even better fit with Kupat Holim's needs and brought yet more money to Kupat Holim's coffers. He did not challenge the Histadrut's right to set, collect, and apportion health insurance fees as it saw fit or publicly question the obligation of the government to pick up the shortfall in Kupat Holim's budget. The Employer Participation Tax Law, which was passed during his term as minister, provided a permanent source of funding earmarked for health, thereby reducing Kupat Holim's dependence on the Ministry of Finance. Under his leadership, the Ministry of Health still did not use allocation to obtain Kupat Holim compliance with government policy and the Histadrut and Kupat Holim determined the level and objects of government support, rather than vice versa.

In regulation, the Ministry of Health was left with little more than declarations it could not implement and agreements it could not enforce. Its dependency on Kupat Holim inevitably caused its regulatory efforts to backfire. In the joint committees established to regulate the health system, the Ministry of Health voluntarily relinquished exclusive control over the long-term investment of its funds and the development of medical facilities, whereas Kupat Holim was able to proceed with its projects with little if any hindrance or supervision and, moreover, was given a determinant say in approving the construction of government health facilities. Moreover, Shem Tov continued his predecessors' policy of informal regulation, justifying it with the idea that the threat of formal regulations would deter Kupat Holim from stepping too far out of line. The threat carried little weight. Kupat Holim consistently outmaneuvered the ministry, and every time the wishes of the ministry clashed with those of Kupat Holim, the ministry backed down.[1] Instead of making regulations that created order in the system, the ministry was trapped into spirals of regulation in which each regulation led to a new one to handle the consequences of the former.

In restructuring, too, little changed. As before, restructuring was the province of the Mapai-held Ministry of Labor and Welfare, and the Ministry of Health played virtually no role. Like Shem Tov's parity principle, the two health insurance bills that were jointly drafted by the Ministry of Labor and Welfare and the Kupat Holim–Histadrut subsystem during this period both aimed at anchoring in law the informal prerogatives that Kupat Holim had accumulated over the years: public medicine based on the existing, voluntary, independent sick funds; Histadrut control of membership and fee collection, along with complete autonomy in the dispersion of the funds; and Kupat Holim's equal status with the government in all areas of public health policy decision making. All indications are that Shem Tov supported these efforts, perhaps not realizing the degree to which they would have yet further empowered the sick fund at the expense of the Ministry of Health.

Shem Tov's efforts to impose core control over Kupat Holim were tentative, incomplete, fraught with contradictions and wishful thinking, and utterly unsuccessful. Yet, despite its failure, his policy was a first step in trying to empower the core and loosen the hitherto almost total grip of the margin. The parameters of utility and ability can also account for this complex state of affairs.

Shem Tov's ability to grant Kupat Holim a formal veto and Kupat Holim's refusal to cooperate with his goal of greater ministerial involvement in health policy were both predicated on the Sick Fund's continuing utility to the Histadrut as a source of members and dues and to Mapai as a source of funding for party activities, as well as on Mapai's continued hegemony as the largest of the coalition parties that governed the state. Both the formalization of the veto and Kupat Holim's free exercise of it would also have been unlikely if Kupat Holim were not generally well regarded by the public and if the socialist ideology it represented were not still in the ascendancy. Also contributing to Shem Tov's inability to bring Kupat Holim into line was the isolation of the Mapam-headed Ministry of Health and its lack of coordination with the Mapai-controlled Ministry of Finance and Ministry of Labor and Welfare.

At the same time, Shem Tov's efforts to circumscribe Kupat Holim's powers can be understood against the background of Kupat Holim's reduced utility to the core and the core's reduced ability to channel to the Sick Fund the powers of the state. By the time Shem Tov took office, the flow of immigrants had slowed and the immigrants who had arrived were settled, so Kupat Holim was less of a vote getter for Mapai than it had been in the 1950s. Israel's basic infrastructure was in place and the stupendous victory in the 1967 Six-Day War ushered in a sense of security and of prosperity. The improvement in the country's material circumstances made Kupat Holim less useful to Mapai in government. Building health care facilities and offering health care services were no longer the urgent matters they had been in the 1950s, and Kupat

Holim was no longer so needed to alleviate the pressures on an overburdened government.

Mapai's ability to permit Kupat Holim to operate without core control was being chipped away from several directions. The changes in the country's material circumstances meant that there was no longer the same justification for massive government support of Kupat Holim and that the flaws in the health services were becoming increasingly glaring, enabling those who objected to Kupat Holim's irregularities and partisan nature to get a better hearing. Politically, cracks were forming in Mapai's cohesion and dominance, as the party was aging and fragmented and the right-wing opposition had gained legitimacy. Occupied with these problems, the party functionaries had less time and energy to spare for matters of health care—as evidenced, among other ways, by the long time it took the party to join in the restructuring efforts. The reduction of Mapai attention created a vacuum in which Shem Tov could try to empower the ministry and place Kupat Holim's autonomy under ministry "supervision."

In addition, the norms of government were changing. One of the legacies of the prestate period was an informal and ad hoc policy-making mode (Horowitz & Lissak, 1978, p. 289), reflected, among other ways, in the cozy "familiness" in the allocation of funds to the sick funds. However, nearly three decades into statehood, pressures were mounting to formalize the conduct of government. Israel's leadership had always seen the country—founded by Europeans and isolated in the Middle East—as belonging to the Western democratic world. It was only natural that pressure would mount to bring the conduct of government into line with the norms in the West by making it more rational and formal. The norms were changing even within Mapai. The younger generation of politicians who rose in the party in the 1970s, among them Yitzhak Rabin, placed greater value on order and rational administration than their predecessors did. These changes too were behind Shem Tov's aspirations to constrain Kupat Holim's power.

Much as in the case of Kupat Holim's informal preventive veto, the human factor was essential in the Sick Fund's acquisition of the formal veto. Here the key person was Minister of Health Shem Tov. Just as Moshe Sorocca, the administrative head of Kupat Holim, was the strategist and driving force behind the sick fund's push for informal power, so Victor Shem Tov, the minister of health, was the strategist and driving force behind the formalization of the veto as a means of empowering the Ministry of Health. In his person he embodied the contradictions that were inherent in the policy. He was sympathetic with Kupat Holim, yet personally fought to rationalize the health system. He had a greater measure of personal independence and integrity than previous ministers. He acted to promote the notion that the Ministry of Health can act independently of the party in power, as a rational bureaucratic agency, and thus started the separation between party, bureaucracy, and body on the margin.

Part III

THE OBSTRUCTIVE VETO

CHAPTER II

Exclusion Under the Likud: 1977–1984

The May 1977 elections swept Labor out of office and the Likud in. After decades in opposition, Menachem Begin, the erstwhile pariah, formed a coalition and became prime minister as head of the Likud, an amalgam consisting of Herut (the party that Begin had formed in 1949), the Liberal Party, and two small factions.

The cooperative relations between Kupat Holim and the government during the decades of Labor rule was one of the first casualties of the electoral turnabout. Begin and his new minister of health, Eliezer Shostak, shared a longstanding antipathy to the entire Histadrut–Kupat Holim ideology and modus operandi. They were determined to clean out the stables, as they saw it, and to institute government control over health care by excluding Kupat Holim from the policy-making process. The immediate result of their determination was a seven-year tooth-and-nail struggle over control of the instruments of policy making, which neither side won and the public lost. Before discussing that struggle, however, it is necessary to provide some grounding in the deep roots of the Likud policy of exclusion.

Ideology Dovetails with Politics
Vladimir Jabotinsky: Ideology of National Health Care

The roots of the Likud's determination to revamp Israel's health care reach back well before either the Likud or Herut, its major faction, was born. They go back almost as far as Kupat Holim does: to Herut's ideological ancestor, the Revisionist Party, which the Polish-born Vladimir (Zeev) Jabotinsky founded in 1925. The name of the party reflected its conviction that to attain a national homeland, the entire Zionist enterprise as conceived by the Labor movement would have to undergo a complete revision.

The focus of the revision was on how to attain statehood. In place of the step-by-step conquest of the land and the slow building of institutions practiced by the various labor parties, the Revisionists advocated militancy against the Arabs and ousting the British by armed force (Arian, 1985, p. 79; Medding, 1990, pp. 61–70). They also differed from the various Labor parties in their economic and social ideology. This ideology was less well articulated, less central to their worldview, and less enduring than the Revisionists' militant nationalism. But it contained the seeds of the health policies that the Likud would pursue half a century later.

The Revisionists generally believed that economic and social issues were secondary to national ones and that economic and social structures had to serve national interests. In their view, attaining the Zionist aim required a single-minded dedication that left no room for other concerns or values. They rejected the idea of the class struggle, which virtually all the Labor parties identified with the building of the new state, as undermining the national revival. In the Revisionists' view, such a revival required not division between labor and capital, as in the Histadrut ideology, but Zionist "monism," characterized by cooperation between labor and capital and the subordination of the class to the nation. The Revisionists even distrusted the very loyalty of socialists to the Zionist idea, seeing socialism—and any other -ism—as a contender for the human spirit (Ofir, 1982, Vol. 1, pp. 22–25; Shapiro, 1989, pp. 26–27).

Jabotinsky and his followers repeatedly claimed that they had a "social" ideology rather than a "socialist" one. In this ideology, the state was the proper body to meet the individual's needs. In Jabotinsky's view, health care was one of five essentials (the others were food, clothing, education, and housing) that the state had a duty to provide its citizens, either through levying taxes or the forced expropriation (i.e., nationalization) of enterprises:

> With respect to each of these five basic needs, every state, at every time, has a known conception of a sufficient minimum . . . and every man who lets it be known that he needs these five essentials must receive them. This is my first social law. From this it can be deduced that the state must always be able to provide these five essentials to all citizens who ask for them. From where will the state take them? The answer is my second law: the state will take them from the people by compulsion, just as today it raises taxes and compels young men to serve in the army. . . . Every year the state will impose an appropriate level of taxes or expropriate an appropriate number of private factories, and draft an appropriate number of young people for social services. (Jabotinsky, n.d., pp. 297–98)

In some respects, Jabotinsky's view resembled Ben Gurion's later statism and derived from a similar rationale: the belief that vital services should be provided by the state to all its citizens rather than by narrow political organizations only to their members. Nor was Ben Gurion averse to state compulsion. On the contrary, he was firmly convinced that the state had the right to oblige its citizens to act for the common good. Most significantly for the issue at hand, the Revisionists no more envisioned private health care than Mapai. The parties did not so much differ in the assumption that the economy and social services had to be organized as in their view of who should do the organizing. In practice, this came down to the state or the Histadrut.

Translating Ideology into Politics

As the *yishuv* began to organize in the early 1920s, their ideological differences and rivalry for power set the Revisionists and the Labor movement on a collision course. Neither was noted for its tolerance. The Revisionists felt that their brand of radical nationalism qualified them for the exclusive leadership of the Jewish national movement (Horowitz & Lissak, 1978, pp. 146–47), and the Laborites were hard put to accept the Revisionists' challenge to their social and political worldview.

The Histadrut was at the center of the fight. The Revisionists saw the Histadrut as an instrument of class power and an impediment to the creation of the state. The Histadrut, for its part, set out to organize the *yishuv*'s entire labor force under its exclusive control, using means fair and foul. The Revisionists and others who were disinclined to accept the Histadrut's protection were excluded from the many workplaces that the Histadrut controlled; more than a few Revisionists were beaten up and some were killed by Histadrut thugs. Kupat Holim refused to give them medical care.

In the early 1930s, during Histadrut-provoked riots at a biscuit factory where a Revisionist laborer was employed (Ofir, 1982, Vol. 1, pp. 95–100), Jabotinsky began to publish articles against the Histadrut monopoly of workplaces. In one article, published after the incident was resolved with the Histadrut's formal acceptance of the right of non-Histadrut members to work, he wrote: "We want to break, and we will break, its [the Histadrut's] claim to a class monopoly and class rule."[1] The declaration would be repeated many times.

The polarization reached its peak after the murder of the Mapai leader Haim Arlozorov in June 1933 (Arian, 1985, p. 80). The Revisionists were accused of the deed (although it was later found that the culprits were two Arabs). Relations between the two movements worsened. Violence against Revisionists at workplaces increased. Revisionist-affiliated administrative and medical staff working for Kupat Holim were called "murderers" and fired from their jobs (Halevi, 1979, pp. 8–9).

These events underscored the need for Revisionist institutions to parallel the Histadrut ones, at a time when the number of Revisionists who were immigrating to Palestine and needed jobs and health care was increasing and the movement was growing. Already in 1931 Menachem Begin had withdrawn from the Labor-affiliated Haganah to form the Irgun Zvai Leumi (the National Military Organization, EZL), which was aligned with the Revisionists. In 1935 tensions with the labor establishment would lead Jabotinsky to withdraw from the World Zionist Organization and to form his own body, the Zionist Organization. In November 1933 the Revisionist professionals who were fired from their jobs in Kupat Holim founded Kupat Holim Leumit (the National Sick Fund). A few months later, in April 1934, the National Labor Federation was founded.[2]

Despite their comparatively small size, these organizations constituted rivals to Kupat Holim and the Histadrut. Although they too were exclusive organizations serving a restricted clientele of party members and meeting party needs in much the same way as Kupat Holim and the Histadrut did[3] (Ofir, 1982, Vol. 2, p. 9), their practical translation of Jabotinsky's philosophy explicitly challenged not only the exclusivity of the bodies aligned to the Labor movement, but their basic assumptions. The leadership of the Leumit Sick Fund, in keeping with the Jabotinskian view that medicine was the province of the state, regarded the Leumit health service as a temporary one to be replaced by a national service when the state was created (Ofir, 1982, Vol. 1, pp. 152–59). The same would apply to Kupat Holim.

The National Labor Federation, for its part, promulgated a set of principles that would have greatly restricted the size and scope of legitimate trade union operations. These principles were outlined at its first convention, held in April 9, 1934 (Ofir, 1982, Vol. 1, pp. 149–50). One principle was the notion that strikes are detrimental to the nation and should thus be outlawed and replaced by compulsory arbitration by a state body—a move that would have deprived the Histadrut of a powerful sanction which it used to great effect to bring both errant employers and national bodies into line and which ran deeply counter to Israel's democracy. Another was the call for politically neutral employment bureaus under national control, which Ben Gurion in fact established in the 1950s.

Two other of its principles are of special relevance. One was that trade unions must restrict themselves to professional matters, while services must be provided by the nation. The services that were named included education, settlement, immigrant absorption, and health insurance. Were this principle ever to be acted on, it would mean a greatly shrunken Histadrut, deprived of all the social service bodies that brought it government money, electoral support, and the prestige and power that went with its playing a major role in the nation's social life. The other principle, which was in fact overlapping but stated separately for emphasis, was that health services be removed from political bodies and transferred to the authority of the state by means of a national health insurance law. These two principles were advocated throughout the prestate period by the leaders of the National Labor Federation and, after statehood, taken up by Herut.

The various principles amounted to a translation of Jabotinsky's ideology into a political agenda to reduce the power of the Histadrut. Revisionist leaders repeatedly called for the dissolution of the Histadrut, the outlawing of strikes, and the transfer of the functions—especially in health and employment—that did not bear directly on the well-being of workers to the state.

The Revisionists had little chance of enacting their program. They were a minority movement, and Jabotinsky's refusal to cooperate with the Labor-organized bodies resulted in its isolation from the sources of power in the *yishuv*. With statehood the Revisionists ceased to function as a political body and were replaced by Herut, the party formed by Begin and his "fighting family" out of the EZL underground movement he had led in prestate days. For reasons outside the scope of this book, Herut formally broke with the Revisionists and rejected all the Revisionist organizations, including its trade union and its sick fund (Ofir, 1982, Vol. 1, p. 14), which continued to operate without the party patronage that sustained their larger Labor-supported rivals.

Moreover, as Herut began to carve out its electorate among the deprived immigrants from the Arabic-speaking countries and the urban bourgeoisie, it shook off the Revisionist demands for a state-directed economy with a major role given to national–public capital. By the late 1950s it had reframed its economic policy in the direction of a more traditional right-wing approach with greater emphasis on individual enterprise and private capital. In the early 1960s this change of direction culminated in Herut's alignment with the Liberal Party in Gahal (Medding, 1990, pp. 186–201).

Nonetheless, Herut was no less hostile to Kupat Holim and Histadrut interests than its Jabotinskian forefathers. Herut continued to present the Histadrut as a tool of the socialists to exploit the workers and continued to attack Histadrut monopolies and the dependence of citizens on party-controlled bureaucracies. Begin himself vowed that when Herut gained power, it would deal with Kupat Holim and institute national health insurance (Ofir, 1982, Vol. 1, p. 224). A few years later Begin brought Herut into the Histadrut (Ofir, 1982, Vol. 2, p. 286), but this in no way indicated any abatement of Herut's deep-seated antagonism to Kupat Holim as the linchpin of Histadrut and Labor power. Why Herut joined an organization to which it was so opposed is a matter of historical speculation. Shostak and other leaders of the National Trade Union saw the act as a betrayal. Begin may have been motivated by a desire for legitimacy or by the wish to influence the Histadrut from within. In any event, the election of the Likud to power in 1977 brought the opportunity to implement the Jabotinskian ideal of national health care while whittling away the bastion of Labor strength.

Eliezer Shostak: Minister of Health

The person Begin chose to reform Israel's health care system was Eliezer Shostak. Shostak, like Begin, was a staunch Revisionist until the establishment of Israel and, afterward, retained the Jabotinskian view of health care as the responsibility of the state. He became minister of health at the end of a long Knesset career, dating back to 1951, during which he served in one or another of the various factions that made up the right-wing coalitions and was active in the Knesset committees that dealt with matters of labor, welfare, and health. More crucially, from the 1940s onward he had been secretary general of the National Labor Federation, the organization which for half a century spearheaded the opposition to Kupat Holim and the Histadrut. Since the National Labor Federation had its own sick fund, this position gave him a long apprenticeship in the ins and outs of the country's health care system and ample opportunity to learn, from the vantage point of the underdog, the advantages that accrued to Kupat Holim through its affiliation with the Histadrut and its ability to mobilize the resources of the state to its own health care services. It also gave him, one should note, a certain conflict of interests. As head of a trade federation, which had its own sick fund, he was compelled to consider the sick fund's survival and well-being. Thus, during the parliamentary debates preceding the passage of the Employer Participation Tax Law in 1973, he put his support behind the Labor initiative, which would have increased Leumit's coffers as well as Kupat Holim's (*Knesset Minutes*, 1972, Vol. 65, pp. 681–82).

With the transition to statehood, the National Labor Federation somewhat modified the Jabotinskian position that health care should be nationalized. Protective of its own Leumit Sick Fund, the federation feared that the ruling Mapai would nationalize the smaller health funds and transfer them to the Histadrut. In the first year of independence, it joined with the other small sick funds in a united stand against nationalization of the health services (Ofir, 1982, Vol. 1, p. 16: 28). But this was only a modification, not a change, of position.

Shostak's October 1959 speech before a National Labor Federation convention makes the same two-pronged attack against the Histadrut enterprises in general and its sick fund in particular that was sounded by the Revisionists and the same objection to the politicization of health services:

> The Histadrut objects to a national health service because such a service would free the worker from the dependence on the tender mercies of its leftist sick fund. . . . The working population bears the burden of taxes because Mapai, which controls profitable enterprises, freed them from the tax burden and placed it on the workers.[4]

The only difference, if any, is that the national health service Shostak proposes may fall short of a "nationalized" health service. The exact nature of the "national" health service seems to have been left deliberately vague; whether it meant eliminating the sick funds and replacing them with a single state-run health service modeled on Great Britain's National Health Service or, less radically, retaining the sick funds as contractors under state control, which among other things would enable the smaller sick funds to compete with Kupat Holim on more equal terms, is not clear. This confusion pervaded the National Labor Federation's and the Leumit Sick Fund's position throughout Herut's years in opposition and was never unraveled. Even the more moderate stance, however, was certainly not one that would have allowed Kupat Holim to continue to function as an autonomous, independent body within the Histadrut.

Throughout Shostak's tenure as its general secretary, the National Labor Federation, along with the Leumit Sick Fund, consistently advocated transferring health care control from the Histadrut to the state. Over the years, Leumit Sick Fund representatives appeared before the various Labor-led committees that discussed the country's health services to put forth their position that the ultimate responsibility for health care should be in the hands of the government. The National Labor Federation and the Liberal–Herut alignment that went by the name of Gahal became increasingly vociferous in their demands (Halevi, 1979). During the 1973 Knesset debate on Almogi's and Shem Tov's national health insurance bill, Shostak himself declared that "the sick funds must be disconnected from the trade unions so as to enable their transfer to the state" (*Knesset Minutes*, 1973, Vol. 68, p. 3935). By the time the Likud came to power in 1977, it had a very clear idea of the changes it wanted to effect in health care; and Shostak, supported by Begin, came equipped with a clear ideology supporting those changes and with long experience and intimate familiarity with the workings of the health care system.

The Policy of Exclusion

Since the Likud's vision of health care was so totally contrary to anything that Kupat Holim and the Histadrut would find even remotely acceptable, the first task for the new minister of health had to be to remove these organizations from the policy-making table at which they had sat during Labor's long reign. Shostak, who held the post during both of the two consecutive terms (1977–1981 and 1981–1984), set out to reduce Kupat Holim's power, separate it from the parent body to which it owed so much of its strength, and bring it under the control of the government. As he described his policy retrospectively in 1985:

Our intention was to give the Ministry ministerial status—to enable it to decide independently on matters of allocation, regulation, and patterns of authority and structures in the health system.

> I wanted to change the [financial] support procedure that gave Kupat Holim preferential treatment. In practice, this meant eliminating what had been and replacing it with a new, methodical procedure for the inspection and approval of Kupat Holim's entire budget. Only after Kupat Holim's total budget was approved would subsidies be allocated, and even then the Ministry would make the final decisions.
>
> The huge gaps in development also had to be changed. For years money was allocated for the development of Kupat Holim facilities, while the Ministry's facilities remained in shacks and turned into slums.
>
> In short, to change the Ministry from a struggling bureaucracy into a real ministry, I decided to put an end to all the frameworks in which Kupat Holim had an equal position in policy formation.
>
> For many years, my personal dream and major aim was to enact a national health insurance law that would detach the sick funds, and especially Kupat Holim of the Histadrut, from the trade unions, so as to transfer them to the ownership of the state.[5]

Shostak's retrospective summary of his aims covers all three instruments of policy making and encapsulates the entire Likud policy during his tenure as minister of health. The ascension of the Likud spelled the end to integration: to the contradictions inherent in the idea of "supervised autonomy" and to Shem Tov's hope that the Ministry of Health would be able to make health policy in cooperation with Kupat Holim.

Step by step Shostak set out to transfer control of all three policy-making instruments from Kupat Holim to the Ministry of Health. As he explains, the Ministry of Health would assume its rightful control of the allocation of the health budget, especially that part that went to Kupat Holim. It would become the sole regulatory power by putting an end to all the joint regulatory bodies in which Kupat Holim had enjoyed parity. It would use its budgetary and regulatory powers to rectify the glaring disparity between the ministry's medical facilities, situated in shacks since the days of the British Mandate, and Kupat Holim's newer and better developed hospitals. And it would work to enact a national health insurance law that would deprive Kupat Holim and the Histadrut of the mutual support that they gave one another and entirely subordinate Kupat Holim to the government.

The vision of control is quite encompassing. If Shem Tov's ideal pattern of interaction between Kupat Holim and the government resembled the corporatistic model, characterized by a voluntary quid pro quo between the core and the margins, Shostak's resembled the hierarchical-elitistic one, in which all authority devolved from the core government and all that remained for the body on the margin to do was to implement its decisions. To attain this vision, Kupat Holim had to be stripped of the policy-making powers it had attained under Labor and totally removed from all areas of policy making. What Shostak set out to put into practice was a policy of exclusion. His understanding was that the Ministry of Health would be able to assume its rightful role as health policy maker only if Kupat Holim were ousted from the table where health policy was formulated.[6]

To implement his policy, Shostak brought to the Ministry of Health a new director general, Baruch Modan. Prior to his appointment Modan had been head of the Epidemiology Department at Tel HaShomer Medical Center, the largest government health center in the country and the major locus of the opposition to Kupat Holim and its entire modus operandi since prestate days. Established by the British Mandate authorities, Tel HaShomer offered a refuge to those physicians who were unwilling to live and work in the oppressive socialist and communal framework that Kupat Holim imposed on its workforce in its early days (Bondi, 1981; Zartal, 1975). Employed at Tel HaShomer, they were able to run private practices, live in their own homes, send their children to whatever schools they wished, and myriad other things that Kupat Holim physicians were forbidden to do in prestate days. The doctors that left Kupat Holim in the late 1930s to go to Tel HaShomer harbored a strong antagonism to the Sick Fund. They became the doctors on whom Ben Gurion could call to head the Military Medical Service during the War of Independence when Sorocca refused to do so and, after the establishment of the state, the physicians who staffed the Ministry of Health. They and their heirs at Tel HaShomer became the physicians and professional bureaucrats who, over the years, consistently urged restructuring the health network to reduce Kupat Holim's power and increase that of the Ministry of Health (Modan, 1985).

Tel HaShomer remained a locus of opposition to Kupat Holim even with the passage of time, and Modan, who joined its staff a generation or so later than the Kupat Holim physicians who had found a refuge there in prestate days, was socialized in the atmosphere they created and the views they held. Echoing Shostak, Modan describes the same determination to endow the ministry with real power by removing Kupat Holim from the policy formation process:

> We simply decided and let it be known that the Ministry is a ministry—and that it will be making policies. Kupat Holim was accustomed to making decisions at 101 Arlozorov St. [its headquarters] and having someone—the Ministry of Health—sign them later. But the state should decide how and where to allocate resources. In principal, the sick funds are good for the state, because they are part of the services that are given to its citizens. But I do not believe that if there were no Kupat Holim—which actively made policies—that people would not have received health services.
>
> We tried to turn the ministry into a ministry by expropriating areas of policy making from Kupat Holim, which, in any case, rightfully belong to the state. Like any public system, the health system must be governed by a Ministry that has the ability to establish rules of allocation, development, and so on.[7]

The bureaucracy thus clearly concurred with the minister's sense that Kupat Holim had to be removed from all areas of policy formation for the ministry to fulfill its policy-making role.

Notably, neither Modan nor Shostak shared any of their predecessors' misplaced optimism about Kupat Holim's understanding of the need for reform under Ministry of Health leadership. Both minister and bureaucrat clearly realized that the views of the core and the views of the margin were at odds. Both also entertained the notion that the solution to the conflict lay in the forced capitulation of Kupat Holim by a ministry unfettered by ideological or political allegiance to the Kupat Holim order and determined to exercise the powers vested in it as a core body to formulate policy.

Modan's version expresses a degree of antagonism that does not come out in Shostak's utterance. In reducing Kupat Holim to a service provider and denigrating Kupat Holim's historical role, Modan added insult to injury. The Kupat Holim leadership was very sensitive to the insult, and Haim Doron, Kupat Holim's chairman during these years, so disliked Modan that he refused to speak with him, although he would speak with Shostak. But the conflict was far more fundamental than personal. The basic issue was the role of Kupat Holim in the formation of health policy. Kupat Holim expected a major role; the ministry was intent on excluding it.

But Will It Work?

The policy of exclusion must have struck those who formulated it as just what the doctor ordered to cure the ills of the health system. Ideologically, it was consistent with the Jabotinskian refusal to brook any rivalry to the state's hegemony and with the Jabotinskian view that the state should be the source of health care and other social services. It made sense administratively in that it would enable the core body to plan the health services rationally and efficiently without being constantly thwarted by interested parties. The failure of Shem Tov's integration to reduce the waste and duplication that plagued the health services could only have reinforced the conviction that order could be brought into the chaos only by central control.

It was also a natural outcome of the deep-rooted antagonism between the camps. Shem Tov's policy of integration had derived from the shared sympathy and shared values between the people in government and those who ran Kupat Holim and the Histadrut. This commonality gave hope that the core and margin could work together constructively toward the same end. The Likud came into office with none of this affinity and, moreover, with grounds for anger and resentment. Begin, Shostak, Modan, and others in the new government had all suffered under the long hegemony of Labor, had themselves been delegitimized and excluded for many long years. They did not feel comfortable enough with the heads of the Histadrut and Kupat Holim to engage in the informal give-and-take that would have been required to work with, rather than without, them.

Finally, whether by design or default, the policy of exclusion served political ends. Empowering the Ministry of Health by excluding Kupat Holim and the Histadrut clearly meant, as these organizations well understood, depriving Labor of the very ground on which its house was built. Exclusion was an ideal means of doing away with, or at least seriously disabling, a long-term political rival.

Implementing the policy, however, would prove a Herculean task. Agencies and organizations whose expectations and patterns of behavior have become entrenched through long habit are notoriously resistant to change (Bell, 1976; Ben Porat, 1982; Kaufman, 1971; Sharkansky, 1983; Sharkansky & Radian, 1981; Suleiman, 1987). The more radical the change, the greater the opposition (Anderson, 1975; Bardach, 1977; Sabatier, 1983, 1986; Sabatier & Mazmanian, 1980). New to office and inexperienced in the business of governing, the Likud came in promising to shake up the health system from its foundations. Its policy posed a clear threat to the independent existence of Kupat Holim and to the interests of the Histadrut. Excluded from the policy-formation process, they would fight for control of policy at the implementation stage.

CHAPTER 12

Government Allocation as a Means of Control

Eliezer Shostak saw control over government support for Kupat Holim as a means of empowering the Ministry of Health, of "turning the office into a ministry," that is, a body which could properly carry out its functions as a core government agency.[1] His time in office was marked by major economic changes in Israel, which began with the liberalization of the country's tight currency laws and proceeded to a significant increase in public spending, which together brought on triple-digit inflation (Sharkansky, 1984, 1987). He worked alongside four different finance ministers, whose attitudes toward Kupat Holim ranged from indifferent to hostile. Throughout it all, he methodically set out to make allocation a tool of policy and policy a tool of governing.

A New Broom
The Laor Committee: Intimations of the New Likud Order

The first tidings of the new order for Kupat Holim came in the Laor Committee on Kupat Holim's budget, set up on August 15, 1977, less than three months after the Likud was elected. The committee was established at the suggestion of the secretary of the Histadrut, Yerucham Meshel, who approached the new Likud Minister of Finance, Simcha Erlich, for help with Kupat Holim's usual budget deficit. Finding top ministry bureaucrats less amenable than before, Meshel asked Erlich for a joint examination of ways of providing government support for Kupat Holim.[2] Erlich agreed.

The committee did not provide the succor that Meshel expected. Chaired by Uri Laor, deputy in charge of the Ministry of Finance's Budget Division, it was a joint committee with delegates from the Ministry of Finance, the Ministry of Health, Kupat Holim, and the Histadrut. Meshel took the inclusion of representatives of Kupat Holim and the Histadrut as indication of their continued involvement in making the health budget.[3] It was not. Coordinated with the Ministry of Finance, which was no longer controlled by Mapai and no longer aligned with Kupat Holim and the Histadrut, the Ministry of Health was finally in a position to formulate policy.

Shostak used the committee not to negotiate with Kupat Holim and the Histadrut, as had been the practice under Labor, but to introduce the new Likud order.[4] The new approach, which was made clear in the working paper that laid out the committee's aims and agenda,[5] was to create a multiannual arrangement for balancing Kupat Holim's budget and to establish procedures for government authorization of its budget and for setting the amount of government participation. These aims signified the ministry's intention to cease shelling out money as Kupat Holim spent it and, instead, to institute procedures for allocation that would give the government a say in how much and on what the Sick Fund spent.

The committee's recommendations were consistent with these intentions. The Histadrut and Kupat Holim delegates presented the committee with the traditional tripartite recipe for funding they had promulgated under Labor, whereby one third of Kupat Holim's funding would come from membership dues, one third from the employer participation tax, and one third directly from the government.[6] This recipe would have obliged the government to provide an indeterminate amount of money to Kupat Holim with no relation to its ability to pay its own way and with no say in what the money was spent on. The proposal was rejected outright. Laor, the committee chairman, informed the delegates that government support would not be detached from the totality of Kupat Holim's fiscal activities.[7] The assertion signaled a radical change in the Ministry of Health's allocation policy; for though the various Labor governments had never formally adapted the tripartite division, in practical terms they did, consistently providing more than one third of Kupat Holim's funding via direct subsidy.

For the first time in Kupat Holim's history, the committee set conditions for government support. These were that Kupat Holim increase its independent income and that it adhere to specified procedures for the discussion and approval of its current and development budgets.[8] In both matters, the committee's recommendations entered into the nitty gritty of Kupat Holim's activities in a way that no Labor government had ever done.

The recommendations referred to two ways of increasing Kupat Holim's independent income, both of which were noted in the agenda. One was that Kupat Holim charge for the medicines it disbursed, a first in the Sick Fund's history.[9] The other, more radical, was aimed at increasing the proportion of membership dues collected via the single tax in Kupat Holim's income. The Histadrut traditionally set the single tax so as to appeal to all segments of the population, including high earners. This resulted in regressive dues, whereby the higher one's income the lower the percentage of it one paid. The committee insisted that the tax brackets be adjusted, that the tax rates be raised, and that the lower rates charged to favored groups such as the religious parties, employees of Histadrut enterprises, and others be abolished. It set as a target an increase of about 30% in the portion of the single tax in Kupat Holim's independent revenues: from 17% (which is what it had been in 1977) to 22%.[10]

With regard to procedures, the recommendations were that government funding for Kupat Holim be contingent on approval of its budget by the Ministry of Finance and the Ministry of Health; that approval be granted only if its budget were drawn up in accordance with the same guidelines that applied to the state budget; and that once the budget was approved, the Ministry of Health be empowered to monitor its implementation.[11] These recommendations were seen as a necessary corrective to the budgetary advantages that Kupat Holim, as an autonomous body on the margin, had long enjoyed over the Ministry of Health. Although the Ministry of Health's budget had to conform to government fiscal policy, Kupat Holim's did not. The budgets for the various government ministries were drafted in accord with government guidelines that covered such matters as wages, manpower, services, development, and so forth. Every fiscal year the Ministry of Finance drew up directives in these matters based on the amount of money the government had to spend. Since Kupat Holim never had to conform to these directives, it could pay its doctors and nurses more than the Ministry of Health could pay its medical employees, build when the government was in a recession and the Ministry of Health had to tighten its belt, and present the bill to the government, confident that the government would fork out. The linkage of support to Kupat Holim's adherence to sound procedure was designed, among other things, to put an end these inequalities.

The two sets of recommendations sounded a death knell to the autonomy and power that Kupat Holim and the Histadrut had hitherto enjoyed and the beginning of the empowerment of the core. The recommendations on Kupat Holim's independent revenues meant giving the government a voice in how the Histadrut distributed its resources, reducing the resources it had available for its own and Labor party activities, and undermining its appeal to the wealthier segments of the population. The procedural recommendations would have imposed on Kupat Holim the same budgetary discipline as applied to core government bodies and sharply curtailed its freedom of operation by giving the government the power to inspect, approve or disapprove, and monitor its budget.

In the end, the recommendations were rejected (*State Comptroller Report on the Audit of Kupat Holim,* 1979, p. 35). Erlich and Shostak refused to endorse them because they were part of a package that included the recommendation that government participation in Kupat Holim's budget come to the same proportion as the employer participation tax.[12] Shostak maintained that the Ministry of Health did not have the authority to commit itself to support Kupat Holim at an unknown rate on a long-term basis.[13] Erlich rejected the idea that the government had any responsibility for Kupat Holim, since it was "run by a voluntary organization."[14]

Nonetheless, the Laor Committee signaled a turning point in the relations among the government, the Histadrut, and Kupat Holim. Its basic premise— that the government was in charge—remained central to the Likud's entire allocation policy, while its willingness to confront the Histadrut similarly remained unabated. Its linkage of government support to Kupat Holim's independent income and adherence to formal administrative procedures signified the withdrawal of the carte blanche that Kupat Holim had hitherto enjoyed. Its various recommendations presaged the budgetary regime that the Likud would try to put into effect from that point on.

Allocation Conditioned on Compliance with Ministry Procedures

On April 1, 1978, the minister of health announced to the Knesset Finance Committee the abolition of the allocation formula. More than any other government device, allocation by administrative routine had enabled Kupat Holim to maintain its privileged position in the health system and severed allocation from policy making. Pointing out that the allocation formula had resulted in the "transfer of 92% of government support [for the sick funds] to Kupat Holim," Shostak declared that, "from now on support will be given on the basis of the examination and approval of [Kupat Holim's] budget framework and each item in it."[15] (*State Comptroller Report,* 1983, p. 156; *State Comptroller Report on the Audit of Maccabi Sick Fund,* 1982, p. 44).

The procedures for this examination and approval were published on January 30, 1979, in the Ministry of Health's budget book and sent to the sick funds (*State Comptroller Report,* 1979, pp. 321–22). They covered the preparation, submission, and review of the budgets, Kupat Holim's independent income, a final approval date for the budgets, and means for settling disagreements (Ministry of Health, *Budget Proposal for 1980,* p. 103).

Budget preparation: A balanced budget consistent with government policies. In keeping with the Laor Committee recommendations, the new procedures required the sick funds to submit a balanced budget consistent with the government's policies on health care development and personnel. They made stipulations on building and construction, which were intended to prevent Kupat Holim from expanding without government approval. They limited the number of positions that the sick funds could fill and the salaries they could pay, to bring the number of Kupat Holim employees into line with the personnel policies that applied to government ministries and to reduce the Histadrut's ability to use Kupat Holim for patronage purposes. They stipulated that the sick funds' budgets include the price increases projected due to the country's high inflation; for when these increases had not been included in Kupat Holim's budget in the past, the government was left to finance them through its system of special supports. Additionally, they stipulated that Kupat Holim's independent sources of income reach a government-set minimum. This was designed to force the Histadrut to relinquish a greater part of the single tax.

Budget submission: To the core. Once the proposed budget was drawn up, the procedure demanded that it be submitted first to the Ministry of Health, where it would be examined by the budget division that Shem Tov had created, and then to the Ministry of Finance's budget division for final approval. This meant that if Kupat Holim wanted government support, it would have to submit its budget for the inspection and approval not only of the Histadrut, as it had under Labor, but also for the inspection and approval of core government agencies, just as government ministries had to do.

Budget review. Approval would not be automatic. Every item of the Sick Fund's income and expenditure would be reviewed by the Ministry of Finance and Ministry of Health. Kupat Holim (like the other sick funds) would be required both to justify every item of expenditure and to show how it would be financed. Government support was designated as the amount needed to cover the difference between the approved expenditure and the government-set level of independent revenues. The review was meant to give the core control over the entire range of Kupat Holim's activities and to enable it to set the level of government support for these activities.

Set level of independent revenues. The Ministry of Health and the Ministry of Finance's budget divisions would determine the proportion of its revenues that the Sick Fund would be required to raise from membership dues and what proportions the government would make sure it received from the employer participation tax and from the national treasury. The single tax ceilings were to be linked to the National Insurance Institute ceilings, without concessions and without expenditure for expensive collection mechanisms, and, in return, the government would raise the employer participation tax.

The idea here was to raise the amount of the single tax the Histadrut channeled to Kupat Holim and to ensure that the portion that reached Kupat Holim added up to a fixed proportion of its revenues. Kupat Holim was specifically instructed to convey to the Histadrut that the government was not interested in the latter's other activities, in the cost of collecting the single tax, or in the discounts that it chose to give to favored groups.

Approval date. Kupat Holim's budget would have to be approved before the beginning of the fiscal year. This requirement was yet another means of trying to keep Kupat Holim from first spending and then submitting the bill.

Dispute adjudication. In the event of disagreement between sick fund and ministry bureaucrats, the matter would be decided by the ministers. This provision was designed to prevent Kupat Holim from exploiting disagreements on the bureaucratic level to do what it wanted.

The new allocation procedures were formulated and dictated to Kupat Holim by the government without any input from the Sick Fund, and they changed the rules of the game in force till then. They constituted a rejection of most of the red lines that Labor neither wished nor dared to cross. They interfered in the hitherto untouchable issue of membership dues, abolished both Kupat Holim's and the Histadrut's financial autonomy, and ended the automatic government support that had made it impossible for the core to regulate the margin while leaving it to bankroll the margin's excesses.

The Imposition of Government Policy

The new allocation procedures were designed to give the Ministry of Health control over the health system. They were used to further a specific policy of health care financing, consisting of a substantial reduction in Kupat Holim's expenditures and considerable increase in its independent income to set off a sharp drop in government support. As Shostak explained retrospectively:

> It [Kupat Holim] will not force its needs on the system. We determine the needs. We approve support not on the basis of an allocation formula, but as part of a general budget framework, after adjusting the revenues and expenditures of the sick fund to our requirements. This gives us control over Kupat Holim's sources of income: we decide on how much from each source, in accord with the demands of the Ministry of Finance. We will endeavor to base Kupat Holim's budget on independent sources of income, while reducing the rate of government support.[16]

Shostak and the various finance ministers who served during the Likud years set out to impose this financial policy over Kupat Holim's and the Histadrut's predictably strong objections.

The Discussions of Kupat Holim's 1978–1979 Budget

Their efforts may be illustrated in the discussions preceding the approval of Kupat Holim's 1978–1979 budget. The discussions took place in three stages between February 1978 and December 1978 (*State Comptroller Report on the Audit of Kupat Holim*, 1979, pp. 38–41). Only the first preceded the April 1 deadline, at the start of the new fiscal year. As the new regulations stipulated, the proposal covered its expenditures, independent income, and direct government support, which Kupat Holim termed its "deficit."

In the first stage, each side presented its opening position (in millions of IL) as presented in Table. 12.1. A considerable gap can be seen in the sides' opening positions. Kupat Holim set a higher expenditure figure than the Ministry of Finance and the Ministry of Health and a lower figure for its independent income—the money it would raise on its own. The result was that the government subsidy it demanded—notably the same one third of its expenditures that it had proposed in the traditional tripartite formula rejected by the Laor Committee—was three times as large as that proposed by the Ministry of Finance and twice as large as that proposed by the Ministry of Health.

To close the gap, a second meeting took place toward the end of May. This time, the Ministry of Finance and the Ministry of Health presented a joint proposal, which raised both the expenditures and the government support they were prepared to authorize but demanded somewhat more independent income from Kupat Holim in exchange. Kupat Holim agreed to raise more in independent

Table 12.1. First Budget Proposal*

	Ministry of Health	Ministry of Finance	Kupat Holim
Expenditure	6,203	5,878	7,291
Revenues	5,151	5,151	4,825
Government support	1,052	727	2,466
Percentage of revenues	83.04%	87.63%	66.18%
Percentage of government support	16.96%	12.37%	33.82%

* In million Israeli Lirot.

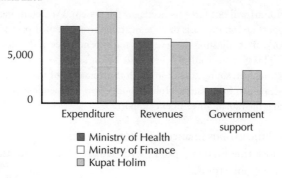

Table 12.2. Second Budget Proposal*

	Ministry of Health and Ministry of Finance	Kupat Holim
Expenditure	6,801	7,840
Revenues	5,281	5,281
Government support	1,520	2,559
Percentage of revenues	77.65%	67.36%
Percentage of government support	22.35%	32.64%

* In million Israeli Lirot.

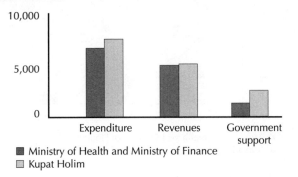

■ Ministry of Health and Ministry of Finance
□ Kupat Holim

income by pressuring the Histadrut for an additional IL 165 million of the single tax, but increased its expenditures and, with that, the amount it claimed in government support, which still amounted to one third of its expenditures. Table 12.2 presents the second proposals. Although the differences had been narrowed, no agreement was reached.

The third meeting took place at the end of December. This time the ministries accepted some more of Kupat Holim's expenditure demands but not its demands for direct government support. But Kupat Holim was unwilling to trim its expenditures to the level the government required, made no offer to raise more in independent income, and continued to insist that one third of its funding come from direct government support. The third proposals are shown in Table 12.3. The third round ended in a stalemate as well, leaving a difference of IL 859 million in the expenditure Kupat Holim claimed and that which the government was willing to approve.

Failing to reach agreement, the government authorized its own third proposal, assuming that Kupat Holim would have no choice but to go along with it. To cover the missing IL 859 million, the Ministry of Finance and the Ministry of Health directed Kupat Holim to cut its budget immediately by IL 277 million (3.5%) and find independent sources of income for the remaining IL 582 million (7.5%). Before Kupat Holim had time to respond, the Ministry of Health presented it with an itemized proposal for the reduction of its expenses. The propo-

Table 12.3. Third Budget Proposal*

	Ministry of Health and Ministry of Finance	Kupat Holim
Expenditure	6,981	7,840
Revenues	5,281	5,281
Government support	1,520	2,559
Percentage of revenues	75.65%	67.36%
Percentage of government support	21.77%	32.64%

* In million Israeli Lirot.

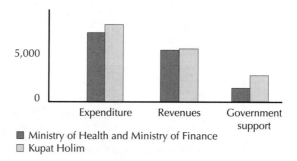

sal stipulated IL 42 million worth of cuts in unapproved appointments and IL 70 million in other items of expenditure, IL 40 million worth of cuts in the Histadrut's Central Tax Bureau collection fees, and the transfer of IL 125 from Kupat Holim's regular budget to its development budget—adding up to exactly IL 277 million.[17] These directives show the Likud government's unwillingness to fund Kupat Holim's activities without a say in what they were and its readiness to specify in considerable detail what they should be. They show its determination to use allocation as a tool of policy and policy as a tool of governing.

Several features of these budget discussions are noteworthy. The discussions were marked by wrangling over the levels of support, independent income, and expenditures, the three components of the government's policy on Kupat Holim's budget. The sides started with completely different assumptions about these components. The Ministry of Finance and Ministry of Health regarded government support as the amount needed to cover the difference between Kupat Holim's approved expenditures and its independent income, and they maintained that the government had the right to determine what those expenditures and independent income would be. They consistently demanded that to obtain government support, Kupat Holim must cut its expenditures and raise more in independent income. Kupat Holim consistently demanded government support to the tune of a third of its expenditures, whatever these were, and saw both its expenditures and independent income as its own prerogative. It regarded government support as its due in payment for its health care services and did not concede the government's right to put a ceiling on its expenditures in exchange for that support. Both sides thus tried to control the components of Kupat Holim's budget that the other regarded as its autonomous domain.

Each side made its calculations on a different numerical basis. Each calculated the percentage of government support in Kupat Holim's budget on the basis of its own determination of Kupat Holim's expenditures. Thus the 22% in subsidies that the government offered Kupat Holim would have amounted to only 18% were Kupat Holim's assessment of its expenditures used as the basis for calculating. Such discrepancies resulted in acrimonious arguments not only over principles but also over the "facts."

Both sides stuck to their guns despite the consequences. To implement its budget policy over Kupat Holim's objections, the government was ready to extend the 1978–1979 budget discussions to the end of the fiscal year, in the meantime depriving Kupat Holim of direct government support. Kupat Holim was equally ready to extend the discussions and forego that support, in order to make the government accede to its wishes. The standoff was brought to an end, but not resolved, by government fiat, with which Kupat Holim never complied.

Despite the government's directives, Kupat Holim never made the adjustments needed to close the gap between the authorized government support and its own demands. This left it with a budget deficit of approximately 10% by government figures.

Much the same scenario was played out throughout the Likud's term in office. The wrangling that marked the 1978–1979 budget discussions became a regular feature of all financial discussions between the government and the Sick Fund. The gap in the sides' starting assumptions was never bridged, the disparity in their calculations never rectified, and the annual deficit in Kupat Holim's budget never funded. While the deficit accumulated year after year, the government persisted in imposing its three-pronged budget policy on the recalcitrant Sick Fund and trade union. As they cut government support, Shostak and the various Likud finance ministers continued to insist that Kupat Holim increase its independent income and decrease in its expenditures. Kupat Holim, along with the Histadrut, would comply to some extent but generally resist.

The remainder of this section examines government efforts to impose its budget policy of reduced government support, increased independent income, and reduced Kupat Holim expenditures on these bodies on the margin.

Reduced Government Support

Reduced government participation in Kupat Holim's budget was both a major aim of the Likud's allocation policy and the lever the Likud would use to pressure Kupat Holim and the Histadrut to comply with its demands on Kupat

Holim's independent income and expenditures. It was the one part of the three-pronged policy on Kupat Holim's budget that the government had the power to effect through unilateral action, and the only part in which it can be said to have been generally successful.

The cuts were made, beginning in the 1980 fiscal year, under three of the four finance ministers who served during the Likud term in office. They were made along with, and perhaps in part as an outcome of, cuts in the government's over-all expenditure on health, which could be justified by the Likud's preelection promises to cut government spending and liberalize the economy (Freedman, 1982; Sharkansky & Radian, 1981). The cuts did not begin immediately. Simcha Erlich (1977–1979), the first of four Likud finance ministers to serve during the period under discussion, was occupied with cutting government subsidies on basic goods and liberalizing Israel's tight foreign currency controls. He went along with Shostak's budgetary procedures, but kept government support for the sick funds at the previous Labor level (Ministry of Health, *Budget Proposals for 1979, 1980, and 1981*).

The cuts began when Erlich left the Ministry of Finance toward the end of 1979 and were made consistently thereafter by each of the three finance ministers who followed him, even though their overall economic policies differed. Erlich was replaced by Yigal Horowitz (1979–1981), whose economic program was aimed at reducing Israel's economic dependence on the United States. This meant an immediate reduction in the standard of living. Horowitz's favorite assertion was, "I don't have," which he translated into an emergency economic program that included reducing subsidies, raising direct taxation, and lowering wages (Ben Porat, 1982; Sharkansky, 1985, p. 38). Government expenditure on health, as on other sectors, was reduced, with a 6% cut in spending achieved in part by a 6% cut in the number of Ministry of Health jobs (Ministry of Finance, *State of Israel Budget Principles for 1980*, pp. 68–70). At the same time, the Ministry of Health radically cut its participation in Kupat Holim's budget. According to Kupat Holim calculations, direct government support was halved from its late 1970's level of more than 25% of its expenditures on average to a mere 13% (Kupat Holim, *Managerial Report to the 12th Convention*, 1988, p. 62).

The next finance minister, Yoram Aridor (1981–1983), changed Horowitz's nostrum to a more generous one: the "correct economy." He increased subsidies on basic goods, froze prices on staples despite the galloping inflation, approved a full cost-of-living wage increase, and reduced the high import levies on cars, electrical appliances, and other imports, producing a burst of consumer spending and artificially bringing up the standard of living. Nonetheless, Aridor's Ministry of Finance continued to reduce government participation in the National Expenditure on Health (*State Comptroller Report*, 1985, pp. 252, 284). In the 1981–1982 fiscal year the Ministry of Health transferred only 8.73% of its budget to the sick funds, in contrast to approximately one fourth of its budget the year before and around one third in the late 1970s (Zalmanovitch, 1991, p. 138).

Of all the Likud's finance ministers, Aridor was particularly hard on Kupat Holim. His bread and circuses economic policy had two aims. One was to attain a second Begin victory in the upcoming elections by easing the hardships of the Horowitz era. The other was to pull the rug out from under the Histadrut, in which he had served in the 1960s as a representative of a right-wing faction and which he hated with a passion. His policy was to undermine the Histadrut by having the government provide the populace with the "goods" that the Histadrut had traditionally fought for in its annual wage negotiations. The Histadrut indeed feared losing its influence among the workers (Ben Porat, 1982, pp. 329 –31).

Of all the Histadrut's "goods," health care was the jewel in the crown, and Aridor's tightfistedness with Kupat Holim, in sharp contrast to his openhandedness in other areas, can be seen as a spoiling tactic. Aridor was deaf to Kupat Holim's complaints that the reduction of government funding during the Horowitz era had already jeopardized its operations.[18] The discussions of Kupat Holim's budget during his term as finance minister were particularly acrimonious. The Sick Fund's budget for the 1981–1982 fiscal year was never approved because the sides could not agree on the percentage of its expenditures that would be financed by direct government subsidies. The discussions of the 1981–1982 fiscal year were not concluded until October, when Kupat Holim consented to accept the Ministry of Finance's offer of 13.6% (*State Comptroller Report*, 1983, pp. 159 –60; *State Comptroller Report on the Audit of Kupat Holim*, 1985, pp. 59 – 60). These delays added to Kupat Holim's financial hardships.

Toward the end of 1983 the skyrocketing inflation and the failure of his correct economy forced Aridor to resign. Yigal Cohen Orgad, who served as finance minister for a single year, succeeded him. To repair the damage Aridor had wreaked, Orgad adapted a conservative fiscal policy and he too sharply cut the Ministry of Health's net budget and forced it to reduce radically the money it allocated to Kupat Holim (Ministry of Health, *Budget Proposal for 1984*, pp. 46 –47). Under Orgad the Ministry of Health allocated less than 20% of its net budget to the sick funds (Zalmanovitch, 1991, p. 138).

In short, although the four Likud finance ministers pursued different economic policies, they all, with the exception of Simcha Erlich, cut government spending on health care and brought about a reduction of government support for the sick funds, including Kupat Holim. In the late 1970s, the Ministry of Health allocated about one third of its budget to the sick funds. In 1980 the portion dropped to about one fourth (Zalmanovitch, 1991, p. 138) and never reached one third again. In Kupat Holim's calculations, between 1980 and 1985 government support declined from more than one fourth of its expenditures to between 11.4% and 14%.[19]

Increased Independent Income

With the exception of Erlich, the various Likud finance ministers consistently demanded that Kupat Holim increase its independent income (Ministry of Finance, *State of Israel Budget Principles for 1980*, pp. 68–70; for 1981, pp. 92–95). The various methods they recommended included setting a fee for services, raising medication charges to keep pace with inflation, streamlining hospital and ambulatory services, and demanding a higher proportion of the single tax from the Histadrut. Their endeavors focused on what the Likud finance and health ministers regarded as Kupat Holim's two stable sources of nongovernmental revenue: the employer participation tax (Ministry of Health, *Budget Proposal for 1982*, p. 129) and the membership dues from the single tax (*State Comptroller Report*, 1987, p. 367). But while the government could cut support unilaterally, it did not have the same direct, exclusive control over Kupat Holim's independent revenues, and its success was only partial.

The Employer Participation Tax

Kupat Holim's revenues from the employer participation tax were relatively easy for the government to increase because its rates and terms were set by the minister of Labor and Welfare. The employer participation tax was raised several times during the Likud term in office: from 3.65% of each employee's gross wages in April 1978 to 4.95% in April 1980, bringing up revenues from this source by around a third.[20] In addition, beginning in April 1984, the National Insurance Institute began to collect the "participation" taxes of the self-employed, many of whom had not sent payment to the Histadrut's Central Tax Bureau.

The Single Tax

In the matter of membership dues, the government was somewhat less successful. The Likud finance ministers all saw the single tax as Kupat Holim's main source of independent income and consistently demanded that the Sick Fund increase its income from this source. Immediately on coming into office, the Likud's second finance minister, Horowitz asserted that he would support Kupat Holim if it raised this tax. With his consent, the Knesset's Finance Committee transferred IL 400 million to Kupat Holim on condition that it hike up the single tax by 150%.[21] In its budget talks with the Ministry of Finance and the Ministry of Health, Kupat Holim was repeatedly pressured to amend its regressive tax rates, raise the taxable income rate, reduce collection costs, and change the tax partners code (which contained the proportions of the tax that went to Kupat Holim and the other tax partners) so that it would receive a larger portion of the dues collected (*State Comptroller Report on the Audit of Kupat Holim,* 1985, pp. 58–60; *State Comptroller Report,* 1986, p. 246).

Posed as conditions for support, these demands in effect pressured Kupat Holim to pressure the Histadrut. In accord with the Histadrut's constitution, the single tax was set and controlled not by Kupat Holim, but by the Histadrut itself. The tax rates, tax brackets, tax ceilings, and tax partners code were all in the domain of the Histadrut. Its Central Committee (i.e., its government) proposed the terms, its Executive Committee (i.e., parliament) had to approve them, and its Central Tax Bureau implemented them.[22]

The government was unconcerned with the formal distinction between Kupat Holim and the Histadrut and did not hesitate to press its demands, which impinged on the trade union's organizational and ideological needs. Rectifying its regressive dues structure and raising the level of income subject to dues could cost the Histadrut its high-income members. Reducing the collection fee and apportioning more of the dues to Kupat Holim would reduce its options for patronage and take revenues away from its politically advantageous social and cultural activities (Becker, 1982, pp. 273–74). The very fact of a government say in the single tax constituted an infringement of the Histadrut's hitherto inviolable autonomy. The stakes were high, and the government was only partially successful.

Tax brackets. As the right side of Table 12.4 shows, the Histadrut amended its tax brackets several times between April 1980 and March 1985, and from 1982 added a third bracket to cover people with high incomes (*Histadrut Report to the 14th National Convention,* 1981, p. 243; Ministry of Health, *Budget Proposal for 1983,* p. 139; 1987, p. 133). Columns A, B, and C cover respectively low, medium, and high incomes. As can be seen, the income in each tax bracket was successively raised (in part to keep up with the three-digit inflation of those years), and the addition of a third tax bracket from 1982 meant that people with higher incomes paid a different rate than those with low and moderate incomes.

Table 12.4. Single Tax Brackets and National Insurance Institute Ceilings*[23]

| Date | SingleTax Brackets per Income Level | | | National Insurance Ceiling (IL) | Ratio | | |
	A	B	C		A	B	C
April 1980	2,000	3,000	—	6,300	31.7%	47.6%	—
April 1982	8,000	18,000	30,000	33,600	23.8%	53.6%	89.3%
April 1983	21,000	46,000	70,000	80,871	26.0%	56.9%	86.6%
April 1984	65,000	145,000	210,000	262,000	24.7%	55.2%	80.0%
March 1985	230,000	490,000	700,000	827,300	27.8%	59.2%	84.6%

* In Israeli Shekels.

Table 12.5. Single Tax Rates: Percentage per Tax Bracket[24]

Bracket	January 1980	April 1983	May 1984	September 1985	November 1985
Bracket A	3.85%	3.9%	3.9%	3.9%	3.9%
Bracket B	1.50%	2.5%	2.7%	2.7%	2.9%
Bracket C	—	1.5%	1.7%	1.7%	2.0%
Bracket D	—	—	—	1.0%	1.3%

On the other hand, as can be seen in the right side of the table, the income level of the high earners taxed at rate C fell short of the ceiling set by the National Insurance Institute for calculating its own monthly insurance charges. Because persons who earned more than the C ceiling paid the same rate as those who earned below it, the Histadrut levies remained more lenient than government social security levies.

Tax rates. Similarly, as Table 12.5 shows, single tax rates were raised several times during this period. However, the rates remained regressive, since high earners continued to pay a smaller percentage of their income than lower earners, just as they had from very early on in Kupat Holim's history.[25]

Collection fee. The demands with regard to the collection fee that the Histadrut charged Kupat Holim for collecting its dues were also met only in part. By somewhat streamlining its organization and firing employees, the Central Tax Bureau was able to cut costs and thereby reduce the percentage of the single tax it charged Kupat Holim as Table 12.6 shows. It did not, however, abolish the fee (*State Comptroller Report,* 1986, p. 288).

Tax partners code. Higher tax brackets, a progressive dues structure, and the elimination of the collection fee were all intended to increase the amount of money the Histadrut raised by the single tax. In addition, the government pressured the Histadrut to apportion more of the pie to Kupat Holim by changing the tax partners code to give the Sick Fund the largest portion. As Table 12.7 shows, the Histadrut slowly but surely relinquished an ever-increasing portion of the single tax.

Table 12.6. Central Tax Bureau Expenditures and Collection Fees, 1978–1985[26]

	1978	1979	1980	1981	1982	1983	1984	1985
Expenditure percent of single tax	7.67%	7.12%	5.99%	5.41%	5.32%	4.68%	4.58%	4.58%
Percent paid by Kupat Holim as collection fee	7.04%	6.80%	6.06%	5.23%	4.52%	4.42%	4.32%	4.24%
Number of Central Tax Bureau employees	790	734	723	711	691	674	672	665

Table 12.7. Reapportionment of the Single Tax: 1978–1984[27]

	1978	1979	1980	1981	1982	1983	1984
Percentage transferred to Kupat Holim	59.79%	59.21%	60.09%	62.29%	64.59%	65.45%	66.54%
Percentage of Kupat Holim's budget	14.40%	14.40%	15.10%	16.00%	18.80%	18.10%	19.20%
Percentage transferred to the Histadrut	40.21%	40.79%	39.91%	37.71%	35.41%	34.54%	33.46%

Although compliance was incomplete and the Histadrut retained approximately one third of the single tax to fund its cultural, social, and political activities, the government did manage to raise the percentage that the single tax constituted in Kupat Holim's budget by approximately one fourth between 1978 and 1984. This represented a sacrifice on the part of the Histadrut, which, in the words of a spokesman, it made "to avoid impairing the high level of Kupat Holim health services" given the reduction in government support.[28]

The Outcome: Increased Independent Income

Up until 1984 Kupat Holim's relative income from the single tax and the employer participation tax increased steadily, as can be seen in Table 12.8 based on Kupat Holim computations.

In the years under discussion, the percentage of independent income in Kupat Holim's expenditure's budget increased by an average of just over 9%. With this the government achieved at least part of its goal of establishing stable, permanent sources of independent income for Kupat Holim.

Decreased Expenditures

In the matter of Kupat Holim's expenditures, however, the Likud had no success. Of the three parts of its policy on Kupat Holim's budget, this was the most important from the point of view of its ability to govern health policy as a whole, for the simple and obvious reason that spending translates into activity. The Likud assumed that its reduction of support would force Kupat Holim to

Table 12.8. Independent Income: Percentage of Expenditures, 1978–1984[29]

Source of Revenues	1978	1979	1980	1981	1982	1983	1984
Employer participation tax	34.0%	39.1%	42.1%	41.7%	44.1%	43.8%	32.8%
Single tax	14.4%	14.4%	15.1%	16.0%	18.9%	19.1%	19.2%
Total	48.4%	53.5%	57.2%	57.7%	63.0%	62.9%	52.0%

cut its expenditures, thereby freeing up money for the government's own priorities and compelling Kupat Holim to comply with the government's overall economic policies.

As bodies on the margin, Kupat Holim and the Histadrut were less interested in government priorities and more interested in the Sick Fund's survival as an active, strong, and autonomous body. Given this imperative, Kupat Holim refused to operate within the reduced government-approved expenditures. As Israel Kessar, who replaced Meshel as secretary of the Histadrut in 1984, put it, "If the government decreases its support for Kupat Holim . . . someone has to finance it."[30] Kupat Holim Chairman Doron articulated the amount needed. With the drop in government support, he said, "Kupat Holim is 10% off its budget, short $80 million to $100 million a year of what it needs . . . to supply the services and develop the facilities expected of it."[31] His 10% figure is consistent with the deficit in Kupat Holim's 1978–1979 budget.

Neither Kupat Holim nor the Histadrut leadership even conceived of contracting the Sick Fund's activities or size to stay within its government approved budget. At most, Kupat Holim made internal administrative changes to cut costs somewhat, reducing the number of doctor's visits and the average annual expenditure per member.[32] But it did not decrease the scope or variety of its activities. While the government pursued its course, Kupat Holim and the Histadrut pursued theirs, no more ready to recognize the authority of the Likud government than they had been to recognize that of the Labor governments.

The Deficit Grew

The result was a growing Kupat Holim deficit, which was not offset by the increase in its independent income. The data in Table 12.9 are based on Kupat Holim computations.

Dialogue of the Deaf

The government's efforts to impose its budgetary policy on Kupat Holim revealed a huge conceptual rift. Not surprisingly, Kupat Holim and the government

Table 12.9. Government Support and Kupat Holim's Deficit as a Percentage of Kupat Holim's Expenditures, 1977–1986[33]

Source of Revenues	1977	1978	1979	1980	1981	1982	1983	1984	1985
Government participation	28.1%	29.8%	24.0%	13.0%	14.2%	13.6%	11.7%	11.3%	6.7%
Budget deficit	6.0%	6.5%	7.1%	13.9%	11.5%	7.9%	10.8%	30.6%	29.2%

each blamed the other for the deficit. Haim Doron, chairman of Kupat Holim, pointed to the unilateral cuts in government support:

> The present government [1981] has us in a stranglehold. It has cut several billions [IL] off our budget. . . . They have cut into our live flesh. First the government suddenly causes a huge deficit, and then the Minister of Health warns that we are about to go under. . . . Who caused this situation? Who brought on this danger? Whose fault is it?[34]

The Ministry of Health held that:

> It is not true that we stopped support for Kupat Holim. This is a mistake and a distortion of the truth. We reduced some of the support but have raised the employer participation tax. So they cancel each other out. The Chairman of Kupat Holim, Haim Doron, plays around with the percentages as suits him. But we have neither stopped nor reduced support. We have only distributed it differently.[35]

Kupat Holim presented figures showing that government support had decreased despite the rise in the employer participation tax. The Ministry of Health and the Ministry of Finance argued that since Kupat Holim's independent sources of income from the single tax and the employer participation tax had risen, the government could legitimately reduce the level of its direct support. [36]

Kupat Holim's basic assumption was that the government "owed" it money for the health services it provided to the public and that it itself was in the best position to know how much money was required. The government's assumption was that Kupat Holim should toe the line on its expenditures and activities while raising more revenues on its own. Neither side grasped the basic premises of the other.

Part of the argument revolved around the employer participation tax. When originally conceived, the employer participation tax was regarded as part of Kupat Holim's independent income in that it did not come directly from government coffers. This was the view of Labor and initially the view of the Likud. The Likud reassessed the tax, however, when it could not get Kupat Holim to accept its dictates on the sick fund's expenditure level.

The finance minister began to contend that the employer participation tax was part of the government's support for the sick funds (*State Comptroller Report*, 1987, pp. 362–63). Kupat Holim argued that it was not, and took out a huge ad in the upscale *Ha'aretz* newspaper stating: "The employer participation tax is not the government's participation in Kupat Holim's budget, but the employers' participation as part of the workers' social benefits."[37] The Ministry of Finance's Budget Division was quick to reply. Director Aaron Fogel declared that "the employer participation tax, intended to fund the health system, is an integral part of the government's participation in Kupat Holim's budget."[38] This dispute became part of the annual discussion of Kupat Holim's budget.

Both the government and Kupat Holim claimed the right to the last word on Kupat Holim's budget, even though each had a different view of the government's responsibility to Kupat Holim, of the funds to which Kupat Holim was and was not entitled as a matter of right, and of the terms for its receiving those funds. The government maintained that direct government support should be contingent on the Sick Fund's conforming to a government expenditure ceiling and should do no more than bridge the gap between the Sick Fund's authorized expenditures and its independent income. Kupat Holim maintained that it was entitled to direct government funding and the proceeds of the employer participation tax and denied the government any say about either its expenditures or the single tax or other independently raised revenues. Arguing that it provided a public service for which the government should pay a substantial part, it considered it the government's responsibility to fund the expenditures it itself determined and continued to demand government subsidies based solely on its own statements of its needs. These different conceptions resulted in different explanations of Kupat Holim's annual budget deficits.

Table 12.10 and Table 12.11 show Kupat Holim's budget deficit from the opposing perspectives. Table 12.10 shows it from Kupat Holim's point of view, based on its own evaluation of its expenditure needs and its own calculations. The upper section of the table shows that while the percentage of the Sick Fund's expenditures covered by the employer participation tax increased during most of this period, the percentage covered by direct government subsidies dropped sharply beginning in 1980—from approximately one fourth in its 1978 and 1979 budgets to somewhat over a tenth thereafter. The result was a decline of about one third in the percentage of its expenditures that was covered by these "external" sources (line 3) between 1978 and 1984.

The lower part of the table shows Kupat Holim's perception of how its deficit was created. Line 4 shows the percentage of the Sick Fund's expenditures that remained to be covered after direct government subsidies and the employer participation taxes were received. As can be seen, as external support decreased, the percentage of its budget that needed to be funded from other sources steadily increased. After 1980, when the first serious cuts were made in direct government funding, close to one half of Kupat Holim's expenditures remained to be funded from other sources as opposed to slightly more than one third in the years before. Line 5 shows the percentage of its expenditures covered by the revenues it raised from fees, the sale of services and membership dues. This increased somewhat over the years, but never by enough to cover the shortfall left by the reduction in government subsidies. Kupat Holim saw no reason that it should.

The deficit (line 6) is the difference between what Kupat Holim needed to run its health services as it saw fit (line 4) after receiving the external support to

Table 12.10. Kupat Holim's View: Deficit Resulting from Reduced Government Support, 1978–1984 (Percent of Expenditures)[39]

	1978	1979	1980	1981	1982	1983	1984
Entitled External Support							
Direct government subsidies	29.8%	24.0%	13.0%	14.2%	13.6%	11.7%	11.3%
Employer participation tax	34.0%	39.0%	42.1%	41.7%	44.1%	43.8%	32.8%
Total external support received	63.8%	63.0%	55.1%	55.9%	57.7%	55.5%	44.1%
Creation of the Deficit							
Expenditures not covered by external support	36.2%	37.0%	44.9%	44.1%	42.3%	44.5%	55.9%
Self-raised revenues	29.7%	29.9%	31.0%	32.6%	34.4%	33.7%	25.3%
Deficit	6.5%	7.1%	13.9%	11.5%	7.9%	10.8%	30.6%

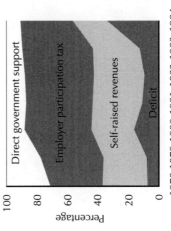

Table 12.11. Government View: Deficit Resulting from Kupat Holim Overspending, 1978–1984 (Percentage of Kupat Holim's Expenditures)[40]

	1978	1979	1980	1981	1982	1983	1984
Entitled External Support							
Employer participation tax	34.0%	39.0%	42.1%	41.7%	44.1%	43.8%	32.8%
Self-raised revenues	29.7%	29.9%	31.0%	32.6%	34.4%	33.7%	25.3%
Total	63.7%	68.9%	73.1%	74.3%	79.5%	77.5%	58.1%
Creation of the Deficit							
Expenditures not covered by stable sources of income	36.3%	31.1%	26.9%	25.7%	21.5%	22.5%	41.9%
Direct government support	29.8%	24.0%	13.0%	14.2%	13.6%	11.7%	11.3%
Deficit	6.5%	7.1%	13.9%	11.5%	7.9%	10.8%	30.6%

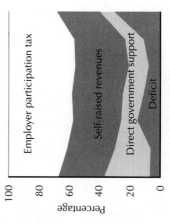

which it was entitled and its internal sources of revenue (line 5). From Kupat Holim's perspective, its deficit began to swell with the sharp reduction of government subsidies in 1980, and the responsibility for the deficit was entirely that of the government.

Table 12.11, based on the same Kupat Holim figures, shows the deficit from the government's point of view. Here the upper part of the table shows what the government regarded as Kupat Holim's stable external sources of income: the percentage of its expenditures covered by the employer participation tax and its self-raised revenues. In the government's version, these were the only funds that Kupat Holim was entitled to as a matter of course. As can be seen (line 3), these funds rose by about 20% between 1978 and 1983.

The lower part of the table shows the government's perception of Kupat Holim's deficit. Line 4 shows the percentage of the Sick Fund's expenditures that remained to be covered after its stable external sources of income were received. Line 5 shows the percentage funded by direct subsidies, which declined. In the government's view, meeting all the funding needs that Kupat Holim claimed was not the government's responsibility. The reduction in direct subsidies was to be matched by a concomitant cut in the Sick Fund's spending.

The deficit (line 6) in this view is the difference between the percentage of the Sick Fund's expenditures not covered by its stable external sources of income and the government subsidies Kupat Holim received. It was the result of Kupat Holim's refusal, beginning in the 1980 fiscal year, to cut its spending to fit its overall income. Kupat Holim, not the government, was responsible.

Obstruction of the Likud Allocation Policy

The Likud's allocation policy meant that Kupat Holim would either have to find alternative sources of funding or pare down its activities: build fewer clinics, purchase less equipment, reduce its workforce, cut down on its renovation and construction, and so forth. This was unacceptable. As Doron told a radio interviewer in 1985: "It is not our way to . . . cut out medical services, shut down medical services, or reduce medical services."[41] Such cutbacks were seen as cutting into Kupat Holim's size and power and as nothing short of a life threat (Becker, 1982, p. 276). Equally unacceptable was the Likud's solution that Kupat Holim pressure the Histadrut to compensate for the shortfall by allocating it a greater portion of the single tax.

To some extent, the Histadrut tried to bargain with the government. One of the major rituals of Israeli public policy was the annual tripartite labor negotiations among the government, the country's private employers, and the

Histadrut. The parties discussed wages and working conditions in these negotiations, as well as a range of matters connected with the country's economy,
from government subsidies (e.g., on food and public services) through interest
rates. These negotiations were de rigueur. Without Histadrut agreement almost
all of Israel's economy would have ground to a halt (Shalev, 1992). For many
years, the threat, sometimes exercised, always hanging like a Damocles sword,
gave the Histadrut enormous leverage, which it could and sometimes did exercise on behalf of Kupat Holim.

Histadrut Secretary General Meshel told that Aridor's hostility forced the
Histadrut to bargain away employees' benefits to sustain Kupat Holim:

> In Begin's and Aridor's time, I acted with one purpose—to keep the Histadrut, Hevrat
> Haovdim [the Histadrut holding company], and Kupat Holim alive, which was a ter-
> rible burden. I toned down the battle [for workers' rights] because I wanted to get
> funds for Kupat Holim. Don't forget, the government in office could decide whether to
> turn its back on me or to help me. If it had turned its back, the situation could have
> been catastrophic.[42]

The more characteristic solution that Kupat Holim and the Histadrut
adopted was to flout government policy. Under Labor, Kupat Holim had often
circumvented government policy. Perhaps the most notable example occurred
in 1976 when it removed Kupat Holim patients from government hospitals
when the government began to charge a realistic price for the beds. But as
long as Kupat Holim had been part of the policy-making process, it had little
need for a head-on collision. After the Likud intentionally excluded Kupat
Holim from policy formation, however, policy obstruction became the sick
fund's modus operandi. Once it could no longer prevent undesirable measures
before they were adopted, all Kupat Holim could do was to try to prevent their
implementation.

The obstruction proceeded along three main avenues: Kupat Holim (1) sabo-
taged the proper conduct of the budget discussions so as to extract more funding and prevent government supervision of its activities; (2) it ran up large debts
and a monumental budget deficit to finance its activities; and (3) it imposed
sanctions to force the government to allocate it more money.

Although the various means of obstruction were ad hoc, adapted as the circumstances demanded or enabled, the policy of obstruction on which Kupat
Holim embarked was a carefully considered one. It was designed to enable
Kupat Holim to maintain itself as a powerful, independent entity in a hostile
government climate and to continue—or expand—its previous level of operations despite government attempts to compel a reduction. It was grounded on
Kupat Holim's confidence that, for all the government's formal powers, it had
the means to force the government's hand.

Sabotage of the Budget Discussions

The new Likud allocation procedure required Kupat Holim to submit data on its activities and expenditures, along with a detailed financial report of the previous year, so that the Ministry of Finance and the Ministry of Health could examine and cross-check the figures against their own and set the amount of government support for the coming year. Between 1978 and 1984, Kupat Holim systematically undermined the procedure.

The budget proposals it submitted were generally slender little booklets no more than a few pages long, whose contents were too vague and unclear for the supervising ministries to comprehend or base decisions on.[43] In an interview I conducted with the Kupat Holim treasurer, he acknowledged that submitting the proposals in this way was an intentional act designed to conceal the activities that the Sick Fund feared the government would not approve.[44] To the same end, the figures that Kupat Holim submitted were often lower than the real ones. This also concealed the scope of the Sick Fund's activities and the size of its deficit, as well as its real income.[45] Various high-ranking and highly experienced Ministry of Finance bureaucrats at the time expressed the feeling that Kupat Holim was in effect working with two budgets: the budget that it submitted for government approval and the actual budget on which it operated.[46]

Kupat Holim also thwarted the budget discussions through delaying tactics. The proposals were often submitted late and the discussions on them punctured by frequent interruptions. Whenever the Ministry of Finance questioned or tried to reject a proposed expenditure, the Kupat Holim bureaucrats would halt discussion on the grounds that they were not authorized to make the changes without consulting the Kupat Holim chairman, thereby dragging out the talks ad infinitum.[47] Kupat Holim also stalled in submitting the required financial reports, making it impossible for the government to assess its cash-flow projections or to hold a proper budget discussion based on up-to-date information on its financial situation (*State Comptroller Report,* 1986, pp. 283, 305; 1987, pp. 362, 367). These delaying tactics enabled Kupat Holim to withhold from the government essential information about its activities and growing deficit and to continue spending without prior approval.

Finally, Kupat Holim tried to exploit, as it had under Labor, the rivalry between the Ministry of Finance and Ministry of Health. Perceiving the Ministry of Health as its archenemy responsible for its financial difficulties, Kupat Holim attempted to circumvent it. Sometimes, instead of following the new Likud procedures, which required Ministry of Health approval for its budget, Kupat Holim tried to move the budget negotiations directly to the Ministry of Finance,[48] which was not always friendly but which controlled the financial resources. At other times, the chairman of Kupat Holim would refuse to talk to the minister of health to resolve disagreements that could not be resolved at a lower level. Things came to such a state that the referent in the Ministry of Finance's Budget Division was not always aware of agreements that Kupat Holim had made with other government bodies.[49] Some of the behavior was motivated by Haim Doron's strong personal animosity toward Shostak,[50] but its ultimate aim was to impede the ministerial coordination necessary to govern the health system.

Under Labor Kupat Holim did not have to submit a budget to obtain government funding. Under the Likud, its loose compliance with the new budget regulations was such that, in the comptroller's words, "the process in Kupat Holim remains . . . the same" (*State Comptroller Report*, 1986, pp. 246, 292, 304–5; *State Comptroller Report on the Audit of Kupat Holim*, 1985, pp. 72–73). Although its various cat and mouse tactics did not get Kupat Holim the allocations it wanted, they made it impossible for the government to exercise the control that its new regulations were designed to give it over Kupat Holim or to create a single, well-coordinated, rationally operated health system in Israel.

Debts, Credit, and Budget Deficits

To keep Kupat Holim operating at full force, its leadership embarked on a policy of running up ever-higher debts. Kupat Holim's National Council, the body that approves and oversees its policy, sanctioned the plan. The report it presented to Kupat Holim's 11th national convention in 1984, with the decisions of several years previous, asserts that: "Kupat Holim has taken upon itself a great burden of debt in order to preserve a reasonable level of service despite the decrease in available financial resources."[51]

According to an internal report prepared by the deputy head of the Ministry of Finance's Budget Division, every year Kupat Holim overdrew its budget by $70 million to $80 million.[52] Although Kupat Holim claimed that this was an "untruthful statement,"[53] the figures coincide with the earlier-cited 10% deficit of which Kupat Holim Chairman Doron complained and are consistent with the state comptroller's report of the 1975–1984 fiscal years citing Ministry of Finance figures showing that Kupat Holim's expenditures grew by of 90% over this period, while the Ministry of Health's grew by only 60%. Even Kupat Holim figures for the same period show that the growth of its expenditures during this period exceeded the Ministry of Health's by 9%. The feat was accomplished despite the drastic reduction of government support (*State Comptroller Report*, 1986, p. 285; 1987, pp. 362–64, 369–75).

To finance its unapproved activities, Kupat Holim took out hundreds of millions of dollars worth of bank loans, mostly from the Histadrut-owned Bank HaPoa-lim, and withheld payments from its myriad suppliers and contractors, knowing that it would not be able to make good on its debts, yet confident that the govern-ment would bail it out. As Haim Doron observed, "Kupat Holim cannot go bank-rupt. It would be like the entire public health system going bankrupt. What kind of government would allow such a thing? They will help. Do they have a choice?"[54]

As described by Aaron Fogel, head of the Ministry of Finance's Budget Di-vision, the strategy involved a systematic exploitation of both Histadrut re-sources and the government's various dependencies:

> What is this system? Kupat Holim arrives at an expenditures framework with the Min-istry of Finance, and the Ministry of Finance assumes that an actual framework budget was thereby established. But this is not the case. Kupat Holim goes directly to Bank Ha-Poalim and asks for and gets credit to finance its expenditures—all of which are beyond the approved budget. . . . Both the bank and Kupat Holim know that the health services cannot cover this debt, but this does not worry them. They assume that at some point, when the debt reaches huge proportions and begins to endanger Kupat Holim and, in-deed, the bank, the government will panic and untie its purse strings. This is the system, which Kupat Holim devised to evade state budget limitations and to maintain a system of unlimited spending.[55]

As the second largest bank in Israel at the time, Bank HaPoalim could not be permitted to go under because of a bad loan. Its bankruptcy would ruin a large proportion of citizens and investors and destabilize the country's entire fi-nancial apparatus. So would the bankruptcy of Kupat Holim. Israel's pharma-ceutical companies (which sold the vast portion of their drugs to Kupat Holim), the manufacturers and suppliers of the enormous quantity of medical supplies that Kupat Holim purchased, and the contractors hired to support and maintain Kupat Holim's services and facilities would all fall in a chain reaction if Kupat Holim defaulted on its payments to them—leading to yet further con-sequences, ranging from damage to Israel's pharmaceutical exports through a serious loss of jobs in a country where high employment is seen as a way of maintaining social cohesion in the face of security challenges. The government could not refuse to bail out Kupat Holim given the domino effect its fall would have on the economy.

Moreover, although the Likud certainly did not need Kupat Holim to help it absorb immigrants or to provide it with political support, as Labor had, it could no more ignore Kupat Holim's monopoly power than could Labor. Kupat Holim still provided the medical care for three fourths of the country's popula-tion and provided the only services available in some parts of the country. Pres-suring Kupat Holim to reduce services was one thing, but letting it founder may have had disastrous electoral results.

Sanctions

When its financial difficulties became intolerable, Kupat Holim imposed sanctions. The sanctions targeted the government hospitals, which were dependent on Kupat Holim patients and payments for much of their budgets. As it had under Labor, Kupat Holim withdrew its insurees from government hospitals and crowded them into their own hospitals, putting them in halls and corridors. It also withheld payment for the hospitalization of patients it did send to government-owned hospitals. These sanctions threatened to paralyze the hospitals' operations. The government soon capitulated and opened its coffers.

The sanctions worked despite changes that the Ministry of Health had made in the way it transferred its subsidies. Under Labor the Ministry had transferred the subsidies to Kupat Holim in their entirety and all at once. Under the Likud the Ministry first deducted the payments for the hospitalization of Kupat Holim members in government hospitals and then transferred the rest to Kupat Holim in monthly installments, at the rate and date the Ministry determined. The purpose of the change, introduced by Shostak, was to stop Kupat Holim from withholding payments for its patients in government hospitals to free up funds for other purposes, as it had done under Labor. The intended deterrence evidently did not work. As Fogel observed, "Kupat Holim knows this sanction pays well. For the government will not allow its hospitals to go under and will give them the missing money."[56]

Its obstructive tactics enabled Kupat Holim to spend as much as it wanted on what it wanted—that is to implement its own policies and priorities. Kupat Holim did not change the level or range of its services, did not sell any of its considerable property to fund its expenditures, and did not significantly decrease the number of its members or employees. On the contrary, as I will discuss in the next chapter, it purchased the most modern equipment, opened huge regional outpatient centers, and even opened facilities in Jerusalem where it had not previously had any.[57] Its refusal to shrink to the size that the cuts in government funding would have enabled it to sustain allowed Kupat Holim to retain for the time being its dominant role in Israel's health services.

Chaos: The 1983 Doctor's Strike

The government's cuts in Kupat Holim funding and Kupat Holim's maverick response led to increasing chaos. Every year, Kupat Holim overspent its approved budget by at least 10%. With the addition of interest and linkage to the hyperinflation, it was $500 million in arrears by 1984.[58] The hospital sanctions imposed in the early 1980s threatened to paralyze the entire government hospital network. In 1983 the chaos peaked in a large doctor's strike, the first medical strike anywhere near its magnitude in Israel. Both Kupat Holim and government physicians walked out of their hospitals and clinics, refusing to treat all but life-or-death cases. They were soon joined by the country's nurses and paramedics. The strike paralyzed the medical services for three months and caused long-term damage to the point of endangering people's lives. Behind it were months of unpaid and late paid salaries in a period of hyperinflation, severe shortages in medication and supplies, and myriad other problems caused by the government's funding cuts on the one hand and Kupat Holim's decision to spend on the maintenance and development of its size and functions at the expense of current needs on the other. Caught in the middle of the often undignified conflict, medical professionals, especially physicians, were demoralized, while the government's general hostility toward Kupat Holim provided them with the opportunity to improve their own, until then relatively low, status and to acquire a say in the management of the health services.

The wildcat strike placed the Histadrut in an embarrassing situation. It was carried out in an aggressive manner without any of the self-restraint or decorum one might expect from highly trained and highly respected professionals. As patients languished without care, doctors appeared on television waving their salary slips to display absurdly low salaries which were in fact sometimes misleading. They evaded a back-to-work order by taking off en masse for a picnic at Lake Tiberius on the morning that they knew the court order would arrive. The theatrics, juxtaposed to the suffering of the sick and elderly, brought home to everyone involved—Kupat Holim, the government, and the public—the turmoil into which Israel's health care system had fallen.

The strike was a painful event in Israel's already strife-filled health care history, and too complicated to discuss here (Ishay, 1986; Modan, 1985). What is noteworthy is that it was the outcome of the conflict between the government and Kupat Holim and both the culmination and epitome of the chaos that reigned in the health services as a result of that conflict.

In the end the strike was settled. The government found that it could not force the doctors back to their posts by depriving them of their salaries. The doctors, who tried to establish private practices in the interim both to tide themselves over and to introduce private health care to Israel, found that very few private patients turned up at their offices. The doctors went back to work, with new powers in running the hospitals in which they worked and fat pay raises, which added to the government's health care costs. Kupat Holim gained nothing.

As with the issue of Kupat Holim's deficit spending, the government and the Sick Fund blamed each other for the strike. Kupat Holim ascribed the crisis to the government's forcing it into deficits by withholding the funding it required.

"The state washes its hands of the issue of health insurance, [and] forces us into a policy of deficits by not participating in our budget,"[59] claimed Doron. The government, represented by Fogel, argued that Kupat Holim ran up its debts knowing that the government would have to bail it out, but that, as a responsible organization, it should have balanced its budget:

> Kupat Holim knows very well that the health services cannot pay debts. But this does not worry them. They suppose that as soon as the size of the debt begins to endanger Kupat Holim, the government will panic, jump in and settle the difference. Responsible behavior on their part would have balanced the budget and we have suggested ways to increase tax collection.[60]

The chaos in the heath system, manifested both in the doctors' strike and in the huge debts and deficits that Kupat Holim had amassed, can be described either as the result of the core's determination to impose its allocation policy on the unwilling body on the margins or as the result of the unwillingness of the powerful body on the margin to comply with the legitimate directives of the core. Kupat Holim and the Histadrut naturally saw it from the first perspective, the government from the second.

CHAPTER 13

Regulation as a Means of Control

The Likud's efforts to exercise control over the health services through allocation paralleled efforts to exercise control through regulation. Between 1977 and 1984, the Likud set out to empower the weak Ministry of Health to enable it to take an independent stand on professional matters. It saw regulation as a major tool in that endeavor.[1]

The precondition for the use of regulation as an instrument of control was the abolition of the parity that Kupat Holim had enjoyed throughout the decades of Labor rule. Shostak told it:

> As soon as I came into office, I called the Chairman of Kupat Holim to inform him that, as of this day, Kupat Holim was like every other sick fund operating in this country, that is a client of the Ministry of Health. Furthermore, I said that as of this moment all the committees in which Kupat Holim had equal representation with the Ministry are abolished.[2]

The Supreme Hospitalization Authority was already defunct. The Supreme Coordination Committee was abolished. And Kupat Holim was soon removed from the Project Approval Committee.

Baruch Modan, whom Shostak had appointed general director of the Ministry of Health, explained Kupat Holim's expulsion from the Project Approval Committee on the grounds of the impropriety of the regulated agency being a regulator:

> The idea was that the Committee's purpose was to regulate and supervise the development of the system; therefore it had to be purely governmental. . . . In our opinion, bodies in the system should not take part in supervising its development.[3]

Modan, like Shostak, was intent on making the Ministry of Health the prime health care policy maker by giving it the practical means to regulate the health system:

The Minister and I simply let it be known that the Ministry would function as a Ministry, and it would decide on the rate of development of the health services. Kupat Holim had been accustomed to making the important decisions on development . . . and then looking for someone in the Ministry to rubber stamp the costs. It could do this because of its enormous power. It could make any decision it wanted, with or without the Project Committee, which was a parity committee with representatives from the Finance Committee, the Ministry [of Health], and Kupat Holim. . . . We made it clear that the State will decide where the resources for renovation and construction are to go, and what the allocation priorities will be.[4]

With Kupat Holim removed from the regulatory mechanism, the Likud proceeded to rewrite the rules for Kupat Holim building and expansion, eliminate government subsidies for these activities, enact secondary legislation on sensitive matters on which Labor had rarely if ever impinged, and introduce a regional hospitalization plan that, had it been implemented, would have seriously undermined the Sick Fund's treasured autonomy in this area.

The National Project Committee: New Rules for Kupat Holim Development

In January 1978 the Ministry of Health formally changed the composition and authority of the former Project Approval Committee. Renaming it the National Project Committee to emphasize the supremacy of the government's role, it restricted the committee solely to government representatives, namely representatives of the Ministry of Health and the Ministry of Finance's health referent; gave it exclusive authority in all matters related to the development of new projects in the health system; and, by requiring that written minutes be kept and relayed to the minister of Health and director general of the ministry, provided a means for monitoring the implementation of its decisions, which the parallel committee had not had under Labor.[5]

In January 1979 the committee's operational procedures were fixed, a form for project approval requests was prepared, and a subcommittee composed of professionals was established to prepare the technical material the committee would need for its decisions.[6] The new working procedures related to four categories: (1) Authority: The committee was made the sole authority for the approval of development projects by all the state's public health service agencies. Because Kupat Holim's enjoyed large government subsidies, it was treated as a public service. (2) Justification: The agency seeking approval would have to justify to the committee of the necessity, location, size, and costs of the project. This requirement meant that the Ministry of Health rather than Kupat Holim would have the last word on the sick fund's development, down to details (i.e., size) that had never been at issue under Labor. (3) Examination: The justification for the project would be examined against committee criteria and on the basis of precise data. (4) Application form: The agency applying for approval would be required to submit precise data concerning the intended project on the newly designed Project Approval Request Form, which required 18 distinct items of information (e.g., square meters, location, financing) on the project (Ministry of Health, *Budget Proposal,* 1980, p. 90).

To these tough specifications, Shostak added yet another requirement: to obtain committee approval, the agency making the request would have to show that it could finance its project.[7] Its purpose was to prevent Kupat Holim from starting projects and then handing the bill to the government, as it had done in the past.

The procedure started with the submission of the completed Project Approval Request Form to the committee secretary. A professional subcommittee consisting of financial and technical experts examined the form without the presence of the client (unless invited), using detailed Ministry of Health criteria (e.g., the number and composition of the proposed catchment area population, building specifications, availability of other facilities in the area). To ensure the need for the proposed project, committee members conducted firsthand field surveys and consulted with relevant agencies.

If the professional subcommittee approved the project, it was then relayed to the District City Planning Commission of the Ministry of Interior, which makes the final decision on all building in Israel. Its approval is contingent on the meeting of zoning, ecological, infrastructure, and other requirements and the adjudication of citizens' objections.[8] Under Labor, Kupat Holim had consistently been able to get retroactive approval for all its projects. The goal of the new regulations was to make it impossible for Kupat Holim to submit applications to the District City Planning Commission without prior approval of the National Project Committee. (With Likud control of other government offices, the necessary permits from other government bodies, such as the Israel Lands Administration could not be obtained either).

The District City Planning Commission examination was also intended to serve as a double check on Kupat Holim. If the commission approved it, the project then went back to the plenum of the National Project Committee, which made the final decision. If the members of this committee disagreed, then the director general and/or the minister of Health would make the decision. The director general also handled any appeals.[9]

The procedure was tight, detailed, and highly centralized. It was designed to reduce Kupat Holim's ability to maneuver and manipulate, to force Kupat Holim to comply with overall government health policy, and to keep the reins firmly in Ministry of Health hands. That Kupat Holim's wings were to be trimmed in the process was inevitable by administrative logic. As the advisor to the minister confessed:

The Project Committee, in its new form, was designed to curb Kupat Holim's development, on the one hand, and to create a situation where the Ministry does not have to ask
Kupat Holim's approval for building and developing our own facilities, on the other.[10]

Termination of Government Funding for Kupat Holim Development

Among the Likud Ministry of Health goals was to bridge the gap between the
government hospitals and the generally newer, better built, better equipped, better maintained, and more comfortable Kupat Holim facilities—the same gap
that had made Labor's Shem Tov so angry when he took office a decade earlier
and that he had failed to narrow through his policy of integration. In the Likud
view, as Director General Modan explained, the disparity created by years of
Histadrut pressure on Labor governments had to be rectified:

> For years there was massive discrimination in building against non–Kupat Holim hos-
> pitals, especially those owned by the Ministry of Health. . . . When Shostak became
> Minister, he found that half of Tel HaShomer [the largest of Israel's government-
> owned hospitals] was operating in old shacks. . . . This was the situation in the govern-
> ment hospitals because Kupat Holim had found a way of exerting pressure to get the
> better part of government resources allocated to the development of its own hospitals.[11]

Between 1977 and 1984 Ministry of Health policy was to ". . . put into effect a
long-term construction plan aimed at eliminating all the shacks in the government owned general, psychiatric and geriatric hospitals and transferring patients to permanent structures, to ensure comfortable hospitalization conditions" (Ministry of Health, *Budget Proposal of 1983*, p. 46). In the 1981–1982 fiscal
year the ministry created a master plan that earmarked funds for the renovation
of the government-owned hospitals.[12] In the 1983–1984 fiscal year renovation
started in six government-owned general hospitals, four chronic care and geriatric hospitals, and five psychiatric hospitals (Ministry of Health, *Budget Proposal
of 1983*, pp. 46, 142–49).

The improvement of the government hospitals was seen as something that
had to be offset by a reduction in Kupat Holim's development. As Minister of
Health Shostak put it:

> I decided there would be no more building of Kupat Holim hospitals. If development
> money were found, we would transfer it all to construction projects in government
> owned hospitals. I decided not to approve budget funds for Kupat Holim so as to freeze
> and put an end to Kupat Holim building.[13]

Financially, the termination of funding for Kupat Holim construction was rationalized on the grounds that there was not enough money to pay for it and the

development of government health facilities as well (Ministry of Health, *Budget Proposal of 1978*, p. 41). Morally, it was presented as a way of redressing the imbalance between the government's health facilities and Kupat Holim's. Politically, it was seen as a way of empowering the Ministry of Health by bringing its assets up to the level of Kupat Holim's.

In fact, Kupat Holim did receive a small development budget from the Ministry of Finance between 1978 and 1983 on the basis of a general needs assessment by its Budget Division (*State Comptroller Report on the Audit of Kupat Holim*, 1985, p. 61). The amount was not enough to meet even Kupat Holim's approved development projects. To pay for these, the Ministry of Finance instructed Kupat Holim to take bank loans. The Ministry of Health's 1978 budget book states that Kupat Holim "will be referred to bank sources to raise the funds to finance the construction of hospitals and clinics for which it received approval" (Ministry of Health, *Budget Proposal of 1978*, p. 41).

For Kupat Holim this was yet another blow. First it was told it could not build without Ministry of Health approval; then it was told that it would have to finance its construction with commercial loans that it would have to repay. At most, in its statement that it would "refer" Kupat Holim to the banks, the Ministry of Health expressed readiness to help arrange favorable repayment terms, a favor that naturally comes with a measure of control over how the money is spent.

Formal Regulation

Labor's strategy of integration had entailed the use of informal arrangements for regulation and enforcement of policies. Legislation was perceived as a sanction to be employed only if the rules were not followed. Under the Likud policy of exclusion, the Ministry of Health bureaucracy set out to formalize its regulations so as to prevent Kupat Holim from circumventing them as it had done under Labor. As Modan told, Kupat Holim's long history of machinations "made it necessary to utilize legal authority and enforce it on all parts of the system, especially on Kupat Holim."[14]

Believing that formalizing regulation would enable enforcement, the Ministry of Health made extensive use of subsidiary legislation to enact rules affecting a wide range of activities.[15] Subsidiary legislation is an auxiliary to primary legislation passed by the Knesset by means of which the relevant minister may make regulations to implement the provisions of the law (Bracha, 1986, p. 77; Rubinstein, 1974, pp. 373–76).

During the Likud term far more subsidiary health legislation was passed than in previous years. Between 1935 and 1984, 53 health regulations that were still in effect in 1991 were made. Of these, 34 (64%) were made in the seven

Likud years between 1977 and 1984.[16] Most, as under Labor, pertained to matters that did not affect the balance of authority between Kupat Holim and the Ministry of Health. Three of the regulations, however, gave formal reinforcement to the Ministry of Health's authority.

The 1979 Amendment to the Public Health Order on Hospital Registration forbid adding or changing the function of hospital beds without the approval of the director general of the Ministry of Health and, furthermore, required hospitals to keep all the documents relating to their physical structure, including construction plans and any changes made in them, as well as the director general's authorizations for the changes.[17] This regulation was designed to curtail the autonomy Kupat Holim had exercised in its building and construction until that time. The prohibition against changing the function of hospital beds without prior approval was intended to prevent Kupat Holim from, for example, closing a geriatric ward and opening up an organ transplant ward in its place. The provision requiring record keeping was intended to enable the Ministry of Health to monitor Kupat Holim's activities. The assumption behind the regulation was that the Ministry of Health, not Kupat Holim, should decide what the needs of the health system were.

The 1979 Amendment to the Public Health Order on Medical Equipment forbid the purchase of expensive medical equipment, including CAT scanners, MRIs, x-ray equipment, and so on, without the direct approval of the minister of health or his designee.[18] Its purpose was to lend formal support to the Equipment Committee that the ministry had established in 1977–1978 to oversee the heavy equipment purchases of all nongovernmental health agencies in order to promote coordination and prevent duplication (Ministry of Health, *Budget Proposal of 1980*, p. 96). Its effect, like that of the regulation relating to hospital registration, would have been to deprive Kupat Holim of autonomy in an area in which it had been accustomed to acting as it saw fit.

The 1980 Amendment to the Public Health Order on Hospitalization required every government-subsidized hospital to treat all persons who entered its emergency room whether or not they belonged to the right sick fund and to hospitalize the patient if needed.[19] This regulation was aimed at limiting the exclusivity of Kupat Holim services, which until then had been restricted almost entirely to its own members despite the tax money that helped pay for them.[20]

Regulation of Hospitalization: Government Regulation Versus Kupat Holim Regulation

Last but not least, the Ministry of Health used its regulatory powers to try to gain control over the hospitalization process. This effort, embodied in a "regionalization" program, was a response to the program that Kupat Holim put into effect after the Ministry of Health had stopped subsidizing the cost of Kupat Holim patients in government hospitals in April 1976. To reduce the suddenly increased costs and exert pressure on the government, Kupat Holim drew up a regionalization plan to regulate the hospitalization in its own facilities (Doron & Ron, 1978, pp. 7–20). In addition to decreasing the number of persons hospitalized, the plan divided the country into 12 districts, each with its own Kupat Holim hospital. Whereas previously patients had been sent to hospitals near their homes and were often diverted to government hospitals, now they were sent only to Kupat Holim hospitals even if a government hospital was in the vicinity where they lived. The implementation of the plan led to a marked reduction of hospitalization days (from 0.97 days per member in 1975–1976 to 0.86 days per member in 1976–1977), to a growth in occupancy in Kupat Holim general hospitals, and to a concomitant decline in Kupat Holim patients in government hospitals and their consequent loss of essential revenues.

Kupat Holim's self-regulation caused considerable hardship to the government hospitals and drew fire even under Labor, when the policy was first implemented. The Government Physicians Association had warned that if Kupat Holim's policy were not quickly nipped in the bud "government owned hospitals will find themselves irreparably damaged"[21] and threatened to use every means at its disposal if something were not done to halt the deterioration.[22] Shem Tov, seconded by his director general of the Ministry of Health, lashed out against Kupat Holim for hospitalizing patients far from their homes without medical justification and often to their detriment.[23] Nonetheless, the only concrete measure Shem Tov took was to increase Kupat Holim's subsidy under the allocation formula in the vain hope that the Sick Fund would send its patients back to the government-owned hospitals. It did not.

Under the Likud, the protests sharpened. In addition to its previous objections, the Government Physicians Association accused Kupat Holim of upsetting the traditional balance between government-owned hospitals and Kupat Holim-owned hospitals and argued that it did not make sense for "hospitalization to continue to be organized according to political considerations. . . . It must be based on a national plan. . . ."[24]

The Likud Ministry of Health responded with its own regionalization program based on the recommendations of the Zohar Committee (which is discussed in the next chapter). Like Kupat Holim's program, the government's program also divided the country into regions, except that the regions were based on geographic and demographic considerations and encompassed both government-owned and Kupat Holim-owned hospitals. Each region contained a "chief" hospital and the remaining "satellite" hospitals. The chief hospital was to be the only hospital in the region that performed sophisticated diagnoses and major medical procedures, whereas the satellite hospitals were to stick to more routine work. Moreover, each satellite hospital was assigned a catchment area to which all persons living in it belonged, regardless of their sick fund membership.

Shostak justified the plan to "put a stop to the self-regulation that Kupat Holim had undertaken" on the grounds of the ministry's "concern for the government-owned hospitals, which kept losing patients and resources." The plan, he noted "prevented Kupat Holim from sending patients from an area that has a government owned hospital to one where there is a Kupat Holim hospital."[25]

The government program, were it fully implemented, would have greatly undermined both the quality and prestige of Kupat Holim's hospitals and curbed its capacity to administer itself and manage its patients. Nonetheless, in 1981 Kupat Holim Chairman Doron put his signature on it. Among the reasons he gave the National Council, Kupat Holim's policy-making body, was that Shostak had promised to help Kupat Holim balance its budget.[26] The Kupat Holim leadership also seems to have regarded the agreement as proof, after four years of practically unmitigated struggle, that "it is impossible to carry out plans unilaterally, without including . . . Kupat Holim" and as "an opening for future cooperation between the government and Kupat Holim" (Kupat Holim, *Managerial Report to the 11th Convention*, 1984, p. 20).

The Response: Obstruction of Government Regulation

Like allocation, the issue of regulation evoked conflict about the position and function of each side in the health system. The Ministry of Health tried to assert control over the country's health care by abolishing parity and unilaterally regulating Kupat Holim, along with the other sick funds, while Kupat Holim persisted in regarding itself as a legitimate and rightfully equal, if not dominant, partner in the regulatory process. Haim Doron's complaint about the Likud's regulatory style conveys Kupat Holim's sense of its right to a say in the formation of government policy:

> Instead of cooperation, separation; instead of institutional debates and joint agreements, a flood of announcements, amendments and bills with no previous discussion. Unilateral committees, unjustifiable investigations and incomprehensible investigations and, to my regret, publications for the sake of publicity. . . . The joy of togetherness in Israeli public health has been dampened.[27]

In support of its rights, Kupat Holim made two major arguments. One was that its "responsibility for providing health services for three quarters of the population compels Kupat Holim to constantly evaluate its services and to plan them in accord with its own principles."[28] This was much the same argument as that by which Doron and others used to justify Kupat Holim's overspending and deficit financing. With regard to regulation, Doron contended that the parity Kupat Holim had enjoyed under Labor in the joint Project Approval Committee was the logical means to fulfilling its responsibilities to its many insured. Thus, whereas the Ministry of Health predicated its ability to regulate on the abolition of parity, Kupat Holim regarded that abolition as a fundamental impediment to its ability to meet its public responsibilities. Its view, as with regard to allocation, was that as the body in the field, which actually provided most of the country's health services, it was in a better position to know what the public genuinely needed than the Ministry of Health bureaucrats in their offices in Jerusalem.

The other argument involved the thorny issue of the regulated agency being a regulator. In response to the Ministry of Health's claim that parity had to be abolished because of the impropriety of the regulated agency being a regulator, Doron pointed out that the Ministry of Health had the same dual role: "When the Ministry enters a debate concerning a Kupat Holim request, it acts not only as a national authority to decide whether to grant a request or not; it is also, legitimately, an interested party. . . ."[29] The claim was that this dual role undermined the Ministry's objectivity and, with that, its right to make health policy on its own.[30] The claim was repeated wherever Kupat Holim wished to delegitimize the Ministry of Health's role as chief regulator of Israel's health care.

At the same time, Kupat Holim had become accustomed to acting as an autonomous organizational entity with a well-developed set of governing bodies, including a legislature, executive, and judiciary, parallel to those of the state government. These bodies acted much like a sovereign government that owed no allegiance to a foreign state. To take a salient example, after the Ministry of Health dictated that Kupat Holim's construction was to slow down, Kupat Holim's National Council declared that "Kupat Holim's development services are the very foundations upon which the Sick Fund exists. They are an integral part of it, today, tomorrow and the day after."[31] Whenever Ministry of Health regulations impinged on Kupat Holim's activities, the Kupat Holim leadership protested that it owed allegiance, first and foremost, to its own governing bodies.

In short, from both a moral and administrative perspective, Kupat Holim regarded the government and its agents in the Ministry of Health and the Ministry of Finance as interlopers on its own rightful turf, who got in the way of its fulfilling its responsibility to the public.

The brunt of the Likud's regulatory drive, as of Labor's efforts under Shem Tov, fell on the area of Kupat Holim's development. Unlike current needs, renovation, construction, and the purchase of expensive equipment could always be delayed and the government could gain credit for saving taxpayers' money without the consequences of an immediate visible deterioration in services. Development was also the area that most called for rationalization.

Kupat Holim considered continuous development unfettered by government regulation essential to the preservation of its organizational identity and existence. For one thing, as part of its responsibilities, it had to maintain its current facilities and build and buy new ones to keep up with the ever-increasing demands made on its services by its (then) growing, diverse, and aging membership; with the wear and tear on its equipment and facilities; and with the rapid innovations in medical technology.[32]

But beyond this impetus, ongoing unimpeded development was an organizational imperative for Kupat Holim. Large organizations (indeed, almost any organization) strive to continue to grow in order to keep ahead of the inevitable upstarts that aspire to cut into their territory; for Kupat Holim both the other sick funds and the Ministry of Health. Such development was also mandated, in the eyes of the Kupat Holim leadership, by Kupat Holim's unique philosophy, going back to prestate days, of comprehensive health services. In contrast to Israel's other sick funds, Kupat Holim had set out to provide all-inclusive services in all areas of medicine, through its own staff, and in its own facilities. To support such comprehensive services, it had to keep renovating, building, and expanding.[33]

To regulate its development, in 1974 Kupat Holim established its own Division of Construction and Maintenance to approve and supervise the carrying out of all maintenance, construction, and development work in the Sick Fund. Since the late 1970s, any Kupat Holim office, service, or body that wished to undertake a building project had to put in a formal application on a three-part form and to meet detailed internal requirements.[34] Kupat Holim's own professionals examined the application, as did the Kupat Holim treasurer and the head of the division. Every project was scrutinized for its necessity, cost, and means of implementation before it was submitted for approval to Kupat Holim's directors.[35] The head of this division considered it something of an internal project committee.[36]

With its own regulatory body Kupat Holim could only have regarded the government's attempts to control its development as superfluous. It regarded the Likud's efforts to curb its development while expanding, renovating, and re-equipping government medical facilities as an illicit exploitation of government power for the purpose of weakening it. It fought all government acts that threatened to impair its ability to provide full, comprehensive, up-to-date medical care to its insurees; that would encroach on the organizational autonomy of its governing bodies; or that might require it to change the philosophy by which it identified itself. These acts included the Ministry of Health's efforts to institute a tight, formal procedure for approval of construction projects; its elimination of funding for Kupat Holim's development budget; and the amendments to the Public Health Order designed to restrict Kupat Holim's ability to make significant changes in its hospitals, to purchase the hospital equipment it wanted, and to provide hospital care only for its own members. They also included the government's new regionalization scheme, which would reduce at least some of the Kupat Holim hospitals to satellite status without the functions of advanced medical institutions that give hospitals their prestige. All these regulations and procedures struck Kupat Holim as calculated threats aimed at imperiling not only its ability to provide adequate health services, but its very existence.[37]

As in the case of allocation, the Likud's exclusion of Kupat Holim from the regulatory processes pushed Kupat Holim and the Histadrut into a corner from which they felt they had no alternative but to obstruct the implementation of the unwanted regulations using whatever powers they had.

Obstructive Maneuvers

Obstruction of the Project Approval Procedure

From Kupat Holim's perspective, the entire project approval procedure was a bureaucratic nightmare with malice aforethought. Kupat Holim saw the detailed examination of its plans by the National Project Committee as inefficient and protracted. The process was further drawn out by the need to obtain the approval of other government authorities, namely the Israel Lands Administration (to obtain a lease on the land) and the Ministry of Interior (to start construction), before receiving final committee approval. Moreover, to submit requests to these committees, the prior approval of the National Project Committee was required. "But by the time you finally get the authorization to build," Doron complained,

> the [Israel] Lands Administration authorization is no longer valid. And that's not all. After this Via Dolorosa, if three years passed and you haven't started to build yet because you have to cope with raising the money . . . selecting the contractors . . . then the Project Committee's authorization is no longer valid, and you have to start the whole process all over again.[38]

The head of Kupat Holim's Division of Construction and Maintenance saw the difficulties as intentional: "The Project Committee is intentionally piling on difficulties for Kupat Holim—sometimes for political reasons, sometimes for financial reasons."[39] Modan, director general of the Ministry of Health, admitted that some of the difficulties were deliberate: "I wouldn't say that in certain cases, and in matters involving development, we did not intentionally trip up Kupat Holim."[40]

On the other hand, some of the delay was undoubtedly caused by Kupat Holim's frequent objections to the new National Project Committee's detailed and, in Kupat Holim's view, intrusive, specifications, which went into such matters as the ratio of doctors per insuree per clinic and the number of doctors per square meter per clinic.[41] A Ministry of Health representative on the committee complained of Kupat Holim's constant arguing over such details.[42]

In possession of its own criteria and its own construction committee, and regarding the National Project Committee's detailed criteria as unrealistic and the entire approval procedure as one huge obstacle to its own delivery of the health services for which it was ultimately responsible, Kupat Holim did not consider itself morally bound to the committee's directives and did whatever it could to circumvent them.

It pointedly did not submit all its construction projects for National Project Committee approval. According to the head of its Division of Maintenance and Construction, it refrained from making requests to renovate or alter functions within clinics or hospitals.[43] This omission, in violation of the 1979 Amendment to the Public Health Order on Hospital Registration, was a way of avoiding government scrutiny of a large portion of its developmental activities. As the Ministry of Health described the maneuver, "Kupat Holim turned renovations into construction and when construction began, they called it expansion and then turned to the Committee for approval."[44] A salient example was a dilapidated structure in the courtyard of Kupat Holim's Meir Hospital in Kfar Saba, which Kupat Holim refurbished and made into a maternity hospital and for which it succeeded in obtaining retroactive approval. Similarly, Kupat Holim started construction of a pediatric oncology ward in its Beilinson Hospital in Petah Tikva while the matter was still under discussion in the committee and the sides were arguing about its size. Here approval was given in medias rex.[45]

Kupat Holim also built several regional professional clinics without prior approval. These well-equipped giant clinics performed a large range of functions, including ambulatory surgery and sophisticated diagnoses, which had previously been the sole province of hospitals. While providing patients with convenient, close-to-home care in nonhospital settings, they posed a threat to the government hospital ambulatory clinics to which Kupat Holim had hitherto sent its members. Kupat Holim built one such clinic in a suburb of Haifa and proceeded to send patients there rather than to the government-owned Rambam Hospital, even though approval had been denied and was not obtained retroactively either.[46]

In two other cities, Tel Aviv and Ashdod, Kupat Holim tried but was not able to do the same. The planned regional clinics in these cities were at the center of a furious row. Kupat Holim insisted that they were needed to meet the growing needs of its membership.[47] The Ministry of Health looked at their size, multiplicity of functions, and technical specifications, and defined them as hospitals in disguise whose purpose was "to cripple the government owned hospitals" that served those regions.[48] Stymied, Kupat Holim responded with a vengeance: it sent persons in need of outpatient care to the ambulatory clinics of the government hospitals, but did not pay for the services.

Obstruction of Development Budget Cuts

According to its managerial report to its National Council, between 1977 and 1984 Kupat Holim constructed 85 new community clinics and 10 health centers totaling 100,000 square meters, expanded its hospital facilities by 30,000 square meters, and made $100 million worth of renovations and changes in its facilities.[49] It did so despite the fact that in 1979 the government severely cut its development budget. Its justification was much the same as that for circumventing the National Project Committee's approval procedures: growth was essential for it to meet its responsibilities and to continue to exist (these were connected in practically one breath), and the government's cutting off the better part of its development budget was a political act clearly designed to harm it. In the words of the Kupat Holim treasurer:

> In the last few years, Kupat Holim has not received one penny from the development budget, yet it took upon itself the grave responsibility of continuing to construct the most important sites, without which the whole institution would be useless today. This is a political problem, which stems from the government's wish to undermine Kupat Holim's foundations.[50]

To finance its development projects, Kupat Holim seems to have had a separate development budget to which the Ministry of Health was not privy. According to the figures Kupat Holim submitted to the National Project Committee, its development budget should have amounted to no more than 3% to 5% of its total budget (Kupat Holim, *Development Budget Proposal,* 1980–1981). These percentages would not have covered the great volume of its projects. Nor did Kupat Holim ever agree to take the development loans that the government offered to help it get from the banks when it stopped its funding (*State Comptroller Report on the Audit of Kupat Holim,* 1985, p. 60).

Its private development budget came from several sources. A major one was huge deficit spending (*State Comptroller Report on the Audit of Kupat Holim,* 1985, pp. 68–69). The Kupat Holim treasurer admitted, "They would rather have a deficit than to have to stop development."[51] In addition, Kupat Holim found other sources of funding. It raised substantial overseas donations both on its own and with the help of Histadrut, which it did not report in its budget books. It channeled funds from the sale of assets to development projects; the maternity hospital in Kfar Saba was built with money from the sale of shares in two hotels.[52] It surreptitiously transferred funds earmarked in its official budget for hospital construction to the construction of community and regional clinics. The regional clinic in Haifa was built in this way.[53]

Above all, Kupat Holim realized its development plans through the aid of the Histadrut, which provided the means that enabled it to renovate and build independently of the government. As noted, during the Likud terms in office, Histadrut's Central Tax Bureau transferred a higher proportion of the membership fees to Kupat Holim than in previous years, and the Histadrut-owned Bank HaPoalim, which provided it with credit on easy terms. In addition, massive assistance was also given to it by the Histadrut-owned building company, Solel Boneh.

Solel Boneh was established by the Histadrut in the 1920s to build roads and public buildings for the *yishuv* and to provide work and income. After statehood, favored by the same political ties to Labor that gave the Histadrut its power, it grew into the country's largest construction company. Up until the Likud period it carried out virtually all of Israel's major public construction, both civil and military, and also engaged in extensive building projects in Africa and Asia. It was thus a wealthy, diversified company with funds to spare. It was also the prime builder for Kupat Holim. Over the years, Kupat Holim provided 3% to 5% of the company's work.[54] The relations, like those between the Sick Fund and Bank HaPoalim discussed in the previous chapter, were very friendly and not quite businesslike. Up until 1979 Kupat Holim channeled "all its construction work, whether large or small," to Solel Boneh "without any public tender" and even without signed contracts (*State Comptroller Report on the Audit of Kupat Holim*, 1979, p. 96).

When Kupat Holim found itself in dire straits, the Histadrut had Solel Boneh give it a helping hand in the form of free construction work, even when the work prevented Solel Boneh from accepting well-paid contracts elsewhere. The tale is told by Yerucham Meshel:

> Kupat Holim did not build, expand or develop anything on its own. Without the Histadrut, I doubt that its facilities could exist. The Histadrut ordered Solel Boneh to build, Bank HaPoalim to lend money, and its Central Tax Bureau to transfer funds and provide guarantees. I had Solel Boneh build for Kupat Holim, even when its directors tried to refuse because they were offered very profitable work [elsewhere].[55]

During the Labor period, Solel Boneh had subsidized much of its Kupat Holim construction, building Kupat Holim facilities on extremely easy credit, while still earning a good profit through its ability to obtain easy credit from banks at home and abroad. When the Likud cut off its development funds, Kupat Holim ceased paying Solel Boneh altogether.[56] Under Histadrut pressure, Solel Boneh continued to build without any profit.[57]

Obstruction of Regionalization Agreement

Although Kupat Holim eventually signed the government regionalization plan, it soon began to obstruct it. Shortly after signing, Doron wrote a letter to the director general of the Ministry of Health asserting that Kupat Holim's responsibilities to its members were anchored in its own Articles of Association and warning that Kupat Holim "cannot and must not honor any bills presented to it by a government owned hospital requesting payment for the hospitalization of any of its members contrary to the directions and procedures that had been in effect till then."[58] From the very beginning, it did not supply the Ministry of Health with the data on its hospitalization and ambulatory services that the ministry needed to implement and monitor the plan.[59]

Furthermore, it continued to send its patients to the hospitals of its own choosing rather than to the hospitals designated for each region in the government plan. A substantial number of patients were sent to Kupat Holim hospitals outside their areas of residence (*State Comptroller Report*, 1986, pp. 259, 260).[60] Baruch Modan, director general of the Ministry of Health, saw behind the violation Kupat Holim's "vested interest to look out for its own hospitals."[61] As he noted in his book *Medicine Under Siege*, "it was clear to the people from Kupat Holim that the implementation of this plan in its complete form would take the direct control over the patient out of the hands of the clerk in the clinic and thus do away with the exclusivity of its hospitals" (Modan, 1985, p. 45). The head of the government-owned Tel HaShomer Hospital put the motive down to the self-interest of Kupat Holim's physicians, who "send the routine cases to government owned hospitals and keep the interesting cases for themselves."[62] Kupat Holim, on the other hand, denied that it had any intent to obstruct the regionalization plan and claimed that the plan was too new for full compliance, which would come gradually.[63]

In fact Kupat Holim saw the regionalization plan very differently from the government. To the government, it was a plan that asserted government authority, gave the government control over hospitalization, and severely limited Kupat Holim's autonomy in that sphere. To Kupat Holim it was nothing of the sort, as Chairman Doron took pains to assure the Histadrut's two major governing bodies, the Executive Committee and the Central Committee:

> The entire agreement is built on the basis of parity. . . . The Ministry of Health's view that every citizen who is insured is linked to a specific hospital and that 17 to 20 regions are to be established was not accepted. The agreement is based on Kupat Holim's outlook. . . . True, there is agreement on the principal of regionality in planning and general hospitalization policy. But it must be emphasized that the doctors in Kupat Holim's regional clinics will respect, as stated in the agreement, the wishes of patients or their doctors that they be hospitalized in a different hospital.[64]

To Doron the plan was an agreement between equals, of the sort common under Labor, and left Kupat Holim a large measure of discretion in implementation.

Kupat Holim outwitted the government in the formulation of the agreement. In the course of the negotiations, it had managed to insert an article, which permitted it to direct its patients to hospitals outside their area. Although the article stipulated that this was to be done only for medical reasons, it provided Kupat Holim with a loophole, which allowed it to send its insurees to the hospitals where it saw fit for whatever reason. Moreover, Doron took pains to inform the Histadrut governing bodies that Kupat Holim's professional clinics were outside the compass of the accord, an exclusion that enabled Kupat Holim to send its patients to its own facilities rather than to government-owned hospitals.

Cardiac and thoracic surgery unit in Carmel Hospital. Kupat Holim also undermined the part of the regionalization plan that distinguished the functions of the chief and satellite hospitals, a distinction which threatened the continuing prestige of Kupat Holim hospitals. In 1982 it opened up a new cardiac and thoracic surgery unit in its Carmel Hospital in Haifa in the northern region. According to the regionalization plan, the region's chief hospital was to be the government-owned Rambam Hospital, whereas Carmel Hospital, Kupat Holim's newest and most modern hospital, was to be a satellite, which by definition would not go into the sophisticated realm of chest and heart surgery. The choice of Carmel Hospital for the new department seems to have been grounded on more than medical reasons. Of all of Kupat Holim's hospitals, Carmel was the only one that was in a region where the chief hospital was government-owned; that is, where a Kupat Holim hospital had to directly compete for status with a government-owned hospital. In addition, Rambam Hospital already had a cardiac and thoracic surgery unit, raising questions about the need for another one.

To add insult to injury, Kupat Holim lured a well-known cardiac surgeon from under Rambam's nose. The surgeon, one Professor Gideon Marin, was in negotiations with Rambam to leave his position at Jerusalem's Hadassah Hospital to head Rambam's department. Before the contract could be signed,[65] Kupat Holim presented him with a better offer. Haim Doron personally went to his home and offered him not only a higher salary and better social benefits than Rambam could give, including housing at Kupat Holim's expense, but also the kinds of things to appeal to a physician of his stature, namely that he would be able to bring to the department any medical or paramedical staff he wished and to purchase whatever equipment he wanted. Marin accepted.

Given Kupat Holim's financial straits, this was an incredible offer. Kupat Holim could make it because of its freedom, as an organization on the margins, from government civil service regulations that put a ceiling on the salaries and benefits of civil servants and limited the freedom of the Ministry of Health both to purchase equipment and to hire and fire staff. Rambam Hospital, subject to government controls that were not binding on Kupat Holim, could not even come close to the offer. Not surprisingly, the director of Rambam Hospital felt that "Kupat Holim opened the department in Carmel Hospital because of medical politics"[66] and that "Kupat Holim [was] waging an open war against Rambam."[67]

Despite the unit's rogue beginnings, its successful management eventually gained it Ministry of Health accreditation, which was initially withheld. About 90% of the unit's operations succeeded and, by working double shifts, it managed to reduce radically the waiting time for heart and chest surgery in the northern region. Its success was particularly impressive because Rambam's heart and chest surgery unit was weak and poorly thought of. Its success induced the Ministry of Health to offer accreditation to a "a joint venture with Rambam Hospital."[68] The offer was rejected, and in 1984 the ministry finally gave its approval without conditions.

Obstruction of Regulations: Kupat Holim's CAT Scanner

Kupat Holim's opening of the cardiac and thoracic surgery unit at Carmel Hospital violated not only the regionalization agreement it had signed, but also two of the Ministry of Health regulations passed under the Likud: the 1979 Amendment to the Public Health Order on Hospital Registration, which forbade adding or changing the function of hospital beds without the approval of the director general of the Ministry of Health, and the 1979 Amendment to the Public Health Order on Medical Equipment, which forbade purchasing expensive medical equipment without the approval of the Minister of Health or his proxy.

The 1979 Amendment to the Public Health Order on Medical Equipment was also violated more directly. Among the items whose purchase required approval were CAT scanners. Initially, the standard the committee set was one scanner for every 650,000 people. Later the number of persons per scanner was lowered, but scanners were still limited. Kupat Holim did not acknowledge such criteria and, without seeking approval, went ahead and equipped most of its hospitals with CAT scanners as soon as they became de rigueur for modern medicine.

Like the construction of professional clinics, the opening of the cardiac and thoracic surgery unit at Carmel Hospital, and other projects that Kupat Holim undertook in violation of government directives, Kupat Holim's purchase of CAT scanners can be seen in two ways. On the one hand it provided Israelis with better health care than they were likely to have received at government facilities; for example, the Ministry of Health did not understand why Kupat

Holim's Carmel Hospital needed a CAT scanner when the nearby government hospital, Rambam Hospital, already had one or why Kupat Holim's Afula Hospital in the northeast should have a scanner before its own larger Sorocca Hospital in the southern desert city of Beer Sheba did.[69] The administrative concern to reduce duplication seems to have blinded the Ministry of Health to the importance of CAT scanners in modern medicine. At the same time, superior patient care using the best equipment, the best physicians, the best facilities, which were often out of reach of the government health network, bolstered Kupat Holim's power and prestige.

Shoring Up Power by Branching into Jerusalem

In one way or the other, all of Kupat Holim's obstructive activities were aimed at preventing the government from diluting its power, whether that power was represented by the size and scope of its facilities, the prestige of its hospitals and physicians, the modernity of its equipment, or its prized autonomy. In February 1984 Kupat Holim took yet another measure to this end. Doing what it had not done in all its years under Labor, it branched into the Jerusalem area, which until that time had been the province of Israel's few voluntary hospitals—the huge Hadassah Hospital and a number of smaller hospitals funded by religious organizations. Without the knowledge of the Ministry of Health, it reached an agreement with Sha'are Tzedek Hospital to enter into a 50% partnership in its administration and management.[70] Sha'are Tzedek was motivated by high deficits, which made its continued operation difficult. Kupat Holim gave as its motives both financial and service considerations. Without its own hospital in the area, Doron asserted, "Kupat Holim spends at least 20% more on its patients in the Jerusalem district than on patients in the same age group in other districts," and added that it needed a hospital affiliation to provide comprehensive clinic–hospital services.[71]

The Ministry of Health, claiming that the new partnership would ruin Hadassah Hospital,[72] demanded the immediate abrogation of the agreement and tried to persuade Sha'are Tzedek's international board of directors to withhold approval.[73] Hadassah Hospital is still standing strong, and whether it was ever threatened is debatable. The chairman of Kupat Holim's National Council pointed to a more pertinent reason for the ministry's objection: "the agreement between Kupat Holim and Sha'are Tzedek will not only benefit the population of Jerusalem, but will also enlarge and strengthen Kupat Holim."[74]

The partnership with Sha'are Tzedek was not an obstructive measure per se, nor did it violate any agreement or government regulation. It is worth noting here, however, because Kupat Holim's entry into the Jerusalem hospital network changed the status quo that had been in effect since the Sick Fund was established. The formation of the partnership at a time of hostility and struggle with the government was a brilliant step by which Kupat Holim expanded its operations into a hitherto closed arena. It can be likened to a surprise rear-end attack in a war, which is carried out while the sides are engaged in a frontal battle. The move catches the enemy unprepared and gives the cunning attacker a tremendous advantage. It reflected Kupat Holim's ingenuity and power, on the one hand, and its need to be constantly on the lookout for new sources of strength, on the other.

The Failure of Enforcement

The Ministry of Health was totally unable to enforce its regulations, notwithstanding the formal powers of enforcement it had as a core government agency. Theoretically, it might have ordered government hospitals to refuse admittance to Kupat Holim patients inappropriately sent, initiated legal proceedings to destroy Kupat Holim's unauthorized buildings, or had Kupat Holim's imported CAT scanners confiscated at customs. But it did none of these things. As is true of government agencies throughout most of the world, its powers of enforcement were more potential than practical. This was true for many reasons, beginning with the fact that total enforcement requires a police state. Israel, moreover, tends to focus on the formation of policy to the detriment of its implementation (Sharkansky, 1985). In the instance here, Modan, the director general of the Ministry of Health who had placed great store in the formalization of the rules, offers an explanation specific to the Ministry of Health: the ministry, which was the operator of most of the hospitals in the country, was "too preoccupied with providing services rather than supervising them."[75] This is the same problem that had plagued the ministry from the time of its formation and gave its rival on the margins the huge advantage that it had always had over it. Moreover— and perhaps this is the most relevant reason for the failure of enforcement—as Labor's Minister of Health Shem Tov was well aware, any attempt to impose government policies on Kupat Holim by force was bound to meet with counterforce, strikes, sabotage, or other sanctions that would turn the muddle and confusion of the health services into total chaos. In his frustration, Modan resorted to reporting Kupat Holim violations to the police. To his regret, he tells, "things did not change" even though he sent memos and talked to high-ranking police officers.[76] Even his colleagues understood that these actions were ridiculous.

CHAPTER 14

Restructuring: National Health Insurance to Establish Government Authority

Throughout the almost three decades of statehood that preceded the first Likud election victory, the Likud's predecessors had vigorously waved the banner of restructuring before hostile Labor forums. At the First Kanab Committee hearings in 1948, David Melamdovitz, chairman of the Leumit Sick Fund, urged that until the government took final responsibility for health care, the various sick funds operate under the direction of the Ministry of Health—not the Histadrut—and that citizens have the freedom to chose their sick fund (Ofir, 1982, Vol. 2, pp. 32–33). At the Second Kanab Committee, Melamdovitz sang the advantages of "general health insurance for the entire population by means of a designated state agency" (Ofir, 1982, Vol. 2, p. 80). The advantages included saving money; avoiding duplication; and providing higher quality, better coordinated, and more efficient medical care (Halevi, 1979, pp. 23–24). Melamdovitz's statement, like similar remarks by Shostak and other Likud party members, leaves exactly what was being advocated rather vague. Whether what was envisioned was the establishment of a single national health service, modeled on Great Britain's National Health Service or fair competition among the various sick funds, which would function somewhat like contractors providing services under the auspices of an impartial national authority, is not at all clear (Rocmer, 1993, pp. 694–698).[1] But the intention to transfer health care from the Histadrut to the government, thereby making it available to the entire population regardless of political affiliation, was clear enough.

In the storm that followed the Second Kanab Committee report, the Liberal—Herut alignment that went by the name of Gahal introduced a private members bill to transfer health care delivery from the sick funds to the government (Halevi, 1979, p. 31). Shortly afterward, Gahal representatives on the Hushi Committee joined the Ministry of Finance and Ministry of Health bureaucrats in advocating transfer of control of the health system to the core government. Similarly, in the Knesset debates prior to the formulation of the National Health Insurance Bill of 1973, the Leumit Sick Fund and the National Labor Federation proposed instituting national health insurance through a state agency (Ofir, 1982,Vol 2, pp 223, 512).

As long as Labor was at the helm the opponents of the status quo lacked the clout to push through their reforms. Shostak, true to his mentor Jabotinsky, who had named health care as one of five essentials that governments were obliged to provide their citizens, made restructuring a "personal dream."[2] He presented his position succinctly in a personal interview:

> I wanted to make these changes for a number of reasons. First, Jabotinski's social theory, which guides me, attests that workers' health insurance is the responsibility of the government, not of a political movement. Second, the structure I found had all the hallmarks of bad management: overlapping, waste and failure. Third, I found that in the existing structure, the field of health was completely neglected in terms of government responsibility. In contrast to education, security and the labor exchange bureaus, the state had shed its responsibilities and abandoned the basic rights of its citizens, forcing them to join a party, trade union or political organization in order to claim their rights to health care.
>
> I wanted to change this, even though I knew that the Histadrut was opposed to a National Health Service, because it would free the workers from their dependence on the left wing Kupat Holim. I saw this change as my main objective in the health system.[3]

Shostak's statement gathers most of the traditional objections to the status quo that protected and favored Kupat Holim: Health care should be available to all citizens whatever their political affinity. Health care is the responsibility of the government and should not be the province of a political party or trade union. The dual structure of the country's health care, marked by overlapping control by Kupat Holim and the government, permitted duplication, waste, and inefficiency.

Shostak embarked on his mission with the hearty backing of the Likud. Menachem Begin had long since promised that when his Herut Party came into power it would deal with Kupat Holim and the Histadrut and institute national health insurance (Ofir, 1982, Vol. 2, p. 224). During the 1973 parliamentary debate on the National Health Insurance Bill, Yoram Aridor, the Likud Minister of Finance who demonstrated so much overt hostility to Kupat Holim, declared that, "The day will come when a non-socialist government will take power in this country, and it will offer national health insurance" (*Knesset Minutes,* 1973, Vol. 68, p. 3919). The Likud election platform promised a reorganization of the health system: that every citizen, regardless of political or trade union affiliation, would be entitled to health care by law; that health insurance dues would be collected by the government; and that health services would be delivered regionally.[4] The last point was a well-understood code that meant that the government would take over the management of the health system, while the sick funds would be relegated to the position of contractors delivering the services.

Shostak and the Ministry of Health worked to implement this platform in three stages. In the first stage, a professional committee was appointed to propose ways of implementing the desired reforms. In the second stage, the Ministry of Health published a declaration of principals of national health insurance. In the third stage in 1981 a National Health Insurance Bill was presented to the Knesset.

Stage I: Laying the Groundwork

The Zohar Committee

In preparation for the sweeping reforms he planned, in August 1977 Shostak appointed a committee of health professionals to examine their implications and means of attaining them. The Zohar Committee, as it was called, was headed by Ezra Zohar, another Tel HaShomer physician who had a long history in public health and for years had been a highly outspoken critic of Kupat Holim's hegemony in the health services (Zohar, 1974, pp. 45–50; 1987, pp. 107–12).

In contrast to the various committees that had met to reform the health services under Labor, the Zohar Committee included not a single Kupat Holim representative; it did not even summon any Kupat Holim representatives to testify. In January 1978 it presented its detailed recommendations for the structural reform of the health system (Zohar Committee, 1978).

In the preface to its report, the committee attributed the problems of the country's health care to the structural division of the health services between the government and the various sick funds. According to the committee, this division, in which a large number of service providers operated without coordination, led to a disparity between the medical capabilities of the health services and the actual care given to the population (Zohar Committee, 1978, pp. 1–3). The coordination necessary to provide proper service was impossible, the committee claimed, in a system comprised of disparate bodies operating under different managements and with separate budgets, even though the major source of most of the funds was the government.

The committee's recommendations thus focused on the unification of the health services under an empowered Ministry of Health (Zohar Committee,

1978, pp. 4, 5). In place of the existent bipolar structure, the committee drew up a new pyramidal structure of authority with the Ministry of Health functioning as the prime policy maker at the top. The lines of authority would run from the ministry to a newly created National Health Authority, and from there first to government regional health centers and then to the various service providers. In the new structure Kupat Holim would be at the bottom of the pyramid, a "client" of the Ministry of Health, no more and no less than other sick fund.

To strengthen the ministry's policy-making powers, the committee recommended that the envisioned National Health Authority would operate as an independent corporate body with sole responsibility for the provision of medical services. This would free the Ministry of Health of the burden of having to provide and supervise its own health services, which undermined its ability to regulate and supervise Kupat Holim. The exact services to be provided would be determined by a future health law and Ministry of Health regulations. The Authority's director and board would be appointed by the government, on the recommendation of the minister of health (Zohar Committee, 1978, pp. 28–31).

To coordinate the disparate health services, the Zohar Committee wrote the regionalization plan discussed in the previous chapter. It recommended that the authority divide the country into 6 health regions, responsible for 22 service areas (Zohar Committee, 1978, pp. 28–29). Each region would be administered by a regional health office with authority over all the medical services, facilities, and personnel in its area, including those that belonged to the sick funds. This recommendation came with a special bite in that it explicitly stated that the sick funds' facilities might have to be leased by the government, raising fears of nationalization (Zohar Committee, 1978, p, 8).

Without so much as asking for Kupat Holim's opinion, the Zohar Committee thus set about pulling the rug out from under it. The National Health Authority and the regionalization plan it recommended were designed to subject Kupat Holim, along with the other sick funds, to Ministry of Health control and to deprive it of its autonomy. Additionally, the committee recommended that health insurance dues be collected by the National Insurance Institute, which could make it difficult if not impossible for the Histadrut to distribute the dues its members thought they were paying for health services to its nonhealth activities.

Histadrut and Kupat Holim Responses to the Zohar Committee

The Histadrut and Kupat Holim regarded the Zohar Committee recommendations as a threat to their existence (Becker, 1982, p. 277). Histadrut Secretary Yerucham Meshel saw the recommendations as "the nationalization of Kupat Holim."[5] He considered Zohar a longtime enemy who "finds it hard to accept the fact that the Histadrut owns Kupat Holim" and "is therefore trying to take it out of the hands of the workers and Kupat Holim employees" (Meshel, 1980, pp. 85–87).

The Histadrut took various steps to prevent the adoption of the Zohar Committee recommendations. It demanded "clear answers to all questions concerning health services" (Meshel, 1980, p. 86), which took up government time and attention. It enlisted the support of Kupat Holim's 27,000 employees by making them aware of "the need to defend their rights."[6] It rallied public opinion by convincing the Sick Fund's members that "the nationalization of Kupat Holim is detrimental to their interests."[7] The first of these steps can be seen as a way of stalling; the second two can be seen as latent threats if the government tried to implement its plan. They represented an amassing of troops, which showed the government the fight that lay ahead if the recommendations were adopted in the face of well-organized public opposition.

At the same time, the Histadrut presented a counteroffer of its own. It was prepared to support a form of health insurance, Meshel declared, that was coordinated with Kupat Holim and relied on Kupat Holim's extensive experience.[8] This proposal obviously had no chance of acceptance and may be seen as the Histadrut's way of presenting itself as ready to cooperate while reminding everyone of its importance and inflaming the debate.

These various actions were not isolated deeds but a fairly well-thought-out campaign of defense. Most of them were detailed in the lecture entitled "The Real Test of Israel's Health Services," which Meshel delivered to the Histadrut Executive Committee in February. If these various steps fail to put an end to the government's designs, Meshel threatened, the Histadrut would wage an all-out counterattack against the politically motivated plan.[9]

Kupat Holim embarked on its own publicity campaign. In an article published in the Labor-supported daily newspaper, *Davar*, the chairman of the Kupat Holim National Council warned that the Zohar Committee recommendations threatened the principle of mutual assistance on which Kupat Holim was founded and subverted the essence of the Histadrut as a social movement.[10] The warnings, which other newspapers reported, seem to have been intended to answer the long-standing objection that the Histadrut appropriated much of the money it collected in the name of its health services for its own purposes. Instead of denying the charge, Kupat Holim legitimized these actions on the grounds that the money went to pay for the mutual assistance in all areas of social well-being for which the Histadrut had always taken responsibility. The warning was that if health were nationalized, Israel's citizens would lose many of the social benefits that the Histadrut gave them.

Kupat Holim Chairman Doron wrote a brochure enumerating the Zohar Committee report's flaws and distortions. The brochure, which Kupat Holim published, attacked the report's failure to tackle Kupat Holim's budgetary problems, charged that the regional hospitalization plan perpetuated waste, and argued that the proposed restructuring of the health services did not address important issues of policy, planning, supervision, coordination, and equipment. It further complained that the recommendations did not provide a formula to determine how much the various parties (the government, the insurees, and the sick funds) would pay for the new health services and did nothing to correct the Ministry of Health's dual role as health service provider and regulator.[11]

In addition, Kupat Holim came up with a detailed counteroffer—a national health insurance bill, which was coordinated with the Histadrut.[12] In this proposal Kupat Holim agreed to "consider" not requiring its members to join the Histadrut and not opposing the establishment of a separate agency to collect health insurance fees. But neither of these offers was in its power to implement because membership and insurance collection were the province of the Histadrut. Then, in exchange for these promises it could not keep, Kupat Holim made demands that, in effect, would preserve the status quo: that health insurance be based on the existing sick funds; that a new health funding formula be created in place of the one that the Likud had abolished, whereby the government would pay one third of Kupat Holim's expenses; and that a health insurance council would be established, with half its members Kupat Holim representatives.[13] This proposal had as little chance of being accepted as Meshel's informal offer and served similar purposes. Moreover, the chairman of the National Council backed the Histadrut's threat of war if the Zohar Committee recommendations were implemented with an analogous battle threat of his own.[14]

The Histadrut–Kupat Holim defense strategy aimed to protect the red lines that demarcated the boundary of the changes that the Histadrut and Kupat Holim were prepared to tolerate. These lines, as recalled, were the provision of public health through the existing sick funds, the Histadrut's control of health insurance fees, dual Kupat Holim–Histadrut membership, autonomous decision making by the two organizations, and their right to a major say in national health policy. Above and beyond Kupat Holim's and the Histadrut's varied and sundry arguments against the Zohar Committee recommendations was their drive to preserve their status, prestige, and power in face of the government's efforts to put order into the country's unwieldy health care system.

Stage II: Pushing Forward with Modifications

"Principles of National Health Insurance"

Undeterred by the threats, in September 1978 the Minister of Health's office issued its "Principles of National Health Insurance."[15] In some ways, the principles were more tempered than the Zohar Committee recommendations. A few of them allowed for Kupat Holim representation in an advisory capacity. Much as recommended by the Zohar Committee, the principles divided the country into service areas, each of which would be managed by a small administrative cadre headed by a ministry-appointed director. But they added in each area a regional health council, which would include representatives of the sick funds to work with that body. Another concession was the stipulation, not included in the Zohar Committee recommendations, that the minister of Health appoint a National Health Council with representatives from the sick funds to advise him on matters concerning health policy. In addition, the principles clearly rejected the nationalization of the sick funds, noting that the National Health Authority would "not purchase or expropriate other agency's medical facilities," but rather sign contracts with the various health care providers, and provided assurance that "the operation and management of the property and institutions of service providers will remain in the hands of their owners, independently and under their sole responsibility, and [that] there will be no change in their status and functions."[16]

At the same time, the principles made no concessions on actual government control of the health services. They supported the creation of a National Health Authority run by a government-appointed administrative committee, which would bear sole responsibility for the provision of medical care to the entire population along regional lines. They stipulated that the health insurance fees be collected by the National Insurance Institute. This would break the financial tie between the citizen and his or her sick fund, eliminate the role of the Histadrut's Central Tax Bureau, and abolish the mandatory dual Kupat Holim–Histadrut membership from which the Histadrut derived so much of its money and power.

For all the Histadrut–Kupat Holim noise, Shostak was intent on pursuing the restructuring of the health services. His office duly relayed the Principles to the Ministerial Committee for Labor and Welfare, a move that in Israel constitutes the first step in the preparation of government bills for presentation to the Knesset.

Kupat Holim and Histadrut Responses to the "Principles of National Health Insurance"

Shostak's embarkation on the legislative route brought the life threat to Kupat Holim and the Histadrut one step closer to realization. This now required a more focused response. The response began, like that to the Zohar Committee recommendations, with words and threats. In a letter to Minister of Health Shostak, Histadrut Secretary Meshel totally rejected the "Principals of National Health Insurance." Opening with elaborate politeness, he suggested that Shostak retrieve the document from the ministerial committee for reconsideration. Then, in a more aggressive tone, he reviewed Kupat Holim's red lines, declaring in no uncertain terms that the Histadrut would not permit them to be crossed. No concessions would be made on Kupat Holim members, institutions, facilities, or employees. The Histadrut "principle of mutual assistance," predicated on the dual membership in the trade union and Sick Fund would be preserved. The Histadrut would not agree to turn Kupat Holim "into a sub-contractor for health services. . . ." And lest there be any doubt in anyone's mind, he warned Shostak against entertaining "any thoughts that it will be possible to maintain this huge complex system, even for one day, without the cooperation of the workers, through their appointed representatives."[17]

Meshel's stand was supported by Kupat Holim's governing bodies. The chairman of its National Council let it be known that he regarded Shostak's Principles as the basis for "a devious political scheme to destroy Kupat Holim and the Histadrut," and warned that "we will not take this persecution lying down."[18] The tenth Kupat Holim convention rejected the Principles by a 75% majority.[19]

In addition to raising the pitch of their verbal objections, Kupat Holim and the Histadrut began to take concrete action to thwart the impending presentation of a national health insurance bill. Once again, they submitted their own proposal to counter that of the Ministry of Health's. Harking back to the various health insurance schemes they had presented under Labor, the major elements of this proposal were diametrically opposed to those contained in Shostak's Principles. Table 14.1 presents the differences.

It is unlikely that Kupat Holim and the Histadrut ever expected that this set

Table 14.1. Likud versus Kupat Holim–Histadrut Health Insurance Proposal

	Kupat Holim–Histadrut Principles	Ministry of Health's Principles
Type of insurance	Not under state auspices	Under state auspices
Insurer	Existing sick funds	National Insurance Institute
Service administration	National Health Council, half of whose members are sick fund representatives in proportion to the size of the fund's membership	National Health Authority in which sick funds have no representation
Insurance fee collection agency	Histadrut Central Tax Bureau and sick fund bodies or, alternatively, a social collection institute run jointly by the state and sick funds	National Insurance Institute
Status of the sick funds	Autonomous organizations that own and manage their services themselves	Service provider and client of Ministry of Health
Freedom of choice	Compulsory joint Histadrut–Kupat Holim membership	Insurees can obtain health care from any sick fund in their area of residence with no reference to labor union membership

of provisions, which had never become law under Labor, to become law under the Likud. On the practical plane, their response to the Principles was to muster the troops to prevent them being realized in the national health legislation that Shostak was planning. To this end, they revitalized the dormant coalition of interests they had with Israel's two major religious parties at the time: the National Religious Party (NRP) and the ultraorthodox Agudat Yisrael Party.

The coalition of interests in health went back to the *yishuv*, when the Labor movement had used the Histadrut to recruit the support of the religious parties. First, it pressured the secular, socialist-based Histadrut to open its doors to the religious trade unions and to make available to their members its health and welfare benefits. Second, it had the Histadrut ensure that the religious parties benefited from the single tax. As recalled, the proceeds of that tax were divided between Kupat Holim and the Histadrut's other "tax partners." The religious parties became de facto tax partners who were permitted to take for themselves almost the entire portion of their members' dues that were not allocated to Kupat Holim. For many years, the religious parties thus kept almost half of what their members paid in the single tax. This money became the main source of their funding.

In 1977 these arrangements were formalized in signed agreements between the Histadrut and the Mizrahi Workers Trade Union (the arm of the NRP) and the Agudat Yisrael Laborers (the arm of the Agudat Yisrael Party; Central Tax Bureau, 1962, p. 39).[20] As a result, the NRP received "tens of millions of shekels a year, for party publicity and organizational needs."[21] In 1981, the sum amounted to IL 70 million.[22]

The religious parties were members of the Labor coalition until 1977, when they joined the Likud coalition. However, they remained tightly woven into the Kupat Holim–Histadrut health network. The end of dual membership spelled the same end to political funding for them as it did for the Histadrut. To protect themselves, they extracted a promise from the Likud that no national health insurance bill would be submitted to the Knesset without the consent of all the coalition partners.[23] They also promised the Histadrut that they would do all in their power to prevent the presentation of the bill even if it meant a government crisis.[24]

Stage III: Legislative Action

The National Health Insurance Bill of 1981

For almost three years after the "Principles of National Health Insurance" were published, the intended National Health Insurance Bill languished in the ministerial committee and the government plenum. The slow pace may be attributed in some measure to Prime Minister Begin's occupation with foreign affairs and especially with the groundbreaking peace accord with Egypt in 1979, so that he did not put his weight behind the bill. Moreover, the Kupat Holim–Histadrut alliance with the NRP paid off. Keeping its promise to the Histadrut to prevent the presentation of the bill, the NRP soon began to stall. When the government plenum was hammering out the draft of the 1981 National Health Insurance Bill, NRP representatives demanded postponing the submission of the bill to the Knesset until their position, which was much the same as the Kupat Holim–Histadrut position, was satisfactorily incorporated. They supported their demand with the coalition agreement that no national health insurance bill would be submitted without the consent of all the coalition partners.[25] The minister of Health, supported by the minister of Finance and the minister of Justice, denied that submitting the bill would violate the coalition agreement and argued that the government's platform committed it to national health insurance.[26] Nevertheless, no progress was made until Prime Minister Begin finally entered the picture and, to circumvent the NRP's arguments, released the party from coalition discipline, allowing party members to vote as they wished on the first reading.[27]

Even so, there were hitches. Just before the first reading, NRP representatives demanded that the prime minister withdraw the bill on the grounds that its submission violated the coalition agreement. Begin refused and reminded the NRP that it could vote against.[28] While this was going on, the general secretary of the Histadrut, the chairman of the Kupat Holim National Council, and the chairman of Kupat Holim, together with the Knesset members from the Labor Alignment, met with Knesset members from various small parties to lobby against the bill.[29]

This politicking was supplemented by a dramatic demonstration of force. On the day the bill was to be voted on, 27,000 Kupat Holim workers went out on strike, shutting down all of Kupat Holim's medical services.[30] Thirteen of the country's major trade unions came to their aid, threatening to support their strike with strikes of their own.[31]

In the end, the bill was submitted to the Knesset on February 10, 1981, four months before the next elections.[32] Still following a lengthy and strident parliamentary debate, the Knesset approved the bill in its first reading by a majority of 56 to 47,[33] representing a setback for Kupat Holim–Histadrut interests. Despite the protests and threats, the bill was based almost entirely on the Zohar Committee's recommendations and the "Principals of National Health Insurance" issued by the minister of Health, and it crossed virtually all of Kupat Holim's red lines.

It was a specifically "national" health insurance bill that put health care under state auspices, although there was to be no nationalization via the purchase or expropriation of sick fund assets, and the various sick funds would continue to run and administer their properties and facilities independently.

The insurer was to be the National Insurance Institute, which would serve as the fee collection agency. It would relay the fees to the Ministry of Health, which would make funds available not to the sick funds but to the various authorities appointed to administer the country's health care and in accordance with the ministry's health services budget.

A national health authority and regional authorities would be created to administer the services. The national health authority would coordinate the services of the various regions. It would be appointed by the minister and report directly to him. To ensure its independence of Kupat Holim, no more than one fourth of its members would be representatives of service providers. The regional authorities would have the job of organizing, planning, and coordinating the health services within the various regions and of signing contracts with service suppliers. They would similarly be appointed by the minister and answer directly to the minister and the National Health Authority. Their independence would be similarly ensured by restricting representatives from the sick funds to 25% of the total membership.

Freedom of choice would be available: health services would be provided equally to all insurees with no mandatory organizational or party affiliation.

With regard to the relative status of the Ministry of Health and the sick funds, the bill would bestow on the ministry the core's powers of allocation and regulation. The ministry would have the authority to authorize and license the service providers, the right to make regulations concerning the preparation of the budget, and the right to set the insurance fees. It would transfer the fees to the national and regional authorities and set the criteria for payment to the service providers. It would appoint the members of the national and regional authorities, retaining the power to ratify the sick fund nominees. It would establish the range and type of services to be supplied and would have the formal right to require that every service provider supply its services according to the minister's directives. All of this meant that Kupat Holim and the other sick funds would become subordinate to the national and regional authorities.[34]

Not surprisingly, Kupat Holim, the Histadrut, and the Labor Party were up in arms, uniformly viewing the bill as intentionally jeopardizing the continued viability of Kupat Holim.[35] In the words of Haim Doron:

> This bill turns the sick funds into service providers. . . . Kupat Holim will be destroyed. It will not be able to supply normal services. It will not be permitted to plan, initiate or develop. . . . The government wants not only to undermine the Histadrut, but to specifically destroy Kupat Holim.[36]

From the Knesset podium, Meshel similarly rejected the plan as an effort to reduce Kupat Holim to a mere service provider.[37] The speaker of the Labor Alignment, who would become minister of Health when the Likud was replaced by a Labor–Likud coalition, contended:

This policy is directly intended to cripple Kupat Holim and subdue it . . . and the main motive for this is age old political acrimony, an attempt to break the Histadrut and weaken its power in the economy and in society. . . . By detaching Kupat Holim from the Histadrut.[38]

In contrast, the Likud were delighted. One of its members termed it "the most important law to be passed by this government in the Knesset in the last four years."[39] Shostak held up the bill as "the depolitization of the health system," although he tried to reassure Kupat Holim that the law, if passed, would "not do Kupat Holim any harm but, on the contrary, frees Kupat Holim from the intolerable burden of huge new debts."[40]

Unassuaged, Kupat Holim's National Council passed a series of resolutions rejecting the bill. Asserting that the bill was aimed at destroying Kupat Holim, it protested that Sick Fund representatives had not been included in its preparation and reiterated the Kupat Holim position that health insurance should be based on the existing sick funds.[41] Haim Doron let it be known that Kupat Holim planned to fight "with all our strength, with all our zeal and with all our energy to stop the tidal wave that threatens to damage the status and power of the Histadrut and Kupat Holim in the health system."[42]

Obstruction of the Legislation

Doron's declaration of war heralded the beginning of the battle against the proposed structural changes in the health system. Under Labor, the Histadrut–Kupat Holim alliance had repeatedly thwarted all plans at health reform from within. The passage of the first reading of the National Health Insurance Bill of 1981 brought perilously close a reform program, which endangered all the attainments. It made it eminently clear to the Histadrut that it would not be able to affect Likud policy by merely the stalling, persuasion, explanation, and gentle pressure that it used until that time.

Obstructive Measures

After the bill was approved, the Histadrut Central Committee called on the Kupat Holim Workers Association to return to work,[43] while the general secretary of the Histadrut announced that the failed struggle to abort the Knesset vote was just the first, inconsequential phase of the battle.[44] The battle plan was created jointly by the Labor Alignment, Kupat Holim, and the Histadrut. Its aim was to kill the bill on its second or third reading.[45] The obstruction proceeded simultaneously along three avenues: creating a broad front against the bill, disrupting the work of the committees appointed to prepare the bill for the second reading, and establishing facts on the ground.

Creating a broad front against the bill, which had begun before the first reading was greatly intensified. To rally public support, the Histadrut took out huge advertisements in the media warning of the bill's dangers. The new law would mean higher fees, reduced services in developing areas and outlying districts, unbearable bureaucracy, and would replace public medicine with private, the ads cried out. The ads also played on public anxieties about the hyperinflation generated by Minister of Finance Aridor's policies, arguing that "the financial turnabout has destroyed the economy and the turnabout in health legislation will destroy the health services too."[46] Kupat Holim Chairman Doron held a news conference in which he called the bill reactionary and declared that its implementation would create anarchy in the health services.[47]

In addition to the support of the Israeli public, Kupat Holim also sought the support of the International Organization of Sick Funds, whose leaders it invited to Israel. This organization's chairman and its general secretary gratefully accepted and went on to state in yet another news conference that they too opposed health insurance plans that nationalized sick funds and supported plans based on insurees' organizations, as were all of Europe's health schemes, excluding Great Britain's.[48]

Kupat Holim was also able to muster the support of its generally disaffected hospital doctors, who took out their own advertisements. These contained an impassioned appeal to the Knesset members "not to give your vote to the National Health Insurance Bill in its present form" and warnings that if the bill became law, the health services would be destroyed without anything to replace them.[49]

In addition, Kupat Holim was able to obtain the backing of the Maccabi Sick Fund and the United Sick Fund. Putting aside the years of resentment and rivalry for government favors, these funds realized that the proposed law also hurt them. Maccabi physicians told the media that "the bill in its present form . . . threatens the existence of their sick fund," and the heads of the fund declared that if the bill became law, "services to their members would become cumbersome."[50] In August 1981, after a meeting with representatives of the Maccabi and United sick funds, the chairman of Kupat Holim announced: "The three sick funds again wish to reiterate their emphatic objection to the National Health Insurance Bill, as put before the ninth Knesset. The three sick funds support national health insurance based on the existing sick funds."[51] The broad front that was developing hovered over the legislators.

The disruption of the legislative process began with the Corfu Committee, which was appointed on February 17, a week after the first reading, to prepare the bill for the second reading. This committee heard testimony from most of the bodies involved in health in Israel but did not manage to complete its discussions and present a revised bill for the second hearing, largely because of the obstructions of the Histadrut–Kupat Holim allies. The NRP, a beneficiary of

Histadrut control of health insurance fee collection, viewed the bill as "a bitter blow to National Religious Party interests,"[52] and its representatives on the committee raised constant objections to minute points in the bill, deliberately did not attend all the hearings and frequently interrupted testimony where they did attend, generating a great deal of noise and an atmosphere of confusion. Members of the Labor Alignment did much the same. Shoshana Arbeli-Almozlino, a Labor Party member who became minister of health under the next government, put intense effort into protracting the proceedings. Her tactic was to constantly demand precise data on complex, amorphous matters on which such data were not, and could not, be available. She demanded figures on the overall cost of the reform, a list of its benefits to the public, information on how the insurance fees would be collected and on contracts made for implementing these arrangements, as well as a detailed comparison of the Ministry of Health's current financial obligations with those it would incur were the bill to become law.[53]

As the proceedings ambled toward nowhere, election time drew near and Shostak tried to accelerate the process. In a meeting with Doron and Meshel, he offered to amend the original provisions of the bill so that the National Insurance Institute would relay money to Kupat Holim and the Histadrut directly, according to a formula, rather than through the Ministry of Health and the national and regional authorities. But the offer was rejected.[54] More wrangling ensued and the committee became paralyzed. The chairman could not produce a version of the bill that had reasonable chances of receiving the majority support required to send it back to the Knesset for a second reading. The bill was not put to a vote.

The ability of the Histadrut and Kupat Holim to mobilize political support to throttle the bill in the committee can be seen as the establishment of facts on the ground. By methodically obstructing the committee hearings and delaying the vote indefinitely, these organizations' political allies effectively tabled the bill while disrupting the Knesset's normal legislative process. Two major factors worked in their favor. One was that the Likud did not have an absolute majority in the committee, so that the opposition of its NRP coalition partner was extremely detrimental. The other was that the committee was established only a few months before new elections were to be held. With pollsters predicting a Labor victory (Arian, 1983), the opponents of the bill probably felt that if they just dragged out the discussions, the entire matter would be dropped in the next Knesset.

Their prediction did not come to pass. The Likud won the 1981 elections, and in early February 1982 the Ulmert Committee was appointed to rescue the bill.[55] Nonetheless, the bill's opponents continued the fight. Not leaving matters to chance this time, the Labor Alignment appointed one of its MPs to coordinate the resistance. The coordinator, as he was called, was dedicated to the familiar Kupat Holim–Histadrut red lines and bent on doing everything in his power to prevent them from being crossed.[56] He appointed a team composed of Labor Alignment MPs, most of them on the Ulmert Committee, and representatives of the Histadrut and Kupat Holim to devise a plan for committee members to demand far-reaching changes in the bill and to keep it from being sent to the Knesset for a second reading.[57]

The team used the same delaying strategy that had been employed so successfully in the Corfu Committee. Only now the delay was professionally organized in Kupat Holim headquarters, where lawyers, accountants, and health system managers combed every item in the bill and prepared virtually thousands of objections. These were gathered in a portfolio, which was given to all the Labor Alignment MPs on the committee. Each MP was assigned the objections that he or she would raise. The tactic worked. In a May 10, 1982 memo to the secretary general of the Labor Party, the coordinator reported that for the four months since the committee was appointed, "we have done everything possible to prolong the debate and delay meetings. Only in the last meeting, which was held at the beginning of May, did we begin to discuss the first items of the bill, and so there is still much work to be done."[58]

As another means of stalling, the team demanded that the Ministry of Health prepare a detailed list of the services that the new law would provide and an itemized estimate of their costs, and that the Ministry of Finance prepare a response to this information. This, the coordinator hoped, would cause the Ministry of Finance to withdraw its support of the bill because the costs—which had hitherto been hidden in the Kupat Holim budget—could not but be sky high.[59] The Ministry of Finance did not withdraw its support, but the promoters of the bill did become bogged down in preparing the demanded itemization and estimates.

Along with dragging out the proceedings, the well-organized opposition solidified and enlarged its political support. The coordinator met with representatives of the Mizrahi Workers and the Agudat Yisrael Workers to obtain their reaffirmation of the agreement, which had committed them to oppose the bill in its current form. In his report to the Labor Party secretary, he gleefully noted that "representatives of the Mizrahi Workers who appeared before the Committee outdid themselves in their vociferous objections to the bill," that one representative of the ultraorthodox Agudat Israel Party suggested returning the bill to the Knesset Speaker for an undiscussed burial, and that one of the NRP representatives boycotted the committee altogether. His boycott, the letter indicated, was supplemented by well-timed absences of other NRP and Agudat Israel representatives, which made voting impossible on numerous occasions because the committee lacked a quorum. [60]

In addition, the Labor Alignment exploited the willingness of small, single-issue parties to make trade-offs on issues that do not particularly interest them to bring their representatives on the committee into the coalition against the bill. The Shinui Party agreed to cooperate on the condition that Kupat Holim make its services available to everyone, not only Histadrut members. The Tchia Party representative, who later became minister of Science, agreed to back the opposition in exchange for Labor Party support for settlements and its agreement not to oppose his nomination as a minister.[61]

The outbreak of the controversial Lebanon War in October 1982 further protracted the proceedings. The high Israeli losses and public opposition to the war so stressed Prime Minister Begin that he withdrew into himself and virtually ceased to function as a leader, while much of his party floundered. The party elite, previously committed to health reform, now turned its attention to healing the party's wounds, and many Likud representatives on the committee stopped attending meetings, which combined with the absenteeism of many of the NRP and Agudat Israel Party members, degenerated into private tête-à-têtes between the coordinator and the representatives of the Labor Alignment.[62]

The morass was so deep that to extricate the bill Shostak proposed compromises more far-reaching than those he had offered during the Corfu Commission hearings. He proposed a revised version of the bill, in which, among other things, health insurance would be based on the existing sick funds; the sick funds would present their budget proposals to the National Health Authority rather than to the Ministry of Health; the regional authorities would only coordinate services, not plan them; and the current level of services would be maintained through a clear statement of the public's health rights and the state's obligations to meet them, a provision that would permit Kupat Holim to continue operating at its current level.[63] Because fee collection was still to be carried out by the National Insurance Institute and mandatory joint Kupat Holim–Histadrut membership was still to be abolished, however, this compromise was also rejected. In the words of Yerucham Meshel, the new version of the bill, like the old, "eliminates Kupat Holim and is worse than nationalization in that it cuts off the insuree from the sick fund and requires us to provide services without enabling us to operate properly."[64]

In the end, the Ulmert Committee fizzed out without results. The professionally planned stalling, the mobilization of the political support of the smaller parties, and the outbreak of the Lebanon War, which diminished the interest of the bill's Likud supporters,[65] all contributed to the committee's slow demise. Following the formation of the National Unity Government in which Labor and the Likud shared power after the 1984 elections, the bill was dropped without the appointment of a new committee to bring it to a second reading.

Interestingly, the Likud's National Health Insurance Bill of 1981 was laid to rest at precisely the same point in the legislative process as Labor's National Health Insurance Bill of 1973. Both were killed in committee, neither reached a second reading, and in both cases the death blow came from a coalition partner whose interests and views in the matter of health were virtually identical to those of the current opposition. Under Labor the threat by the Independent Liberals, who wanted to separate sick fund and trade union membership and to have the National Insurance Institute serve as the fee-collection agency, to leave the government and dismantle the coalition if the bill were passed led to a stalemate. Under the Likud, the NRP's affinity of interests with Labor in the matter of Histadrut control of Kupat Holim money and membership made the NRP an ardent fifth column in the coalition ranks. This type of end to bills is not uncommon in the Israeli political system.

The outcome of Kupat Holim's obstruction was the preservation of the status quo in the health system at the three points that were most vital to Kupat Holim and the Histadrut: control over insurees, control over fee collection, and complete sick fund autonomy in making health policy and setting priorities. This preservation represents the failure of the Likud to wield the major instrument of government—restructuring—insofar as health policy was concerned and the power of Kupat Holim and the Histadrut to impose health policy.

CHAPTER 15

The Obstructive Veto

Between 1978 and 1984, Kupat Holim exercised an obstructive veto in the implementation stage of the policy-making process. Unlike the preventive veto, the obstructive veto was neither informally permitted nor formally given to it by the core, but was wrenched from the core in a fierce political struggle from outside the government. It represented a shift in approach, after the friendly and accommodating Labor Party lost the elections, by means of which Kupat Holim endeavored to continue to control health policy in the hostile environment created by the Likud, a longtime foe of the entire Labor apparatus and worldview.

The obstructive veto was manifested in Kupat Holim's effective blocking of the implementation of the measures that the new Likud Minister of Health Eliezer Shostak took so as to enable the ministry to exercise what he saw as the right of a democratically elected government to wield the tools of policy on its own, without the participation of a body on the margin. In all three policy-making tools, Shostak unilaterally changed the procedures that had enabled Kupat Holim to exercise a preventive veto in the formative stage of the policy-making process. He replaced allocation by a routine administrative formula, which mirrored Kupat Holim's needs with detailed procedures that linked support to government supervision and approval of Kupat Holim's expenditures. He abolished parity in regulation and the committees in which it was exercised; established new regulatory structures in which Kupat Holim had no place; and made formal, detailed, and often intrusive regulations impinging on the most sensitive areas of Kupat Holim's operations: its hospital renovation and admission, its heavy equipment purchases, and its ability to regulate the uses of its hospitals and the flow of its patients. He introduced the first bill designed to make real changes in the structure of the health system and to subordinate Kupat Holim to the Ministry of Health. Crossing all the Kupat Holim–Histadrut red lines, the bill sought to sever the link between the insuree and the Histadrut and

Kupat Holim, transfer fee collection to the National Insurance Institute, reduce Kupat Holim to the status of a service provider, and bestow concrete authority and practical power upon the Ministry of Health.

In none of these measures did Shostak even consult with Kupat Holim, much less include it. He had the advantage, which his predecessor did not, that his party was not enmeshed with Kupat Holim, and that the Ministry of Health was relatively well coordinated with the other key ministries. The Ministry of Finance, out of Labor's grasp, no longer worked hand in glove with Kupat Holim to control the allocation process. The Ministry of Labor and Welfare, which under Labor had consistently sought to anchor Kupat Holim's privileged position in law, kept out of health care altogether. These advantages gave the Likud-run Ministry of Health greater control over the policy-formation process. So did the fact that Shem Tov had raised the institutional caliber of the ministry and had set his sights beyond the family, or what LaPalombara terms "parantella," modus operandi (1974). But policy formation is only one part the policy-making process.

Instead of accepting the new rules of the game, Kupat Holim waged a life-or-death struggle to obstruct their implementation. In allocation, it stalled and obfuscated the Ministry of Health–mandated budget discussions, established facts on the ground in the form of an ever-increasing deficit with mounting debts to suppliers and banks, and imposed sanctions on the Ministry of Health by defaulting on payments for its patients in government-owned hospitals. It adopted similar strategies to obstruct the implementation of the Likud's new regulations. It dragged out and disrupted the government-set procedures for approval of its activities by withholding information and raising endless objections to the government-set standards and criteria, and it established facts on the ground through unapproved construction, renovation, and equipment purchases, the unapproved opening of a cardiac and thoracic surgery unit at Carmel Hospital, and the independent referrals of its patients to hospitals of its own choosing. And it embarked on a fierce struggle to derail the government's restructuring initiatives, first to prevent the presentation of the bill to the Knesset, and, when that failed, to block its second reading.

In essence, the dispute between the Likud and Kupat Holim was over who had the right to make health policy: the government or Kupat Holim. This issue had been implicit in the under the surface tension that had always existed in Kupat Holim's relations with the preceding Labor governments. With Shostak's determination to exercise exclusive control of the tools of policy, the issue rose to the surface. Driving its obstructive measures was the fervent conviction of Kupat Holim's leadership that it, not the government, had the right to make health policy. Kupat Holim's contention was that the government had no right to impose policy on its own and that it itself had a legitimate place in the policy making process. In the words of Chairman Doron:

This is a government which discusses and makes decisions on the state budget and the health budget without first discussing the matter with the largest supplier of health services in the country. They make arbitrary budget decisions detached from reality, and then cut them [the budgets] yet further without any examination of their effects and without obtaining our agreement either before or after.[1]

The assumption behind this and many similar Kupat Holim assertions is that being the body that actually delivered the health care, Kupat Holim was in a better position than the government to determine what was really needed. It, not the government, was on the front line contending with the daily realities of providing health care. It, not the government, had to supply medical care to the patients who arrived at its clinics, hospitals, pharmacies, diagnostic centers, and so forth, and who expected treatment—whether or not there was money to pay. It, not the government, knew what was needed and what had to be done to meet the needs. And this close responsibility and intimate knowledge gave it a right to a determining say about how the country's health care should be financed; about what medical facilities should be built, where they should be built, how they should be equipped, to what hospitals its insurees should be sent; and the way the system as a whole should be run—in short, to the right to a determinant role in health policy.

The obstruction was temporarily successful. Despite drastic reductions in government support, Kupat Holim continued to spend as it saw fit, while forcing the government to pay for its activities with no say in what they were. The Likud's efforts at unilateral regulation ended in a stalemate, with Kupat Holim imposing its own preferences on the government through the wholesale violation of Ministry of Health regulations. The Likud-run Ministry of Health could no more enforce its formal regulations than the Labor-run ministry could coax Kupat Holim into voluntary compliance with its vision of a well-ordered health system. Kupat Holim built and bought as it wished, creating modern and prestigious facilities far superior to the government's. The Likud's inability to restructure the system meant that Kupat Holim remained the authoritative body in the health system.

To attain these ends, Kupat Holim exploited its many advantages as a monopolistic body on the margin in a vital service area in Israel. It made use both of its own internal resources and of the prevailing social attitudes and cultural norms in the country during this period.

Of its internal resources, which included a large, highly skilled workforce, a well-developed organizational structure, and a network of ambulatory clinics, hospitals and other facilities unmatched by any of the other sick funds, perhaps the most significant in the fight was the deeply entrenched dependency of both the Israeli population and the Israeli economy, which it had systematically nurtured over the Labor years. Not only did Kupat Holim insure 80% of the population, but until the mid-1980s, when the smaller sick funds began to expand, few alternatives existed. In the major cities, people could join one of the smaller sick funds, but in many of the outlying towns and villages, Kupat Holim was the only medical service available. On the economic front, the country's pharmaceutical companies and manufacturers and suppliers of medical equipment and supplies relied on Kupat Holim for a major part of their business; a large medical and nonmedical workforce depended on Kupat Holim for their livelihood; and the solvency of what was at the time the second largest bank in Israel, the Histadrut-owned Bank HaPoalim, was connected with Kupat Holim's solvency.

Kupat Holim parleyed these dependencies into the threat of paralyzing the health system and of wreaking havoc on a good portion of the country's economy by defaulting on its debts and deficits. These are strange threats from the perspective of a liberal market economy in which with rare exceptions private-sector organizations are left to fend for themselves. They were effective in Israel largely because, despite the beginnings of the public's disaffection with socialism that the Likud victory revealed, the government was still expected to bear ultimate responsibility for both the health and the economic welfare of its citizens. Health care in Israel was—and is—still regarded as a public utility, which the public expected the government to provide. Private health care was not economically feasible for most Israelis and not part of the culture. Israelis' expectations that their government see to their health needs meant that no government could let Kupat Holim founder. On the economic front, in the course of Israel's history, various governments had paid the debts of a large list of other bodies, including local municipalities, kibbutzim and moshavim, banks, and large private companies. It was virtually inconceivable at this point that the government would abandon Kupat Holim, along with the many enterprises and individuals whose solvency were linked to its own, to the consequences of its fiscal irresponsibility.

Three other assets that Kupat Holim brought to the fight are also noteworthy. One was its fervent entrepreneurialism, manifested in the flexibility and ingenuity of the tactics and strategies that it used to obstruct the Likud's policies. Entrepreneurialism is a quality highly valued in Israeli culture, which respects leaders and organizations that are able to improvise and get things done, even if that means pushing the boundaries of the law (Arian, 1985; Caiden, 1970; Nachmias & Rosenbloom, 1978; Sharkansky, 1979; Sharkansky & Zalmanovitch, 2000). This culture made it possible for the heads of Kupat Holim to thumb their noses at the government and to enjoy public support as they did so.

Another asset was its continued popularity. Through the early 1980s Kupat Holim was still a well-thought-of organization. During the 1983 doctors' strike, when the chaos was at its peak and Kupat Holim's services shut down, a poll showed that only 10% of the public was unhappy with Kupat Holim, whereas 81% understood the importance of the Sick Fund, 74% of those polled said that it was worth their being members in Kupat Holim, and 84% said they would not change sick funds as a result of its strike policy.[2] A year later, in 1984, opinion polls showed that 70% of the adult Jewish population had a positive attitude toward Kupat Holim and its activities, that 66.5% preferred it to any other sick fund, and that the public supported its actions.[3] Its support in the population shielded it from the consequences of its own egregious acts and from the Likud's determination to make it comform.

The third asset was the fervent sense, possessed by Kupat Holim's leadership, that Kupat Holim had the right to make health policy. Kupat Holim's job was to deliver health care. The government's job was to finance it to the sum that Kupat Holim deemed necessary and with no strings attacked. As Doron argued:

> Kupat Holim fills a position of national importance in addition to its social and medical functions. This sick fund, with its 3.2 million members and its attainments and achievements, has the moral right to demand from the Israeli government pre-agreed rules on how the financial burden should be divided. . . ."[4]

This sense of right infused everything Kupat Holim did, from its overspending to its prevarication, manipulation, and flouting of government regulations. It was a major source of Kupat Holim's obstructive energy and ingenuity in this period.

The assets that Kupat Holim brought to the veto and the cultural factors that enabled it to behave as it did were vital, but in and of themselves they do not adequately account for its ability to obstruct government policy for these seven years. The obstructive veto was as much the work of the subsystem as the preventive veto had been and would have been impossible without the active support of the Histadrut and Labor Party.

The Histadrut helped Kupat Holim to raise money from foreign donors and, confident that the government would come to the rescue, provided it with easy credit through the Histadrut-run Bank HaPoalim and virtually free construction by the Histadrut-run building company Solel Boneh. In its annual labor negotiations with the government and the country's private employers, the Histadrut bargained away employees' benefits to sustain Kupat Holim. It used its financial muscle to propagandize against the restructuring bill and its trade union membership to launch demonstrations and to threaten labor unrest should the bill be presented to the Knesset.

The Labor Party lent Kupat Holim its political muscle from the opposition. Its main contribution was to organize, along with Kupat Holim and the Histadrut, an intense, well-planned, and well-coordinated campaign to torpedo the Likud's restructuring bill in the Knesset. It organized its MPs to filibuster the

bill and kill it with endless petty questions. It mobilized some small, independent parties to the cause by calling in favors. Above all, along with the Histadrut, it enlisted in the battle the country's two main religious parties which like
itself benefited politically from the Histadrut apportionment of the single tax.
Reminding these parties of what they would lose if the bill became law, it got
them to obstruct the preparations and readings of the bill from within the Likud
coalition, of which they were pivotal members.

Without this assistance from its partners in the subsystem, it is questionable
that Kupat Holim would have been able to buy, build, renovate, and otherwise
maintain and expand its facilities in excess of government allocation and in violation of government regulations, and doubtful that it would have been able to
ward off restructuring that was detrimental to its interests.

The question here is why the subsystem came to Kupat Holim's aid at this
point in time. Kupat Holim's utility to the subsystem was not nearly as self-
evident as it had been in the past. The Likud's economic strangulation of Kupat
Holim forced the Histadrut to transfer to it increasing proportions of the single
tax: from 58% in 1977, when Labor still set the figure, to a high of 67% in 1983–
1984.[5] The transfers were particularly burdensome because with the Labor out
of office, the Histadrut could no longer compensate for the shortfall by exploiting the national treasury. By the second Likud term, Histadrut General Secretary Yorucham Meshel found Kupat Holim more of a burden than an asset.[6]

Nor was Kupat Holim the vote getter for Labor that it had once been. The
1973 Yom Kippur War had robbed Labor of its glamour and given the public its
first real view of the rot in the Labor establishment. Voters' concern shifted to
security issues, on the one hand, and to revamping the Labor-led system that
had apparently failed the country in its hour of danger, on the other. In addition, these years saw the eruption of long-smoldering resentments by the
country's relatively deprived Sephardi population (of Middle Eastern and
North African origin) against Israel's ruling (Labor–Histadrut) elite of Ashke-
nazi Jews (of European origin). This resentment was translated into votes for
the Likud and the concomitant devaluation of the Labor ethos, enterprises, and
social accomplishments. Although public health care was still important to
most of the population, many no loner considered a Labor government necessary to its provision.

Numerous reasons can be adduced for the subsystem rallying to Kupat
Holim at this point in history, including long habit; ideological affinity; the insistent, unabashed demands of Kupat Holim's leadership; and the Histadrut's
trade union commitment to Kupat Holim's employees. Equally, if not more important, the motive may be found in the political dimensions of the struggle. All
three members of the subsystem saw the Likud measures as a threat to themselves individually and to the subsystem as a whole.

Most of the Ministry of Health's new measures had sound administrative rational. The budget-approval procedures Shostak introduced were good management and essential if the government were to cease being hostage to Kupat Holim and the Histadrut as it had been during much of the Labor period. The abolition of parity and the removal of Kupat Holim from the Ministry of Health's regulatory bodies was essential to eliminate the anomaly of the regulated body making and enforcing the rules that governed it. The formulation of clear, tight and detailed procedures for the approval of Kupat Holim building, expansion, and purchase of heavy equipment—most of it with government money—and provisions for monitoring Kupat Holim's compliance were necessary to plan and coordinate the development of the health services and to reduce waste and duplication. Written rules and procedures are more transparent and more difficult to evade than the informal regulations that Kupat Holim had virtually ignored under Labor. In the area of restructuring, allowing people to join the sick fund of their choice and separating health insurance from trade union membership and political affiliation are more consistent with democratic values and procedures than the arrangements these provisions sought to replace.

Thus presented, the Ministry of Health's measures can be seen as a continuation of Shem Tov's efforts to rationalize the health system. The radicalism of the measures, the exclusion of Kupat Holim from the process, and the determination to subordinate the sick fund to the ministry can all be justified by the failure of Shem Tov's gentler policy of integration and accommodation to accomplish this aim.

The administrative rational, however, converged with the Likud's longstanding political interest in breaking Kupat Holim and the Histadrut as the basis of Labor's power. The changes in the allocation and regulatory procedures were accompanied by systematic reductions in financial support for Kupat Holim's current budgets and the cessation of financial support for its development. These measures jeopardized the scope and quality of Kupat Holim's services and, with that, its consumer appeal and continued hegemony in the health system. They also jeopardized the membership and the dues that came to the Histadrut via Kupat Holim. Moreover, the changes in procedure were accompanied by intense and successful pressure on Kupat Holim to force the Histadrut to allot it ever larger portions of the single tax—a measure that impaired the Histadrut's autonomy and cut into Histadrut funding for the cultural, social, and political activities whereby it attracted voters for Labor. The National Health Insurance Bill was a direct attack on the legal and financial arrangements that held the subsystem together.

Although the Likud denied political motives, the subsystem viewed the Likud's measures as politically motivated gambits to enfeeble and ultimately destroy not only Kupat Holim but the entire Labor–Histadrut edifice. According to Israel Kessar, who served as Meshel's righthand man in the Histadrut (and in 1984 replaced him as secretary general), "The Likud governments set themselves the task of crippling the Histadrut and the Labor movement through Kupat Holim. . . . The administration's aim was to break Kupat Holim, which is the Histadrut's soft underbelly."[7]

The obstructive veto was the response that the entire subsystem chose to counter the Likud's attack. Theoretically, it was not the only possible response. Other responses might have been to forego expansion, to cut back on its social commitment and reduce services in the outlying areas, or to otherwise adjust to the changed environment. The choice of the obstructive veto was a gut choice, which rested on three foundations: Kupat Holim's deep sense of its mission, the failure of the entire subsystem to relate to the rational of government by the core or the administrative logic of the Likud's demands, and the failure of the subsystem to grasp the depth of the disaffection that had brought the Likud to power. In retrospect, Israeli political scientists recognize that the loss of the 1977 election spelled the end of Labor dominance (Arian, 1985). At the time, though, the partners in the subsystem saw it as a temporary setback. They expected a speedy return to government and looked forward to the day when they would be able to refill Kupat Holim's coffers and recoup their own losses from the public treasury.

By nature, an obstructive veto is a temporary measure. It ultimately backfired. In embarking so assiduously on the path of obstruction, neither Kupat Holim nor its partners in the subsystem addressed the need to clean house and the chaos caused by their maverick tactics eventually alienated much of the public and paved the way for rescinding the veto.

Part IV

THE EROSION OF THE VETO

CHAPTER 16

Erosion of the Veto

In mid-1994 the Knesset passed the National Health Insurance Law, 1994 (Chinitz, 1995; Chernichovsky & Chinitz, 1995; Zalmanovitch, 1997). This law, which took effect on January 1, 1995, crosses all of Kupat Holim's red lines, save the ideological one that public medicine be provided by the sick funds. It shifts fee collection from the Histadrut's Central Tax Bureau to the National Insurance Institute. It puts an end to compulsory dual Kupat Holim–Histadrut membership, thereby allowing people to be members of Kupat Holim without joining the Histadrut, and Histadrut members without joining Kupat Holim. It draws up a uniform, fixed package of subsidized health services to be provided by all the sick funds, thereby limiting Kupat Holim's functional and decision-making autonomy and greatly reducing its ability to do what it wants with the government money it receives. And it defines the sick funds simply as service providers and makes no stipulations whatsoever to include them in any health policy-making forum. The law is a watershed in the history of Israel's health care legislation. It is the first health insurance legislation that Kupat Holim and the Histadrut did not succeed in squelching, and it spelled the end of Kupat Holim's veto power.

The law was the culmination of a long process of erosion, which changed Kupat Holim from a political, social, and economic power to be reckoned with into a self-contained body with the most limited social or political role. Its passage shows that for all the difficulty of rescinding it, a political veto is not carved in stone. Just as its nature can change from preventive to obstructive with changing exigencies, so too it can be eroded and the powerful organization that exercised it become so debilitated that it can no longer protect it, or itself.

This chapter shows and attempts to account for the progressive chipping away of Kupat Holim's control over the tools of policy up through the restructuring of the balance of authorities in Israel's health system.

Erosion of the Veto in the Transitional Decade: 1984–1994

In September 1984, elections were held and the Likud was replaced by a rotating national unity government, headed in the first two years by Labor's Shimon Peres and in the second two years by the Likud's Yitzhak Shamir. In 1988 another national unity government was voted into office, in which Shamir served as prime minister and Peres as his deputy. In 1990, a vote of "no confidence" brought down this government, and Shamir formed a minority government that lasted until the election of 1992, when Labor, headed by Yitzhak Rabin, finally returned to power on its own (Korn & Shapira, 1997, pp. 308–58). Two years later the National Health Insurance Law was passed.

Erosion of Kupat Holim's Control of Allocation

During the 1977–1984 Likud terms, Kupat Holim had effectively vetoed the Likud's allocation policy in the implementation stage by taking out loans it could not repay, amassing deficits, and obtaining resources and assistance from Histadrut affiliates. It held its breath, so to speak, in the expectation that when Labor returned to office, it would cover the debts and bring back the good old days of allocation determined by its own demands and unlinked to the control of health policy.[1]

To its astonishment and chagrin, nothing of the sort happened. When Labor's Shimon Peres became prime minister in the 1984 National Unity Government, he had more pressing matters on his agenda. These were pulling the Israel Defense Forces out of the mire of the Lebanon War and salvaging the ailing Israeli economy, which was suffering from hyperinflation of almost 24% per month, swelling budget and balance of payments deficits, and the near collapse of the banking system stemming from the manipulation of bank shares by the collusion of banking and government officials (Beilin, 1992, p. 57; Keren, 1995; Korn, 1994, pp. 140–42; Sharkansky, 1987, pp. 4–6).

In former times Kupat Holim would have been able to force a change in priorities. Now it no longer could. For most of the period under consideration, the Likud held the Ministry of Finance, while Labor held the Ministry of Health. The Likud finance ministers had no interest in channeling funds either to the Labor-run Ministry of Health or to the Labor-affiliated Kupat Holim.

The days of the preventive veto were gone. In its efforts to restore Israel's foundering economy, the National Unity Government embarked on the Economic Stabilization Program, a major component of which was the reduction of government expenditures. Among other things, the government cut its part in the national expenditure on health: from about 58% in the early 1980s to 51% in the mid-1980s and 47% at the end of the decade.[2] This was a reduction of about

20% over the course of the decade. As the government cut back its funding, the Ministry of Health channeled less and less of what it got to the sick funds, from 18. 5% in 1985 to 7% in 1987, 3% in 1988, and 1. 5% in 1992.[3] All of this was happening in a decade that saw skyrocketing increases in the cost of medical care throughout the world. To make matters worse, during these years Israel experienced a huge influx of about 750,000 immigrants (more than 15% of its population) from Ethiopia and the former Soviet Union, which was placing yet added strain on the health care facilities.

Instead of shifting priorities to restore Kupat Holim to its former self, Peres, with the Likud watching closely, appointed the Gadish Committee to examine the size of Kupat Holim's debt, apportion responsibility, and recommend ways of repaying it. The chairman of the committee, Yakov Gadish, was a former director of the Ministry of Finance's Budget Division who had a reputation for probity. But he was also a member of a kibbutz affiliated with the NRP, which like the Labor Party depended on the Histadrut for a sizable portion of its funding. The report he presented on March 4, 1986, reproduced the Kupat Holim–Histadrut claim that a vital service that provides health care to the better part of the country's citizens must be properly funded, and it pointed an accusing finger at the government and the banks:

> A sick fund that provides health services for 85% of the population in this country and is on the verge of becoming inoperable, must raise money to finance its activities, without regard as to the cost. It is to be regretted that the system has taken advantage of this situation and charged high interest rates. The situation cannot be allowed where a vital service has gotten into a financial trap and the public is burdened with completely unacceptable additional payments. The budgeting system must solve the problem before it snowballs and begins to pile up useless expenses on the national treasury.[4]

Kupat Holim leaders gloated that the report confirmed its contention that its financial distress was caused by circumstances beyond its control, not by bad management or insubordination.[5] The Ministry of Finance countered with its own report claiming that no more than one third of the debts could be put down to high interest rates and that the other two thirds (about half a billion dollars) were the result of Kupat Holim's budget irregularities. [6] With Labor back at the helm, the Gadish report was accepted.

Although it exonerated Kupat Holim, the committee did not allocate funds, however. It recommended that Kupat Holim take measures to rehabilitate itself as a condition for government support.[7] The blueprint was set out in the the Kupat Holim Recovery Plan signed in October 1986 by representatives of Kupat Holim, the Histadrut, the government, and the Ministry of Finance. This plan punctured Kupat Holim–Histadrut autonomy more radically and effectively than the Likud had succeeded in doing when it was in office alone. Rather than assuming Kupat Holim's debt burden, as previous Labor governments had done, the National Unity Government agreed to cover only a small portion of it and required Kupat Holim to repay the rest by itself. The plan required Kupat Holim to sell assets and to reduce its workforce and other expenditures, and the Histadrut to transfer more money to Kupat Holim from the single tax. It forbade the banks to grant Kupat Holim credit without government authorization. It stipulated that if Kupat Holim did not do as required, the government would deduct money from the employer participation tax and establish a monitoring procedure to ensure that Kupat Holim fulfilled the terms of the agreement (*State Comptroller Report,* 1987, pp. 365–67).[8]

Kupat Holim responded in character by trying to obstruct the plan's implementation. Although it stopped building hospitals and clinics for lack of funds, it did not sell assets or substantially reduce its workforce, and the Histadrut did not transfer the required amounts of the single tax.[9] A June 1989 follow-up report disclosed continued operational deficits, surplus manpower, overdrawn bank credit, delays in the Histadrut's transfer of the single tax, and deliberate procrastination in selling off assets.[10] Kupat Holim responded with a letter arguing that it had been required to expand its activities to improve its medical services and tacked on a list of financial demands.[11]

The days of the obstructive veto were gone, however. The government would not bail out the Sick Fund with generous infusions of state funds. The Recovery Plan became a stick to beat it with. Every time Kupat Holim representatives approached the government with requests for assistance in making repayments or to cover new deficits, the Ministry of Finance cited the latest monitors' report, which showed the Sick Fund's failures in implementation and let them know, again and again, that without compliance no funding would be forthcoming. Here and there, the Ministry of Finance, and on some occasions the Knesset Finance Committee, came through with small sums, but no more than a shot in the arm to enable the Sick Fund to limp along for another month or two (Barzilai, 1996, pp. 111–12). At the same time, the Ministry of Finance continued to demand, as it had between 1977 and 1984, that Kupat Holim pay its way by charging for doctors' visits and hospitalization and by increasing its charges for medicines. Only this time when Kupat Holim refused to comply, the Ministry of Finance, still in Likud hands, calculated the revenues anticipated from these charges and deducted the sum from its transfers to Kupat Holim (Barzilai, 1996, p. 109).[12]

The ongoing conflict between the government and Kupat Holim resulted in turmoil. As Kupat Holim tried to maintain its former magnitude and level of operations, its day-to-day services were shunted to second place. Kupat Holim went from crisis to crisis: long waiting lists for treatment, critical shortages of medicines and equipment, and continuing unrest among its demoralized workforce (*State Comptroller Report,* 1988, pp. 170–278). Because of Kupat Holim's great size and centrality, the turmoil within translated into turmoil in the health services as a whole, and ultimately undermined the Sick Fund's veto in regulation.

The Erosion of Kupat Holim's Veto over Regulation

The continuing turmoil raised Kupat Holim's operations to the top of the public agenda. The media, politicians of all parties, the two Israeli doctors associations (the Israeli Medical Association and the Organization of Kupat Holim Doctors), the public and even the president of Israel, Chaim Herzog, were all screaming "enough": enough strikes, enough sanctions, enough suffering.[13]

There was a feeling that Kupat Holim's problems were not mere symptoms but rooted in the entire workings of the health system. These had to be righted, it was understood, and new regulations were not deemed adequate. Of course new ordinances were passed during this period, but they were directed to routine administrative ends and dealt with new diseases, nutrition, hospitalization, equipment, and so forth. There was a widespread sense that new regulations that tried to restrain Kupat Holim's expansion or organize its hospitalization were not to the point and that radical measures were required. Things were so bad, it was felt that only a major change in the rules of the game could right them.

Regulation was thus moved to a new plane, from passing ordinances that Kupat Holim could flout to subjecting the organization, for the first time in its history, to invasive scrutiny by bodies it could not evade: first the State Comptroller's Office and then a nonpolitical State Commission of Inquiry. Until 1977, Kupat Holim's affairs were closed to the state comptroller because Israel's State Comptroller Law (1958) applied only to government agencies. Soon after the Likud took office, the law was amended to extend the state comptroller's audits to nongovernment bodies that received state funds. In 1977 the State Comptroller audited Kupat Holim. In 1979 it issued a general, rudimentary report whose importance lies in its being the first objective and reliable public account of Kupat Holim's structure, relations with the Histadrut, finances, workforce, and development (*State Comptroller Special Report on the Audit of Kupat Holim,* 1979).

In the mid-1980s, the State Comptroller subjected Kupat Holim to repeated incisive probes. Within three years the State Comptroller issued four reports on Kupat Holim: a separate report on Kupat Holim in 1985 and three reports on Israel's health system in its 1985, 1986, and 1987 annual reports (*State Comptroller Report,* 1985; 1986, p. 244, 1987, pp. 362, 380, 1988, pp. 170–278). These reports did far more than simply audit Kupat Holim's finances. When it deems necessary, Israel's State Comptroller extends its work to examine the policies of the audited bodies. In the case of Kupat Holim, it deemed it necessary. Its reports made a frontal attack on the entire health system, castigating both the government and Kupat Holim. The gist of the reports was that the health "system" lacked order and that a clear health policy was needed.

The visible continuation of the crises, epitomized by repeated health services strikes between 1985 and 1988, led to the appointment in June 1988 of a State Commission of Inquiry to examine the efficiency of the health care system.[14] This commission was a highly respected, nonpolitical, nonpartisan body whose recommendations are traditionally heeded. Its members are appointed not by the political party in power but by the president of the Supreme Court, and it has judiciary powers, including the power to subpoena data and witnesses. Its chairman was Supreme Court judge Shoshana Netanyahu, after whom it was named, and its members were the directors of two non–Kupat Holim hospitals (Hadassah and Tel HaShomer) and two university professors.[15]

Kupat Holim, the Histadrut, and the then Labor Minister of Health, Shoshana Arbeli Almozlino, naturally objected to the commission, since it was not a body they could hope to dominate or even to influence. They asked Shimon Peres, as deputy prime minister, to prevent its establishment, but he could not.[16]

The commission issued its report on August 20, 1990. Like the State Comptroller it too called for a consistent, overall health policy. The majority opinion, endorsed by four of the five members, emphasized the need for a national health insurance law that would put an end to the compulsory dual membership in Kupat Holim and the Histadrut and transfer fee collection from the Histadrut's Central Tax Bureau to the National Insurance Institute.[17]

The significance of the Comptroller's and commission's reports is that they were issued by objective, nonpolitical entities with ties to neither the government nor the subsystem. These bodies were able to obtain more information about Kupat Holim's finances and activities than the Ministry of Health and the Ministry of Finance had been able to obtain in the Likud years. More important, they lifted the discussion from the infighting between a self-interested core and a self-interested margin. This reduced Kupat Holim's ability to use the core's self-interests as a justification for obstruction and gave their recommendations unprecedented stature.

The Erosion of the Kupat Holim Veto over Restructuring

Preparations to implement the *Netanyahu Report*'s recommendations were begun under the minority Likud government headed by Yitzhak Shamir, but the government fell before the work was completed. The 1992 elections brought Labor back to the helm without having to share power with the Likud. This Labor government, headed by Yitzhak Rabin, passed the National

Health Insurance Law, which finally changed the structure of authority in Israel's health system. Of all the setbacks to Kupat Holim's veto power, this was the greatest. The irony is that it was struck by the Sick Fund's erstwhile political ally and protector.

The remainder of the chapter discusses how the governments that led Israel between 1984 and 1995 could do what no previous government had been able to: that is, how they eroded Kupat Holim's veto power and restructured the health system.

The Loss of Labor Dominance

The erosion of Kupat Holim's veto was a gradual, incremental process. Every bit of erosion enabled further erosion, so that the progressive decline became a cause of further decline, until the process became self-perpetuating. To take the most salient example, the complications resulting from loss of the veto in allocation led to the abrasion of its veto in regulation and from there to the rescinding of its veto over restructuring. At the same time, the veto was chipped away in nonlinear fashion simultaneously from all sides, making it difficult, on the microlevel, to separate the erosion process itself from the factors that contributed to it.

On the macrolevel, the precipitating factor was Labor's loss of dominance. Duverger (1967, p. 308) points out that a party can lose an occasional election without losing its dominance. But 15 years had passed before Labor was re-elected to office in 1992 with the capacity to form a coalition without the Likud. Its seven years in opposition were followed by another eight of governing along with the Likud, which held the powerful Ministry of Finance, over-looked all of its moves, and constrained the freedom of action it had enjoyed as a dominant party.

The loss of dominance has many ramifications. The inability of a party out of office to channel state resources to bodies with which it has reciprocal interests and to regulate on their behalf has already been emphasized. Yet another is the loss of the ability possessed by a dominant party through its long control of government institutions to cloak its doings and those of its partners from public awareness. Both these ramifications were directly exploited by the Likud.

Two other aspects of the loss of dominance formed the background in which the Likud could exploit these ramifications. One is that the no longer dominant party ceases to set the social and cultural tone of the society. The other is that it loses the control it had once had of key institutions. In Israel, the first change preceded and was accelerated by Labor's loss of office, while the second issued from it.

Change in cultural values and social climate

The 1977 Likud victory first marked and then accelerated the deep shifts that were taking place in Israel's cultural values and social climate. The Kupat Holim–Histadrut–Labor Party subsystem was built on common socialist values, which were shared as well by much of the Israeli public. The comprehensive health care system that Kupat Holim and the Histadrut developed epitomized the prevailing societal values of social solidarity, equality, mutual dependency, and help to the needy. These values gave legitimacy to the Histadrut's and Kupat Holim's activities and underpinned the public support for them.

During the transitional decade, the spirit of socialist collectivism gradually gave way to a spirit of capitalist liberalism not too different from that in the United States. Various developments contributed to the process. Up until the 1980s, Israel saw itself as a garrison society endangered on all sides. With the signing of the peace treaty with Egypt in 1979, this feeling gradually gave way to the feeling that it was a normal country that could enjoy the benefits of peace with its neighbors. In peace and security, the sacrifices of collectivism seem not so necessary and may become irksome. The 1980s also saw the start of a movement away from the welfare state in Europe and the United States with the election of such leaders as Margaret Thatcher, Helmut Kohl, and Ronald Reagan (Kickert, 1997; Peters & Savoie, 1995; Savoie, 1994). With the Likud in government, Israel was plainly moving in the same direction. Moreover, as Israelis became wealthier and traveled abroad more (Israel Yearbook and Almanac, 1996; World Bank, 1996), they were exposed to competing ideologies and ways of doing things from other countries. In particular, Israel underwent an Americanization of outlook. The apparent wealth, free market, and individual rights in the United States became highly regarded objects of emulation. Self-fulfillment, personal attainment, and the market values of competition, efficiency, wealth and consumerism became the new totems (Aronoff, 1989; Barzilai, Yuchtmann-Yaar, & Segal, 1994; Eisenstadt, 1985; Horowitz & Lissak, 1989; Mahler, 1990; Mautner, 1993; Zalmanovitch, 1998). Although this shift has not been examined empirically, it is evident in such things as the continuing reduction of government subsidies on basic foodstuffs; the increasing acceptability and availability of private education, private security services, private employment services, and private medicine (Lehman-Wilzig, 1991, 1992); and the election and reelection of the Likud and Labor's difficulty in regaining office. The sharp cuts in spending on health care in general and in Kupat Holim in particular in a decade of massive immigration may also be attributed to the shift in values and cultural climate.

Development of Constraining Institutions

During the long unopposed rule of the Labor-led subsystem, Israel's Supreme Court, state comptroller, bureaucracy, and media remained undeveloped. They were closely connected in outlook with the ethos of the subsystem and did not fulfill their inherent potential to monitor, supervise, disclose, and criticize government conduct or to define norms of good government. In the early through mid-1980s, when the economic crisis was at its height and revelations of corruption on the part of politicians in both the main parties eroded public trust in the entire political establishment, these institutions came to be seen as reliable institutions that served the interests of the citizens and provided alternative forums for solving problems that had previously been dealt with within the subsystem.

Until the early 1980s, Israel's Supreme Court had contented itself with interpreting laws and handing down judgments consistent with the ethos of the governing elite. It restricted its review of government bodies mainly to the questions of whether their activities were legal and nondiscriminatory. During the transitional decade, responding to the vastly increased number of appeals to it in the wake of the subsystem's demise, the court adopted a new judicial activism committed to liberal, democratic values. Its judicial opinions increasingly emphasized citizens' rights, government transparency, proper management, and what it termed the "reasonableness" of government decisions.[18] To be judged reasonable, a measure had to be based on a sound factual foundation, be the best of the available alternatives, and balance contending interests. Laws, regulations, and policies that did not meet these criteria were struck down.

The State Comptroller extended its audits to objectives of policy. In the late 1970s and early 1980s it audited for the first time bodies that were part of the subsystem. Then in the mid-1980s, it introduced a new, expanded type of audit which replaced the "classical," after-the-fact financial audits it previously had conducted.[19] The audits were comprehensive investigations of broader policy issues across several years and public agencies. These enabled identifying problems of coordination, duplication, waste, and cost benefit, and supervising activities in process. Its application led to conclusions that could imply the need to cease, formulate, or alter policies.[20] Israel's health system was among the many matters thus audited.

In the wake of demands for accountability and correct procedure by the Supreme Court and State Comptroller, the bureaucracy underwent a process of formalization. In place of its informal, arbitrary, and self-favoring modus operandi under the subsystem, it began to act on the basis of written procedures and universal criteria, which met the principle of reasonableness. This change strengthened the bureaucracy by loosening the hold of political interests and made channeling subsidies, tenders, and other state favors to their proteges more difficult for politicians.

Among the government offices thus strengthened was the Ministry of Finance. Although it had always been a powerful ministry in Israel, so long as it was controlled by the Labor-led subsystem it had to struggle to contain the spending of a government committed to social values. In the 1980s, the economic crisis, the elevation of economic thinking over social ideology, and Israel's move, along with that of the international community, toward a market economy gave legitimacy to its natural inclination to put economic values first.[21] The Ministry of Finance became the policeman of the public services, putting obstacles in the way of funding costly legislation. It linked funding for Kupat Holim with its compliance with the Recovery Plan.

The Israeli news media grew in size, independence, and importance. In 1985 Israel had only one television channel. In 1989 a second channel funded by advertising, began to operate, and cable television was introduced. As in the United States, the competition for ratings, readers, and viewers made the media increasingly investigative and uninhibited in the information they researched, broadcast, and published. Increasingly, hitherto well-hidden political processes were made public, corruption exposed, and issues of public interest raised for discussion.[22] Together, the two sets of developments facilitated the Likud's using its powers in office, whether alone or in the national unity governments, to vitiate Kupat Holim and the Histadrut and, thereby, to pry apart the subsystem.

The Disintegration of the Subsystem

In the context of these ongoing changes the Likud used its powers in office, both when it governed alone and when it governed jointly with Labor, to launch a concerted assault against Kupat Holim and the Histadrut. Armed with its core control over allocation and regulation, it set about to impoverish and to delegitimize these bases of Labor power in the eyes of the public.[23] Its attack ultimately brought each of the partners in the subsystem to abandon its social vision and to set on a course of self-transformation to accommodate the new economic, social, and political realities. It made Kupat Holim a burden and a liability to its partners in the subsystem and made them unable and unwilling to help it.

When the National Health Insurance Law, 1994, was passed, Kupat Holim still possessed major resources that had enabled it to exercise both its preventive and obstructive vetoes. It was still the country's largest—and in some areas the only—provider of health care, and Israel's people and economy were still highly dependent on it. As the public turned away from Kupat Holim, however, these dependencies, rather than serving as sources of leverage, became sources of resentment and grounds for acting against the Sick Fund. Kupat Holim's argument that as the country's major health care provider it required commensurate funding and privileges soured as the quality of its services declined and its public image tarnished. Once Kupat Holim was out of public favor, the government no longer feared that harming the Sick Fund would lose it votes. On the contrary, these dependencies provided good reason for shifting authority in health care from Kupat Holim, which had proven unreliable, to the government, which had not yet been put to the test.

The Impoverishment and Delegitimation of Kupat Holim

Government transfers to health care in general and to the sick funds in particular dropped precipitously over the two Likud terms. In 1977 the Ministry of Health allocated 34% of its budget to the sick funds, in 1984 it channeled only 18%, a drop of almost 50%,[24] without a concomitant rise in the ministry's budget or any meaningful adjustment for the rising cost of medical care or the hyperinflation that reached its peak at the end of the Likud's second term. As described, the cuts in health care funding continued in the transitional decade.

The financial strangulation led to a progressive deterioration of services. As long as Kupat Holim could pay for its activities with credit and borrowed money, the public did not feel the constriction. As Kupat Holim continued to expand, renovate, and build without the influx of government funds, drawing more and more from its current budget to do so, the quality of its day-to-day services declined. Its members, subjected to long delays for appointments, tests, and operations, expressed their dissatisfaction by leaving the Sick Fund. Between 1984 and 1994, Kupat Holim membership declined from about 81. 3% of the insured population to 63. 5%, a drop of more than 20%, most of it among the younger, better educated, and higher earning members, who joined the smaller sick funds (National Insurance Institute, *Annual Survey,* 1995, p. 222; Rosen & Steiner, 1996).

The Likud's unrelenting exposure and populist propagandizing discredited Kupat Holim in the eyes of the public. Up until the Likud took office, Kupat Holim's modus operandi was kept under wraps. People were aware that Kupat Holim was part of the Histadrut–Labor Party subsystem, but the details of the relationship were well hidden. They did not really grasp that their health insurance fees paid for other Histadrut activities. Nor did they know that Kupat Holim employees consistently received higher wages than government medical personnel with the same qualifications and in the same positions. The Likud made all of this public knowledge and, furthermore, used the information to deflect attention from the role of the sharp funding cuts in the deterioration of

Kupat Holim's services. With this exposure, Kupat Holim ceased to be perceived as the all good, all caring health fund, which looked after the interests of
the common man.

The many problems with which Israel's health care was plagued in the 1980s
and 1990s—soaring costs, poor service delivery, shortages of supplies and equipment, repeated work stoppages or slowdowns, demoralized personnel, and an
overall sense of chaos—were thus placed at the door of the Kupat Holim–Histadrut alliance. Kupat Holim's adversaries could blame its financial straits and
deteriorating services on the generous salaries it paid and the diversion of its
funds to the Histadrut, and could convincingly (although not entirely accurately) claim that its members would get better health care if all their insurance
money went to that purpose and no other.

Over time, Kupat Holim came to be perceived as a lumbering, mismanaged,
inefficient, and overly political organization, and tying health care to trade un-
ionism and politics became increasingly unacceptable in the public mind. The
switch in public opinion seems to have occurred between the late 1980s and early
1990s. Up through the mid-1980s most Israelis still sided with Kupat Holim in
its conflict with the government. As late as 1986, 71% supported Kupat Holim's
borrowing from the banks to provide services, more than two thirds were against
providing additional government subsidies.[25] In 1987 fewer than 25% of Israelis
supported compulsory national health insurance.[26] By late 1993, shortly before
the government approved the draft of the National Health Insurance Bill, two
polls of Histadrut members revealed very different attitudes. The first, conducted in late November, showed that 70% of Histadrut members favored getting rid of the compulsory dual Kupat Holim–Histadrut membership. The second, held in mid-December, showed that almost 50% supported the health
reform bill, whereas only slightly more than 20% supported the Histadrut's opposition to it (Barzilai, 1996, pp. 328–32).

The Impoverishment and Delegitimation of the Histadrut

The noose was similarly tightened around the Histadrut. As long as Labor was
dominant, the Histadrut enterprises were seen as part of the process of nation
building and as instruments of social welfare and social cohesion. Among their
major functions was to provide employment, especially but not only in parts of the
country where private entrepreneurs would not venture. Profitability and efficiency were secondary motives. Like Kupat Holim, they depended on government
funding and preferential regulation. While Labor was the dominant party, it made
sure that both were forthcoming. Among other things, the Histadrut companies
were protected by stringent import disincentives and favorable government-
mandated exchange rates. From the 1960s on, the Histadrut enterprises received a

good part of their working capital from the Histadrut pension funds. These were at the time almost the only pension funds in the country and they accumulated considerable sums. By a special arrangement with the government, the pension funds were permitted to transfer 46% of their capital to an investment company created for that purpose by the Histadrut-owned Bank HaPoalim, which, in turn, distributed the money among the various Histadrut companies.

The Likud reduced the import taxes and foreign currency controls, opened up the market to competition, and canceled the special arrangement, exposing the enterprises to the consequences of their nonprofit management (Barzilai, 1996, pp. 92–95). With the high inflation and economic instability of this period, by the mid-1980s most of the Histadrut's major enterprises—its bank, its construction company, its holding company and subsidiaries, as well as the kibbutzim and moshavim—were on the verge of financial collapse.

The Likud also discredited the Histadrut, both as a trade federation and an industrial body. Since prestate days, Israel's right wing bashed the Histadrut as a Bolshevik organization opposed to the interests of the state and its citizens, and Menachem Begin and others continued that line of attack from the opposition. When the Likud took office and unearthed Kupat Holim's relations with the Histadrut, it added that grist to the mill. It emphasized the Histadrut's transfer of health money to political purposes and pointed to the Histadrut's readiness to sacrifice employee benefits to obtain benefits for Kupat Holim.

Moreover, after having pulled the rug from under the Histadrut enterprises, it exploited the natural ill will created by their financial straits. As companies were closed or downsized, everyone sought culprits and casting the Histadrut as the villain was easy. The Likud could point a collective finger at the failings of the Histadrut management and claim that the Histadrut was more interested in preserving its own interests than those of the workers it purported to protect. Its arguments were brought home by the television cameras poised on hapless men and women waving dismissal slips or locked out of factories where they had worked all their adult lives. The Histadrut came to be seen as irrevocably outdated, a remnant of the socialist past, while the inherent contradiction between its dual role as trade union and employer rankled, as did the membership requirement for health insurance.

Parting of the Ways: The Beginning

Under this battering, by the end of the 1980s both Kupat Holim and the Histadrut were impoverished, discredited organizations. Kupat Holim had become a liability to the Histadrut just as the Histadrut's enterprises were collapsing; and the Histadrut had become progressively less able and less willing to support

Kupat Holim's mounting deficits as it flouted the Recovery Plan. Moreover, both organizations became exhausted with their futile, debilitating struggle with the government. They moved away from their socialist mission and proceeded to remake themselves in a capitalist image.

Before the mid-1980s, the Histadrut holding company, Hevrat Haovdim, abandoned its original social orientation and started on the road to self-support. It replaced the socialist company managers from the old-boy network with managers with business school training or proven success running large private enterprises. It shut down factories, fired employees, rationalized operations, and courted foreign investors. And it stopped transferring money to Kupat Holim. Solel Boneh, a Hevrat Haovdim subsidiary, went bankrupt and stopped providing Kupat Holim with free construction (Bartal, 1989, pp. 105, 107, 109, 126, 131; Barzilai, 1996, pp. 95–101; Goldberg, 1992, p. 152; Margalit, 1994, p. 28; Shalev & Grinberg, 1989). Bank HaPoalim, which was removed from Histadrut control after the 1983 bank notes crisis, was no longer prepared to give Kupat Holim loans it could not repay. With its empire dwindling and Kupat Holim continuing to flout the Recovery Plan, in 1986–1987, the Histadrut was compelled to pay 75% of the single tax to Kupat Holim, a hike of some 12% over the 67% when the Likud had last held office alone.[27]

In November 1987 several younger members of the Histadrut's Central Committee formally proposed wide-ranging reforms of Kupat Holim's structure and administration. They blamed Haim Doron, the mastermind of the obstructive veto and Kupat Holim's last ideological leader, for the chaos in the health system. In December Doron announced his resignation at the end of his current term. On May 31, 1988, the proposed reforms were brought before Kupat Holim's 12th Convention, which approved the key measures. These transformed Kupat Holim's structure from one reflecting its erstwhile aspirations to be a state within a state to one befitting a corporation, and which would foster its operation as a professional and economic body rather than as a politicized, ideological one. Following a short interim, most of the old-style, ideologically oriented management was replaced, as they had been in Hevrat Haovdim, with new managers hired from the army and business sector, who had no allegiance to the Histadrut and no driving sense of social mission.[28] Committed to sound finance and sound management, they proceeded to implement the Recovery Plan and began to integrate services, reduce duplication and waste, and make Kupat Holim more efficient.

Countdown to Restructuring

These reforms came too late to repair the damage that had been done to Kupat Holim and the Histadrut and to their relations with the Labor Party. By the end of the 1980s Kupat Holim and the Histadrut had both become embarrassments to the Labor Party (Barzilai, 1996, pp. 109–12).

Labor's loss of office (in 1977) after so many years in power was traumatic for it, and the trauma intensified with every subsequent election it did not win. As long as it was the dominant party, Labor had represented, or could believe it represented, the beliefs, ideals, and values of most of the electorate. The longer it remained out of power, the clearer the message that it no longer did.

In its bid to regain public support, Labor gradually retailored itself to the new mode that was developing. It abandoned its traditional socialist stance in favor of more liberal, market-oriented, and democratic values. It tried to create a new image of itself as a modern, innovative vibrant party and as an open rather than machine run party. And it determinedly distanced itself from the ailing, discredited Histadrut and its Sick Fund, which it came to regard as major impediments to electoral victory (Margalit, 1994, p. 146).

The National Health Insurance Law was passed as the Labor Party remade itself. In the vanguard of its self-transformation were the party's younger generation, a coterie of bright young men who came of age in the new cultural climate and, moreover, understood that if they were ever to attain power in the party, they would have to get around the Histadrut dominance of the party machine that supported the entrenched senior leadership. The Histadrut exercised considerable control of the party through the multitude of salaried functionaries it employed to run the party's day-to-day affairs and to serve in its decision-making bodies. It was they who had the major say in party nominations and party policy. Before these ambitious young men could rise in the party, this control would have to be broken.

The way to break it was to attack the Histadrut and its role in the party. Among the leaders of the attack was Haim Ramon, who would eventually author and push through the National Health Insurance Law. Much like the Likud, Ramon and his group presented the Histadrut as a lumbering behemoth woefully out of step with the times. He spoke against its outmoded socialist philosophy and claimed that it was more concerned with protecting its assets than promoting the social values it expounded, that it put the interest of its pension funds above that of their members, the interests of the companies it owned above that of their employees, and the interests of Kupat Holim above those of its insurees. The Histadrut, he argued, was causing Labor to lose votes, and the party would have to disencumber itself if it wanted to regain power (Barzilai, 1996, pp. 233–43).

The longer Labor was out of office and the worse the Histadrut's and Kupat Holim's plight, the more convincing the argument became. So long as the Labor Party and Histadrut had shared the same socialist values and the Labor Party found the Histadrut serviceable in advancing its electoral interests, the ability of the Histadrut to promote its interests in the party (and while the party was in power, within the state) was acceptable. When these two conditions ceased to exist, the entire Histadrut role in the party came into question.

The unencumbrance was effected mainly through revisions in two-party regulations. The first, in July 1990, was the introduction of party primaries. Prior to that, the party's candidate for prime minister and the party list for Knesset were chosen within the party itself. Until 1984 they were chosen by a very small committee of senior politicians with strong ties and commitments to the Histadrut and the party machine it dominated. In 1988 the decisions were transferred to the "party center" consisting of several hundred persons, a good portion of whom were from Histadrut institutions. The primaries, billed as a measure that would democratize the party and win back voters, gave party members who had not been handpicked by the Histadrut a much greater say in party nominations. The second change, in July 1991, was the severance of party membership from the hitherto compulsory Histadrut membership. The new regulations permitted persons to join the Labor Party without belonging to the Histadrut, thereby diluting the power of the Histadrut-paid party functionaries through the influx of new, non-Histadrut members. Together these changes reduced the political dependence of Labor Party office seekers on the Histadrut and greatly weakened the power of the Histadrut-run machine within the Party (Barzilai, 1996, pp. 189–94, 218–21; Goldberg, 1992, pp. 42, 53, 1994).

The two changes were also behind Yitzhak Rabin's election as prime minister in 1992 and, with it, the passage of the National Health Insurance Law. Shortly before the 1991 primaries, some 50,000 people signed up for the Labor Party who formerly would not have been able to vote in them (Barzilai, 1996, p. 221). Their votes led to Rabin's victory over Shimon Peres in the primaries.

This victory can be seen as the triumph of the new values over the old. Peres, an active Labor Party leader from prestate days, drew his power from the Histadrut-linked party apparatus. European born, he was comfortable with the Histadrut, with its roots in Eastern Europe, and its functionaries in the party. Although he was forced to go along with the Kupat Holim Recovery Plan, could do nothing to prevent the incursions of the State Commission of Inquiry, and even promoted the privatization of state-owned enterprises, he retained loyalties to the old order that Rabin never possessed.

Rabin was a native born Israeli, a latecomer to the party who had spent most of his adult life as an army professional. He was elected to his first term as prime minister in 1974 at age 52. He owed his nomination then to the party's search for someone new, who was not associated with the failure of the old political leadership to prepare the country for the surprise Arab attack that launched the 1973 Yom Kippur War. He came into office as a war hero, the general who in 1967 had recaptured east Jerusalem and liberated the Western Wall. Although of necessity he was nominated with Histadrut support, he was not beholden to or committed to the Histadrut and had little rapport with the Histadrut functionaries in the party. In his new bid for power, he drew his support from the younger party members and, with them, regarded Histadrut control of the party as a barrier to political advancement. Ideologically, too, he was far from Histadrut-style socialism. Shortly after he left the army, he served as Israel's ambassador to the United States, where he developed an appreciation for its market economy and more open political processes (Arian, 1985, pp. 64, 65–66; Rabin, 1996).

Prime Minister Rabin appointed as his minister of health none other than Haim Ramon, who had been active in the anti-Histadrut campaign in the party and instrumental in the inauguration of party primaries and the severance of party from Histadrut membership. Although the health portfolio is not particularly prestigious in Israel and Rabin was willing to give him a post with more status, Ramon expressly asked to be minister of health (Barzilai, 1996, p. 251). Like Shostak, he was eager to tackle Kupat Holim and the Histadrut.

The State Commission of Inquiry recommendations gave him the opportunity he sought. Within a short time, he had a draft of the new bill. Unlike all previous Labor-sponsored health legislation, it was drawn up without any input from Kupat Holim or the Histadrut. When the draft was finished, he sent it to them, as he did to other bodies in the health system, but he ignored the alternative drafts that they proposed.

In February 1993 the government approved Ramon's draft and on July 6 the law passed the first reading in the Knesset (Barzilai, 1996, pp. 268–73). This was the point at which the two previous health insurance bills, under Shem Tov and Shostak, were killed in committee. For a while, it seemed that the same fate awaited the new bill. The Histadrut launched an energetic media campaign against it and warned Rabin that if it were passed, the bill would destroy the Histadrut and with it the Labor Party. A special gathering of the Labor Party Convention, whose decisions are binding, voted against it, and the government withdrew the bill (Barzilai, 1996, pp. 315–17).[29]

But this time the Histadrut victory was short lived. Something happened that had never happened before in Israel's history. On February 8, 1994, an enraged Ramon resigned from the government, and on April 11 proposed his candidacy for, of all positions, the secretary general of the Histadrut. The move can be likened to a hostile corporate takeover, where the aim of the buyer is to diminish or absorb a competitor. Ramon created his own political party, Ram, to which he drew some of his supporters from Labor's young guard, and formed a bizarre, opportunistic coalition with the Sephardi ultraorthodox Shas Party and the Ashkenazi-based, hotly antireligious Meretz Party. With the Histadrut in decline and its members blaming the traditional, Labor-affiliated Histadrut establishment, Ramon won the May 10 Histadrut elections (Barzilai, 1996, pp. 337–94).

This was the first election in the Histadrut's history that the Labor Party, which had founded and fostered the organization, lost. With Ramon at its head and his coalition partners behind him, the Histadrut was no longer the same body it had been. It no longer opposed national health insurance. Because the majority of the Labor Party did not oppose it either, Rabin returned the bill to the Knesset. On June 15, 1994, the Knesset approved the second and third readings (Barzilai, 1996, pp. 397–98).[30]

The National Health Insurance Law that was finally passed closely resembled the Likud-sponsored National Health Insurance Bill, which a very different kind of Labor Party had helped to torpedo in 1981. Its passage can be traced directly to the changes in party ideology and procedure that followed upon the cultural and political changes in Israel. From the party's new perspective, removing Kupat Holim from the trade federation, giving people the freedom to choose their sick fund, restricting the money people paid for health care to health care, and divorcing health from party politics seemed only right. In other words, in the new cultural climate and new political realities, the Labor Party had come around to the Likud point of view on Israel's health system.

The major lesson of the erosion of Kupat Holim's veto power is that, for all its strength, the veto power of a body on the margin can be revoked. Over the long haul the core is stronger than the body on the margin. The fact that the tools of policy are legally in the hands of the core ultimately enables it to repossess those tools and then to use them to chip away yet further at the body on the margin's veto power. Yet veto power cannot be rescinded in one go, with a clean cut. The revocation of veto power is a long and slow process, something akin to a war of attrition, in which the core hacks away at the resources of the body on the margin from all directions and at every opportunity, and during which the cultural, social and political conditions that supported the veto power inevitably change, as does the body on the margins itself.

Although having a preventive veto strengthens an organization on the margin, the extensive use of an obstructive veto enervates it over the long run. To exercise an obstructive veto, the organization on the margin may have to dig deep into its own resources. If these are not unlimited or renewable, they will depreciate and eventually be exhausted. This happened to Kupat Holim's financial resources, its public support, and its trade union and political backing.

CHAPTER 17

Stateness in Health

The struggle recounted in this book was a struggle over who would control health policy in Israel: the government or the body on the margin. It was not a struggle over health policy as such, but over who would make it—over *stateness,* defined by Tilly (1975) as "the degree to which the instruments of government are differentiated from other organizations, centralized, autonomous, and formally coordinated with each other" (p. 32). Tilly does not delineate what he means by the "instruments of government." In this study, they are defined as the tools of policy: the struggle was over the degree to which the Ministry of Health would exercise the tools of policy on its own or with the not-so-remote control of Kupat Holim.

The struggle began in the transition to statehood, when Kupat Holim's administrative head refused to accept core authority during Israel's War of Independence and set the Sick Fund on a course of expansion expressly designed to prevent the new state from curbing or controlling it. It continued in the fight between Israel's first Prime Minister, David Ben Gurion, and the Mapai Party functionaries over the nationalization of health care, as Kupat Holim took advantage of the perceived needs of the new state and the government's overburdened agenda to deepen and spread its influence. When Ben Gurion lost to the functionaries, the issue lay smoldering beneath the surface, as Ministry of Health bureaucrats chafed under virtually unlimited Kupat Holim control of health policy. It arose again as Minister of Health Shem Tov locked horns with Kupat Holim in his efforts to obtain a greater Ministry of Health say in health policy. During the Likud terms, it exploded in the two sides' contending claims. Kupat Holim argued that, as the country's largest insurer and health care deliverer with accumulated knowledge and daily responsibility for the citizen's health, it, not the government, had the right to make health policy. To this, government officials countered that the "dual control" of health care by the government and a body on the margin was inefficient and, moreover, undemocratic in that it undermined government by the country's elected officials.[1]

The passage of the National Health Insurance Law, 1994, put the struggle to rest. Although billed as health care reform, the law was largely a political measure aimed at establishing core control over an important social service. For all ostensible purposes, Israelis continued to receive and pay for their health care in much the same way as they had before. Health care remained a public service available to all and the responsibility of the government. It continued to be provided by the same four sick funds. It continued to be financed by the familiar three-part arrangement consisting of an annual government subsidy, an employer participation tax, and a graduated, income-based tax on the population, which, as far as the citizens were concerned, was not materially different from the fee previously paid, only higher. The law also preserved Kupat Holim's service package, using it as the basis for the government-defined package of services to be provided by all the sick funds.

The monumental changes were on the political level. The law firmly consolidated health care policy in government hands. It was the first piece of primary legislation in Israel that laid out the authority of the Ministry of Health to supervise the quality of care, demand information, and authorize development budgets and additions to the service package. Equally if not more important, it created the conditions that would enable the ministry to exercise its authority. Of particular importance in this respect were the replacement of the Histadrut–Kupat Holim single tax with a health insurance tax collected and distributed by the government-run National Insurance Institute and the stipulation of a government-defined service package. The change in tax collection greatly reduced the independent income that Kupat Holim had to spend at its discretion and also made it impossible for the Histadrut and Labor Party to divert health care money to political purposes. The government-defined service package embodied the government's health policy and put a cap on government spending for health. It was presented as a means of clarifying the health services to which all sick fund members were entitled, should the sick funds try to economize by cutting services. It was not only a minimum package, however, but also a maximum one. Any extra services that the sick funds wanted to provide or extra projects they wished to undertake were not to be funded. In the absence of alternative, independent funding, the package serves as an effective curb on sick fund activities. The law thus stripped Kupat Holim of the powers and resources that had enabled it to be a prime health policy maker, subordinated it to the core, and transformed it into a mere service provider.

Inextricably interwoven with the struggle over the control of health policy was the political struggle between Israel's two major political parties, in their various forms. Labor's ongoing efforts to create, improve, or maintain a favorable balance of power and authority between Kupat Holim and the Ministry of Health were motivated to a large extent by the political and financial benefits that accrued to it from its partner in the subsystem. The Likud (and its precursors) drew upon the logic of stateness to oppose the politicization of health care and the practices that went with it, and, once in office, to defend the measures it took to realize its vision of exclusive core control of health policy. But the Likud had a store of animosity for its Labor rivals and as clear a political interest in strengthening the core and disempowering Kupat Holim, the linchpin in the Labor–Histadrut subsystem, as Labor had in empowering Kupat Holim and keeping the core in health weak. The struggle was as much over political power as over principle.

The National Health Insurance Law, the product of the Likud victory, achieved stateness in health. But the principle over which the rival parties fought is still an issue in other areas of the Israeli polity. The principle was the question of what kind of state Israel would be: a party-run state, in which the powers and resources of the state are channeled through the party machine, or a state in which these powers and resources issue from the core. Half a century after its formal establishment, Israel is still a state in the making, and this battle is still being waged over other social services, by other political parties.

The Rise and Fall of a Political Veto

The four cases trace the development of three types of veto before its final demise, each exercised with different government input and each inherently weaker than the one before. The first, exercised with the collusion of the government, was an informal preventive veto, whose strength lies in its being silent, amorphous, and taken for granted. Its existence, legitimacy, and scope are not public issues. The second was a formal preventive veto exercised with the accommodation of the government. Formalization of a value brings with it definition of the rights and prerogatives of its holder, and although this may increase the veto's legitimacy, it inherently circumscribes it and also brings it to public awareness. The third was an obstructive veto exercised as a weapon of defense against government efforts to subordinate Kupat Holim. Like other types of force, an obstructive veto can work for only so long before the suffering and confusion it causes create antagonism and its exercise consumes the energy and the resources of its wielder. The loss of the veto was the final blow in a long process of erosion that was accelerated in the decade or so prior to the passage of the National Health Insurance Law, but which had actually started much earlier.

Kupat Holim's veto was a political veto. A political veto differs from a structural or constitutional veto in that it is not anchored in law and predefined, but fluid and contingent. It is won and lost in the give-and-take of the political game. Its strength varies with the changes in the material, ideological, institutional, and political context of the polity in which it is exercised and with the resources, leadership, and conduct of the organization itself.

The cases argued that the changes in the veto were a function of Kupat Holim's utility to the subsystem and of the subsystem's readiness and ability to support it. These were the veto's essential conditions. Separately and together, they varied with the same circumstances as the veto itself did. This section identifies the main factors that entered into the dimensions of utility, readiness, and ability.

Utility is a multidimensional concept. At the simplest level, it refers to the direct benefits that an organization brings the party that supports it. Kupat Holim provided its partners in the subsystem with financial and electoral benefits. Its financial utility was anchored in the single tax. Its utility as a vote getter was more complex. To serve as a vote getter over a long period of time, a body on the margin must be perceived as essential, or at least highly beneficial, not only to the party, but to the populace. The service it provides must be regarded as necessary and the government be considered responsible for providing it; the alternatives to the organization must be limited, whether these take the form of competing providers or other means of structuring the service (e. g., in Israel both private health care and nationalized health care were early ruled out); and the way that the organization operates must be accepted as legitimate by most of the population.

Kupat Holim's utility, in this definition, changed with the material, cultural, ideological, and institutional development of the state, as well as with its own actions and capacities. Kupat Holim was perceived as most essential and legitimate when (1) the government of the infant state was overburdened with the exigencies of absorbing masses of immigrants, building a basic infrastructure, and securing the country's defense; (2) the prevailing socialist ideology supported the view that health care was a vital public good that the government had to make sure was supplied; (3) norms of good management were underdeveloped in Israel, the state bureaucracy was an extension of the political parties, and the constraining institutions of the state, namely the courts, the state comptroller, and the media, showed little inclination to penetrate or reveal the workings of the government and its related institutions; and (4) Kupat Holim provided well-run services to a grateful public.

Its perceived utility was progressively diminished as the state built its infrastructure, settled its early immigrants, and advanced economically, and as Israelis felt less immediate peril to their physical security; as the prevailing socialist values were gradually displaced by values that put the individual and the marketplace ahead of the collective; as norms of proper management and good government developed, the state bureaucracy became formalized, and the constraining institutions of democracy placed checks on the behavior of the political parties and their affiliates; and as Kupat Holim's deficits so grew and its services so deteriorated that it was perceived as more of a hindrance than a help in providing public health care. These developments helped to make Kupat Holim seem increasingly less essential to the populace, to delegitimize Kupat Holim and the Histadrut in the eyes of the voting public, and to make the politicization of health care increasingly unacceptable. They reduced Kupat Holim's electoral utility to Labor and helped to make the party less willing to support it. This analysis underscores the importance of the material, ideological, and institutional underpinnings of a political veto.

The readiness to support a veto is a function of the utility of the body that exercises the veto to the body that supports it. The ability to support a veto rests in the political realm. The more cohesive the party that supports it and the greater control it has in the polity, the stronger the veto and vice versa. Concomitantly, the stronger the veto, the weaker the level of stateness in the relevant core body.

Kupat Holim acquired and exercised its informal preventive veto during the early years of the state, when Labor was at its most cohesive and dominant and, in the absence of an effective political opposition, could freely channel the resources of the state to augment the powers of all its partners in the subsystem. Mapai functionaries prevented the nationalization of health care and created a structurally weak, poorly institutionalized Ministry of Health, which was financially dependent on Kupat Holim, and subordinate to the Ministry of Finance and the Ministry of Labor and Welfare, both of which were under tight party control and consistently favored Kupat Holim's interests. The Ministry of Health, for its part, made few if any efforts to control the tools of policy in any but the most politically neutral matters.

The attempt of the Ministry of Health to assume greater control in health in the early 1970s occurred as cracks formed in Labor's cohesion and control: following a temporary split in the party, its inclusion of the hitherto outcast opposition leader Menachem Begin in a National Unity Government, and its loss of public trust with the 1973 Yom Kippur War. The Ministry of Health adopted a policy of accommodation as the price that it had to pay to augment its role in the making of health policy, to which end it also raised the level of its institutionalization and sought cooperation with the other ministries involved in health. These administrative measures represented key weapons in the struggle for core control of health. Accommodation turned out to be unattainable, foiled by Kupat Holim's unwavering aspirations to control health policy, the great disparity between Kupat Holim's powers and those of the ministry at that point in history, and the continuing strength of the Labor-led subsystem, despite the cracks. Nonetheless, the formalization of the veto during this period can be seen as the beginning of the core's extrication from the control of the margin.

Labor's loss of the election in 1977 meant that the party could no longer channel the resources of the core to its partners in the subsystem, protect them from harmful regulation, or guard their and its own secrets. It also meant that for the first time in Israel's history, there was a clear differentiation between core and margin, since the party in control of the core was no longer the party affiliated with the body on the margin. This differentiation cleared the way for the Ministry of Health to set out to subordinate Kupat Holim: to centralize the tools of policy in its own hands, to coordinate its activities with a non-Labor Ministry of Finance, to upgrade its level of institutionalization, to formalize its allocation procedures, to enact formal regulations, and to formulate health policy, even in the vital area of restructuring, without Kupat Holim–Histadrut input. It also enabled the ministry, in coordination with the ministry of Finance, to impoverish and discredit both Kupat Holim and the Histadrut, thereby reducing Kupat Holim's utility to is partners in the subsystem and the readiness of its partners to support it. On the other hand, the Labor–Histadrut subsystem still had enough financial and political resources to support Kupat Holim's obstructions of government policy.

The loss of the veto followed a decade of its accelerated erosion as Labor was returned to office only with the Likud looking over its shoulder. The result was a stalemate in which Labor's ability to maneuver on behalf of Kupat Holim, as well as on behalf of the Histadrut, was sharply curtailed. It could not repair the damage that had been done to Kupat Holim and the Histadrut, and it was compelled to lend a hand to the measures that were taken to divest Kupat Holim of its remaining control of the tools of policy. Moreover, failing to return to office on its own in election after election, it became demoralized and fragmented and, in the hope of regaining its former glory, abandoned its erstwhile partners. The veto was finally revoked when the Labor Party was in such a state of internal disarray that maverick elements in its midst, motivated by a combination of personal ambition and the belief that the party's association with Kupat Holim reduced its electoral appeal, joined with the Likud and a fortuitous coalition of small parties to pass the National Health Insurance Law, 1994.

Two approaches have been advanced to explain health care reform in Europe, where resistance to change was also very great. One is Day and Klein's (1992) systemic approach, which holds that major health care reform can only follow upon changes in the wider political, social, and economic environment. The other is Immergut's (1992) institutional approach, which holds that the ability to overcome strong resistance to change depends on the institutional and political context in which political decisions are made. Although each of these theories tends to deny the importance of the other, they converge in accounting for the restructuring in the Israeli health system. Kupat Holim's veto over health policy was revoked only at the end of a long process of material, cultural, institutional, and political change, in the course of which Kupat Holim became an impoverished, delegitimate organization and a liability and embarrassment to its partners in the subsystem, and the subsystem itself was gradually depleted and enervated, and finally dismantled.

Although the analysis has focused on the contextual factors involved in Kupat Holim's veto, the role of the body on the margin itself must also be recognized. As the cases have shown, until only a short while before its veto was revoked, Kupat Holim's leadership was driven to control health policy and invested enormous entrepreneurial energy and ingenuity in doing so. Not all organizations are as intent on power as Kupat Holim was or as adept at seizing the opportunities that are available to attain and exercise it. Although its will for control, ingenuity, and entrepreneurialism did not enable Kupat Holim to preserve its veto in the face of persistent government determination to revoke it, these qualities seem to be essential for acquiring and maintaining of a political veto.

Bodies on the Margin, Policy Making, and Stateness

Political scientists in the United States and Europe are concerned about the apparent hollowing out of strong states by bodies on the margin created by the state. This study shows that a body on the margin that is not created by the state can hinder the development of stateness in its domain. It validates the concerns that a body on the margin can expropriate policy-making powers from the core. It shows that neither allocation nor regulation is an effective means of government control as long as the service that the body provides is considered essential and the government is held responsible for ensuring that the citizens receive it; as long as there are no viable alternatives to the body; and as long as the body is popular, esteemed, viewed as legitimate, and protected by a strong political party. It also shows that once a body on the margin acquires veto power, it may take decades, and considerable turmoil and pain, to restrict its powers and bring the domain under state control.

Tilly (1975, pp. 81–82) points out that the European state-building experiences will not repeat themselves in new states and that we cannot infer the events and sequences in contemporary states from an informed reading of European history. The struggle traced in this study is instructive about "modern democratic" state building.

The essays in Tilly's *The Formation of National State in Europe* (1975) show the vital role played by things such as the building of armies and police, the taxation to support them, and the recruitment of administrative and technical personnel in the development of the European states. The need for these things,

Tilly points out, is assumed by modern state builders. In Israel, most of them became givens within a few years after the state was declared in 1948.

In Israel, health was a tool for consolidating the state and bolstering its legitimacy, as were other social services. In this, the development of Israel differs from that of the classic European State. The Israeli experience suggests that in the "modern democratic" state, the provision of social services, which in Europe came at later stages of the state-building process, is an essential element in establishing control over the tools of policy, whether by the core or a rival power. Health care is not necessarily one of the services—education or any other service that the citizen expects would do as well—but in Israel it was, largely because of the prevailing consensus, not shared by all countries, that health care should be provided by the public sector and not the private sector.

The designation *democratic* to describe the state in which social services become a means of consolidating power is important. Tilly points out that democracy came late to the European states after the instruments of force were centralized. In Israel, as in other new countries, the army and police were centralized immediately. But once it was secured, force ceased to be the major, or even an important, means of holding the state together. Its place was taken by desired social services, which bestowed public acceptance and legitimacy on the body that provided them, whether the party or the government. It may be that the role of services is what distinguishes those developing countries that are democratic from those that are not.

Tilly's (1975, p. 70) definition of *stateness* is essentially a territorial one: stateness is marked by the consolidation of control and the acquisition of autonomy, centralization, and coordination within a specified territory. The Israeli experience, in which geographic stateness was established with the receipt of sovereignty in 1948, suggests that the territorial concept is inadequate to the "post-European" state. It shows that sovereignty and independence within a specified territory do not necessarily guarantee stateness, defined as core control over the tools of policy, in all facets of the core's functioning in the geographic area.

On the contrary. The Israeli experience suggests that even where the modern state comes into being with relatively well-defined borders, is relatively well unified, and its government is recognized by the populace, a long struggle for stateness in specific policy areas may ensue; that different levels of stateness may be attained in different policy areas; and that political parties within the government may have interests in thwarting stateness.

At the same time, the Israeli experience also suggests that however strong the margin, the core of the modern state is ultimately stronger. Once it sets out to centralize the tools of policy—and is willing to pay the high cost in human suffering that the process inevitably entails—it will eventually be able to do so.

Core Control and Retreat from Responsiveness

The establishment of core control over health policy in Israel follows trends in Western Europe and elsewhere toward increased state autonomy in health care in the name of cost containment, with a similar triumph over effectively mobilized providers. The success of these countries in containing costs is closely monitored and widely applauded in the literature (Allsop, 1995; Hurst, 1991; Marmor, 1994; Saltman & von Otter, 1992; Schut, 1995; Wilsford, 1995). At the same time, we find growing awareness that some of the methods of cost containment—especially the rationing of health care, the main method—may involve trade-offs with equally important values such as responsiveness, equity, access and possibly even the long-term health of the poorer groups in the population (Abel-Smith, Figueras, Holland, Makee, & Mossialos, 1995).

Much of this book has documented the abuses and shown the vulnerabilities of Israel's politicized health care system. It is obvious that politicized health care cannot serve as a model to be followed. Linking health care to a political party makes it an instrument of political control while subjecting it to the vicissitudes of the normal partisan struggle.

At the same time, Israel's politicized health system was both singularly responsive and relatively cost efficient, claims to the contrary notwithstanding. It allowed for voluntary insurance, which covered more than 96% of the population and provided reasonably accessible and available universal coverage of almost all the citizen's health demands (other than dentistry, mental health, and long-term geriatric care) with no relation to the person's ability to pay. The four sick funds, which doubled as health care deliverers and insurers, competed on their premiums and services; and the expenditures of the system were modest relative both to Israel's economy and to the outlays on health care in wealthier Western countries (State of Israel, *Netanyahu Report*, 1990, p. 47). Even after its responsiveness and efficiency declined with the intensification of the struggle for control of health policy beginning in the Likud years, Israel's health system still met most of the public's demands.

Its responsiveness can be attributed to the convergence of values and politics in Israel. The conviction that health is the responsibility of the society is deeply rooted in Israel. Its roots lie not only in the collectivist values of the country's pioneers, but also in long-standing Jewish tradition of mutual aid. It was accepted by both political blocs, which disagreed not on the principle, but on how it should be implemented. It was backed by the readiness of the Israeli taxpayer to pay for health and other social services. As long as this conviction prevailed, Kupat Holim and its partners in the subsystem were able to use it to their advantage: Kupat Holim to expand and accrue power, the Labor subsystem to win elections. These advantages, in turn, augmented their interest in making sure that health care was provided and paid for. Kupat Holim's veto power was also instrumental to the responsiveness of the health system. Under both Labor and the Likud, it used its veto power to make sure that public resources continued to be channeled into health even where the government might have preferred spending them on other goods.

The health system was restructured in the wake of the worldwide crisis in health care in the 1980s, as burgeoning health care costs forced governments to find ways of making their health systems more efficient. Although the politicization of health in Israel promoted responsiveness, it also made it impossible for the government to use allocation and regulation to rationalize the health system. The crisis was concurrent with the Likud's rise to power in Israel and provided justification for its politically based determination to curb Kupat Holim's power.

The National Health Insurance Law was promoted as the means to improve health care delivery, lower its cost, and stabilize its financing. Health care reform is an extended and dynamic process, however, and constant adjustments are still being made to the law as this text is being written. It is thus still too early to determine its ultimate impact. Nonetheless, this section looks at the patterns that can be discerned.

On the positive side, several accomplishments can be noted. The law makes health insurance compulsory for all Israelis. It enables persons to join any sick fund they wish and to move with relative ease from one sick fund to another. It removes the former entrance barriers imposed by the smaller sick funds, and requires all sick funds to accept all applicants, regardless of age, general health, or previous illnesses. The result has been a more equal distribution of elderly members among the sick funds (Rosen & Shamai, 1998). The new tax structure is more progressive than Kupat Holim's dues structure had been, in that persons with higher incomes now pay proportionately more. In addition, the law replaced the previous allocation formula, which mirrored Kupat Holim's needs with a per capitation formula which takes into consideration, in addition to the number of members, only their age and certain chronic diseases. This change equalized government funding for the various sick funds. This, in turn, has encouraged competition for members from peripheral areas, low-income areas, and the Arab sector, resulting in better facilities and improved service levels in areas previously neglected by the sick funds (Rosen & Shamai, 1998). On the positive side, then, the law extends protection, increases freedom of choice, and adds fairness.

In addition, Kupat Holim's service delivery has improved. The improvement has been appreciated. Whereas in the past the members of the smaller funds had generally been more satisfied with their services than the members of Kupat Holim, a survey conducted in September 1996, nine months after the law was put into effect, indicates that Kupat Holim members were then more satisfied than the others (Berg, Rosen, Gross, & Chinitz, 1996).

These benefits have had a downside, however, in particular, the increase in freedom of choice of sick funds is offset by a reduction in what to choose from. With its funding by capitation and its fixed package of services, the law introduced managed competition in the delivery of services. Such competition has been hailed as contributing to better patient care, equity, and customer satisfaction (Saltman & Figueras, 1997; Saltman & von Otter, 1992). The law's version of managed competition, however, also means that the services of the various sick funds are virtually identical. Thus, although consumers can now shop around more for good service delivery, they have less opportunity to shop around for the content of the services.

Moreover, the improvement in Kupat Holim's services has been offset by deterioration in the services of the smaller funds,[2] which now have as their members more than 40% of the population.[3] The smaller funds have not been able to expand their infrastructures and increase their medical manpower to keep up with their rapidly growing membership. The result has been the same long lines, delays, and demoralization that previously plagued Kupat Holim. Nor, it may be noted, is the improved quality in Kupat Holim's service delivery necessarily the result of the law. A good deal of it may be attributed to the radical loss of membership in the late 1980s, which increased the ratio of personnel and facilities to patients, and to measures taken by the new leadership that was installed at that time.

Most important, the reform's promise of better health care at lower cost has not been kept. The argument was that this would be attained through stopping the diversion of funds to political and trade union activities and by cutting the waste and duplication that were the products of the dual control of health care. In retrospect, these claims can be judged to have been populist propaganda, which cynically exploited the public's limited understanding of a very complex issue.

The National Health Insurance Law has not given the public less costly and more competitive health care. Modern health care is expensive, and good, universally accessible health care such as Israel still has costs money. Israeli doctors and other medical personnel are relatively low earners; they are paid on a combination salary and capitation basis, which contains little incentive for excess referrals or authorizations, and Israel has no medical industry middlemen such as those found in the United States. For all Kupat Holim's unbridled spending and the diversion of funds, there was not nearly as much waste or extra in the system as had been claimed.

In the name of efficiency, the law introduced rationing and privatization. The rationing, embodied in the services package, was adopted with no public or professional discussion. In certain countries in Europe, among them Holland, Denmark, and Sweden, similar rationing was preceded by an elaborate process of priority setting, involving the government, politicians, and bureaucrats, as well as representatives of the public, the medical profession, the business sector, and other groups with relevant knowledge or interests (Danish Council of Ethics, 1997; Dunning, 1992; Swedish Parliamentary Priorities Commission, 1995). In Israel, as noted, the law's services package was based on Kupat Holim's 1993 package, taken as it was, although the packages of the smaller sick funds contained more services.

The rationing of health care has continued. Although data are not available on clinical outcomes and access to expensive treatments after the restructuring (Rosen, 1998), visible cutbacks have been made in several areas. Ambulatory clinic hours have been cut by all the sick funds. Hospital facilities have not been expanded, although Israel's population grew by approximately 20% in the early 1990s as immigrants poured in from Ethiopia and the former Soviet Union. Monitoring has been tightened on physicians, who are being pressured to limit their authorizations (Gross, Greenstein, Greenberg, Tabenkin, & Harison, 1999). The services package has not been updated, with the exception of some medications being added and others being removed.

Private health care, long taboo, has become part of the system. The law permits the sick funds to offer supplementary insurance to cover medical services (excluding long-term care) that are not included in the basic services package. Commercial insurance companies, which in the past hardly offered health insurance at all, also entered the arena. By 1999, 40% of the adult population had supplementary insurance purchased from the sick funds and 17% had additional insurance purchased from private insurance companies. Not surprisingly, those who bought the extra insurance were in the higher income brackets.[4] Although the trend toward the marketization of health care saves public money and follows that in Europe, it reduces equity.

The law has not stabilized health care financing. Ever since the law was passed, health care costs have exceeded allocation. In 1997 the sick funds incurred a deficit of NIS 1.3 billion (about $360 million) with spending 8% over revenues (Rosen & Shamai, 1998). The deficit exists despite the fact that about one half the population pay more in health taxes than they formerly paid in membership dues[5] and derives from the government's progressive retreat from responsibility for health care.

The first step backward occurred immediately with the law's passage. According to the law, government funding for health care, the third part of the tripartite financing arrangement, was supposed to cover the difference between the cost of providing the health services package and the amounts raised from the citizens and employers. The sum was determined annually on the basis of Ministry of Finance projections. Yet, from the beginning, large gaps existed between the projected costs and the real ones. In particular, the smaller sick funds are finding themselves in ever-growing arrears, with the same debts to suppliers and government hospitals that Kupat Holim used to accumulate. The sick funds maintain that the Ministry of Finance has not taken into account the growth and aging of the population, the rising cost of medical technology and supplies, or the increase in per diem hospital rates. The Ministry of Finance accuses them of profligacy and demands that they operate more efficiently—much as it had formerly demanded of Kupat Holim.

The second regressive step was taken through the Arrangements Law of 1997. Arrangement laws are a special category of legislation in Israel, which are formulated by the Ministry of Finance and consist of highly detailed regulations meant to complement the annual budget. This law, passed under Benjamin Netanyahu's pro-business government, eliminated the employer participation tax and stipulated that the resulting missing funds were to be supplied by the Ministry of Finance from the state budget. This measure replaced a relatively reliable, earmarked source of income for the sick funds with one subject to the Ministry of Finance's discretion. Needless to say, it reduces the stability of health care financing.

Stateness in health has increased the core's ability to regulate the health system, but it has not increased its sense of responsibility for health care. On the contrary, it seems to have enabled the government to continue to withdraw from health care. In actual terms, health policy has become the province not of the Ministry of Health but of the Ministry of Finance, whose interest, by definition, lies in cutting costs. With the 1994 law, Ministry of Health approval is required to add new services to the package; but the actual addition of the services is contingent on Ministry of Finance authorization that resources are available. Moreover, since the passage of the law, unremitting pressure has been placed on the sick funds to raise copayments for doctors' visits and medication, to cut and privatize more and more health services, and to introduce regressive financing methods (Rosen & Shamai, 1998).

By depoliticizing health care, the reform effectively dismantled the veto structure by means of which Kupat Holim, working through the Labor Party and Histadrut, kept health care at the top of Israel's political agenda and ensured that, one way or another, it received the funding it needed. Today, Kupat Holim no longer carries the banner. In keeping with the spirit of the times and the curbs on its powers, it has ceased to be an ideologically driven organization with a sense of social mission and has become an inward-looking economic organization, dedicated to the rational use of its resources and the efficient provision of a consumer good. It has even changed its name to signify its metamorphosis: As of November 1999 its new name is *General Health Services* to emphasize its new consumer orientation.[6] Israel's politicians—Labor politicians included—have similarly disassociated themselves from the social implications of health care.

In depriving Kupat Holim and the Histadrut of their previous powers in setting the country's health care agenda, the new law has destroyed the only lobby Israelis had for high-quality public health care. Although the law has not enabled the government to contain the real costs of health care, it has enabled it to avoid providing the funding that is truly needed.

With the achievement of stateness in health, Israel's health system has moved from an ideological and politicized model to an economic, managerial one. This model weighs efficiency more than responsiveness. It has not resolved the crucial issues of health care financing and of the best way to balance the contradictory requirements of containing costs and meeting health care needs. Core control was essential to regulate the health system at a time of confusion and runaway costs. Now the need is for a new countervailing force to put health care back on the public agenda, to remind the core of its responsibility, and to restore the health system's waning responsiveness.

Appendix

Israeli Currency

As a result of inflation and devaluations, the Israeli currency has undergone a number of changes in name and value, as follows:

Year	Name of Currency	Value at the Time of Change
1948–1980	Israeli lira (pl. Lira) (IL)	
1980–1985	Shekel (IS)	1 IS = 10 IL
1985–2001	New Israeli shekel (NIS)	1 NIS = 1,000 shekel

Approximate Dollar Exchange Rates: Selected Years (Amounts in Israeli currency equivalent to $1. 00)

Year	Month	Exchange Rate	Year	Month	Exchange Rate	Year	Month	Exchange Rate
1948		IL 0.25	1979	Mar.	IL 21.42	1986	Mar.	NIS 1.49
1949		IL 0.36		Dec.	IL 35.35		Dec.	NIS 1.48
1955		IL 1.8	1980	Mar.	IS 4.15	1987	Mar.	NIS 1.60
1962		IL 3.00		Dec.	IS 7.55		Dec.	NIS 1.53
1971		IL 4.20	1981	Mar.	IS 8.87	1988	Mar.	NIS 1.55
1974		IL 6.00		Dec.	IS 15.60		Dec.	NIS 1.68
1975	Jun.	IL 6.12	1982	Mar.	IS 19.16	1989	Mar.	NIS 1.81
	Nov.	IL 7.10		Dec.	IS 33.65		Dec.	NIS 1.96
1976	Jan.	IL 7.24	1983	Mar.	IS 39.58	1990	Mar.	NIS 1.99
	Dec.	IL 8.90		Dec.	IS 107.77		Dec.	NIS 2.04
1977	Jan.	IL 9.07	1984	Mar.	IS 153.26	1992	Mar.	NIS 2.40
	Dec.	IL 15.39		Dec.	IS 638.61		Dec.	2.77
1978	Mar.	IL 16.42	1985	Mar.	IS 858.50	1994		NIS 3.01
	Dec.	IL 19.02		Dec.	NIS 1.49			

*Source: The Accountants Calendar for 2000–2001, published by the Bureau of Israeli Accountants

Notes

PART I: THE INFORMAL PREVENTIVE VETO

Chapter 3:   The Formative Stage: 1947–1949

1. The largest prestate underground defense organization, identified with the Labor movement.

2. The original letter is not available to the public, and the cited source does not supply a date.

Chapter 4:   Health as a Political Resource: The First Two Decades of Statehood

1. I gathered the information about the operation of the Ministry of Health through several interviews with bureaucrats at the ministry headquarters in Jerusalem because no available written material existed. With regard to the Israeli health system, interviews serve as the major source of information, which Arieli (1986, p. 4) noted.

2. O. Tokatly, interview, February 14, 1984.

3. A. Kover, interview, June 16, 1985.

4. The Hebrew name of the tax is the *mas makbil* or the *parallel tax*. The name expressed the idea that employers would pay for Kupat Holim in tandem with the insurees.

5. Laws of the State of Israel, *National Health, Public Health*, Vol. 4 (p. 1567 by Ordinance).

6. Cited in N. Baruch, 1973, p. 44.

Chapter 5:   The Informal Preventive Veto

1. O. Tokatly, interview, February 26, 1984.

PART II: THE FORMAL PREVENTIVE VETO

Chapter 6:   Accommodation Under Labor: Vision of Supervised Autonomy

1. The information on Shem Tov comes from in-depth interviews because no other reliable sources were available.

2. V. Shem Tov, interview, May 20, 1985.

3. V. Shem Tov, interview, September 15, 1985.

4. V. Shem Tov, interview, May 20, 1985; R. Uri, interview, June 17, 1985.

5. S. Haber, interview, December 18, 1983.

6. S. Haber, interview, December 18, 1983.

7. S. Haber, interview, December 18, 1983.

Chapter 7:   Expropriation of the Allocation Process

1. O. Tokatly, interview, February 15, 1984.
2. Y. Brandeis, interview, October 9, 1984.
3. S. Haber, interview, December 4, 1983.
4. V. Shem Tov, interview, May 20, 1985.
5. O. Tokatly, interview, February 15, 1984.
6. For the 1954–1962 and 1963–1970 code N. Baruch, 1973, p. 77; for the 1970–1977 code *State Comptroller Report*, 1979, pp. 317–18.
7. O. Tokatly, interview, February 26, 1984.
8. The data were obtained from several sources and combined in Table 7.2. For Kupat Holim Clalit: Report to the 9th convention, 1974, p. 62; *State Comptroller Report*, 1979, p. 151. For United Sick Fund: Auditing firm Leevai and Leevai, Reports for December 31, 1972, March 31, 1975, March 31, 1977; *State Comptroller Special Report*, 1979, pp. 13, 57. For Maccabi Sick Fund: Maccabi Sick Fund, Research and Statistics Department, 1975; Auditors Kost Lev-Ari and Furer-Summary of Income, 1977. For Meuhedet (United) Sick Fund: Meuhedet Sick Fund–First National Convention (1976); Second National Convention (May 1981); *State Comptroller Report* on Meuhedet Sick Fund, 1982, p. 68. The data were collected from the various sick funds, resulting in difficulties in calculating the actual support the sick funds received. It is important to mention that I found no data for 1970 for the Maccabi and National sick funds. The United Sick Fund first began operation in 1975.
9. A. Ben Ya'akov, interview, August 7, 1985.
10. Data for 1970–1974: *State Comptroller Report*, 1975, p. 244. For 1975–1977: *State Comptroller Report*, 1977, p. 277.
11. *Ha'aretz*, June 13, 1976.
12. Y. Meshel, interview, July 31, 1985; V. Shem Tov, interview September 15, 1985.
13. The data relevant to the number of employees, to collection fees, percentage transferred to the Hisdatrut and Kupat Holim are from the Histadrut Central Tax Bureau, *Reports and Budget Proposals, 1970–1977*. The data relevant to the percentage transferred to the Kupat Holim budget are from, For 1970–1973, *Kupat Holim Report to the 9th Convention*, 1974, p. 62; For 1974–1977, State Comptroller, *Report on Kupat Holim Clalit*, 1979, p. 151.
14. The data for Table 7.5 derive from the same sources cited in note 13.
15. The calculation is based on the sources cited in note 13.
16. Y. Almogi, interview, December 11, 1987.
17. Y. Almogi, interview, December 11, 1987.
18. The National Insurance Institute, 1984, Table 2; Yosef Tamir, January 7, 1987 memorandum.
19. The data presented in Table 7.7 derive from: The Histadrut Central Tax Bureau, *Reports and Budget Proposals, 1970–1977*. The data relevant to the percentage in the Kupat Holim budget was taken from, For 1970–1973, *Kupat Holim Report to the 9th Convention*, 1974, p. 62; For 1974–1977, State Comptroller, *Report on Kupat Holim Clalit*, 1979, p. 151. Each of the four sick funds calculated the percentages in this table. Given politics in Israel, they do not necessarily coincide with figures held by the National Insurance Institute, the Ministry of Health, and the Ministry of Finance.

Chapter 8:   Regulating Through Parity in Joint Regulatory Bodies and Through Informal Agreements

1. V. Shem Tov, interview, May 20, 1985; S. Haber, interview, December 18, 1983.
2. O. Tokatly, interview, February 15, 1984.

3. O. Tokatly, interview, February 15, 1984.

4. O. Tokatly, interview, February 15, 1984.

5. V. Shem Tov, interview, May 20, 1985.

6. V. Shem Tov, interview, May 20, 1985.

7. O. Tokatly, interview, February 15, 1984.

8. V. Shem Tov, Interview, May 20, 1985.

9. V. Shem Tov, interview, May 20, 1985.

10. V. Shem Tov, interview, May 20, 1985.

11. O. Tokatly, interview, February 15, 1984; and S. Haber, interviews, December 4, 1983, June 17, 1985.

12. Ministry of Health Archives, Kupat Holim file (letters, memorandum, meeting minutes), marked 1/15/5, 1973.

13. Ministry of Health Archives, Kupat Holim file (memorandum, meeting minutes), marked 1/15/5, 1973, 1974, 1976.

14. Ministry of Health Archives, Kupat Holim file 1/15/5, 1971–1972.

15. Ministry of Health Archives, Kupat Holim file (issues on the agenda with Kupat Holim, memorandum sent from Kupat Holim to the Ministry of Health), marked 1/16/5, 1975.

16. O. Tokatly, interview February 26, 1984.

17. A. Yadlin, 1980, p. 181; Archives of the Labor Party, Beit Berl, Minutes of party bureau meetings 1976, document 25/27, Vol. 2, March 24, 1976.

18. Ministry of Health Archives, Kupat Holim file (memorandum), marked 1/15/5, 1973, 1975.

19. Ministry of Health Archives, Kupat Holim file (meeting minutes), marked 1/15/5, February 14, 1975.

20. S. Haber, interview, December 18, 1983.

21. The information derived from several interviews with Uzi Keren (Project Committee secretary), July 26 and 28, 1985, August 14, 1985.

22. R. Hareuveni, interviews, August 1, 1985, August 7, 1985.

23. O. Tokatly, interview, February 26, 1984.

24. V. Shem Tov, interview, May 20, 1985.

25. Ministry of Health Archives, Kupat Holim file (memorandum) marked 1/15/5, 1973, 1975.

26. S. Haber, interview, December 4, 1983.

27. S. Haber, interview, December 18, 1983.

28. V. Shem Tov, interview, May 20, 1985.

29. S. Haber, interview, December 4, 1983.

30. U. Keren, interview, August 14, 1985.

31. U. Keren, interview, July 26, 1985.

32. O. Tokatly, nterview, February 26, 1984.

33. S. Haber, interview, December 18, 1983.

34. S. Haber, interview, December 18, 1983.

35. Pinchas Lavon Institute for Labor Party Research, Labor and Hechalutz Archives (minutes of the Histadrut Executive Committee meeting), meeting 17/72, April 30, 1972.

36. O. Tokatly, interview, February 26, 1984.

Chapter 9: *Restructuring the Health System*

1. Y. Almogi, interview, December 11, 1987.

2. Archives of the Israel Labor Party, Beit Berl (minutes of party bureau meetings 1970), file 25/70, April 29, 1970, and a memorandum written by Moshe Sorocca (1970), Kupat Holim at a Time of Change.

3. Minutes of the Labor Party, April 29, 1970.

4. *Davar,* February 14, 1971.

5. A statement delivered to the Knesset Finance Committee chairman, February 24, 1974. Gzebins's wife provided the text.

6. Y. Almogi, interview, December 11, 1987.

7. *Ha'aretz,* June 30, 1976, July 13, 1976; G. Haika, interview, October 2, 1985.

8. Archives of the Israeli Labor Party, Beit Berl (minutes of party bureau meeting), file 25/76, November 24, 1976.

9. *Ma'ariv,* July 26, 1976; *Davar,* July 26, 1976; Becker, 1982, pp. 167–69.

10. V. Shem Tov, interview, May 20, 1985.

11. V. Shem Tov, interview, May 20, 1985.

12. Y. Almogi, nterview, December 11, 1987.

13. V. Shem Tov, interview, May 20, 1985.

14. The Israel Bureau of Statistics defines national expenditure on health (NEH) as the sum of current expenditures and fixed-capital formation. Current expenditure is calculated on the basis of the production costs (excluding credit costs) of the services supplied free or at subsidized prices to households by the government, national institutions, sick funds, local authorities, and other nonprofit institutions with the exception of the army, and the value of the goods and services purchased by households directly from commercial bodies. Fixed-capital formation consists of expenditure on construction of buildings and purchase of equipment for provision of services (*Statistical Yearbook of Israel,* 1976, Vol. 27, p. 637). Both definitions are extremely complex, involving many factors and parties, who do not always transmit reliable data. This means that the NEH is extremely difficult to determine and the figures inevitably rough estimates. We use them, however, for lack of better figures.

15. Ministry of Health, *Budget Proposal for the Fiscal Year,* 1985, p. 53.

16. Ministry of Health, *Budget Proposal for the Fiscal Year,* 1986, p. 53.

17. The National Bureau of Statistics defines each sector's relative part as its total outlay on goods and services, along with subsidies, grants, and transfers to other sectors. Low-cost loans and subsidies are not included in its calculations, but would obviously increase the figures.

18. *Statistical Yearbook of Israel,* 1988, Vol. 39, p. 671. Supplement to Israel Statistical Monthly, National Expenditure on Health for 1979–1980, and Preliminary Estimate for 1980–1981, No. 2, p. 11.

19. Ministry of Health, *Budget Proposals for 1972–1979.*

Chapter 10: The Formal Preventive Veto

1. O. Tokatly, interview, February 26, 1984.

PART III: THE OBSTRUCTIVE VETO

Chapter 11: Exclusion Under the Likud: 1977–1984

1. The citation is from Y. Ofir 1982, Vol 1, p. 103.

2. A detailed account of all the mentioned developments can be found in Y. Ofir, 1982, Vols. I, II.

3. In contrast to the arrangement between the Histadrut and Kupat Holim, the Leumit Sick Fund channeled funds to the trade federation. See A. Ben-Ya'akov, interview, August 7, 1985.

4. Quoted from Y. Ofir, 1982, Vol. 2, p. 245.

5. E. Shostak, interview, July 8, 1985.

6. E. Shostak, interview, July 8, 1985.

7. M. Baruch, interview, October 1, 1985.

Chapter 12: Government Allocation as a Means of Control

1. E. Shostak, interview, July 8, 1985.

2. Y. Meshel, interview, July 25, 1985, July 31, 1985.

3. Y. Meshel, interview, July 25, 1985, July 31, 1985.

4. E. Shostak, interview, July 8, 1985.

5. Ministry of Finance, Laor Committee Report of 1977 on Kupat Holim's Budget. Ministry of Health Archives, Kupat Holim file marked 1/15/5, 1977.

6. Y. Meshel, interview, July 25, 1985.

7. Laor Committee Report of 1977 on Kupat Holim's Budget. Ministry of Health Archive, Kupat Holim file marked 1/15/5, 1977.

8. Laor Committee Report, 1977, p. 4.

9. Laor Committee Report, 1977, p. 6.

10. See table 7.5, chap. 7, herein.

11. Laor Committee Report, 1977, p. 7.

12. *Ma'ariv*, October 12, 1977.

13. Reply from the minister of health to the secretary general of the Histadrut, Ministry of Health Archives, Kupat Holim file marked 1/15/5, 1977.

14. Reply from the minister of finance to the secretary general of the Histadrut, Ministry of Health Archives, Kupat Holim file marked 1/15/5, 1977.

15. E. Shostak, interview, July 8, 1985.

16. E. Shostak, interview, July 8, 1985.

17. Data supplied by Y. Nevo, interview, February 5, 1984.

18. *Ha'aretz*, February 12, 1982.

19. Kupat Holim, *Managerial Report to the 12th Convention*, 1988.

20. Data supplied by Y. Tamir, interview, May 25, 1987.

21. *Ma'ariv*, December 27, 1979, and July 29, 1980; *Ha'aretz*, July 29, 1980.

22. A. Kover, interview, June 16, 1985; Y. Meshel, interview, July 31, 1985, Histadrut Constitution, Tel Aviv, 1985.

23. Table 12.4 data is from Ministry of Health, Budget Proposals, 1985, pp. 124, 1987, p. 133.

24. Table 12.5 data is from Ministry of Health, Budget Proposal, 1983, p. 139, 1987, p. 133.

25. Compare *State Comptroller Reports*, 1986, p. 305 and 1987, pp. 367–68.

26. Data in Table 12.6 were given to me by the head of the Division of Accountancy, Histadrut Central Tax Bureau, June 7, 1990.

27. See note 26.

28. Report of the Histadrut to the 16th National Convention, 1990, p. 293.

29. Sources for Table 12.8, Zalmanovitch, 1991, p. 150; Managerial Report to the 12th Convention of Kupat Holim, 1988, p. 62.

30. Archives of the Israeli Labor Party, Minutes of Party Bureau Meetings, September 19, 1985; Pinchas Lavon Institute for Labor Party Research, Histadrut Central Committee Decisions, August 10, 1986.

31. Archives of the Israeli Labor Party, Minutes of Party Bureau Meetings, December 12, 1985; Pinchas Lavon Institute for Labor Party Research, Histadrut Central Committee Decisions, August 10, 1986.

32. See H. Doron, December 24, 1984, Speech to the delegates of the 11th Convention of Kupat Holim.

33. Managerial Report to the 12th Convention of Kupat Holim, 1988, p. 62.

34. *Ma'ariv*, February 13, 1985.

35. B. Modan, interview, October 1, 1985.

36. A. Fogal, interview, December 16, 1985.

37. *Ha'aretz*, January 18, 1987.

38. A. Fogal, interview, December 16, 1985; *Ma'ariv*, January 23, 1987.

39. The data for Table 12.10 are from Managerial Report to the 12th Convention of Kupat Holim, 1988, p. 62.

40. The data for Table 12.11 are from Managerial Report to the 12th Convention of Kupat Holim, 1988, p. 62.

41. Kol Israel Radio, Channel B (2), December 20, 1985.

42. See Y. Meshel, interview, July 25, 1985.

43. A. Rivka, interview, February 5, 1986.

44. S. Eli, interview, November 4, 1985.

45. A. Rivka, interview, February 5, 1986; A. Snapiri, interview, August 13, 1985.

46. A. Fogel, interview, December 16, 1985.

47. A. Snapiri, interview, August 13, 1985.

48. Conversation with H. Doron, the outgoing chairman of Kupat Holim, *Meida Larofeh [Information for the Physician]*, 1984.

49. A. Rivka, interview, February 5, 1986; A. Snapiri, interview, August 13, 1985.

50. See A. Fogel, interview February 5, 1986.

51. Report to the 11th Convention of Kupat Holim, presented by the National Committee 1984, p. 5.

52. *Ma'ariv*, March 27, 1986.

53. *Ma'ariv*, March 27, 1986.

54. *Ha'aretz*, April 11, 1986.

55. A. Fogel, interview December 16, 1985; *Ma'ariv*, January 23, 1987

56. A. Fogel, interview, December 16, 1985.

57. Kol Israel Radio, Channel B (2), December 20, 1985.

58. *Yediot Ahronot*, March 27, 1986.

59. *Yediot Ahronot*, January 18, 1987.

60. A. Fogel, interview, February 5, 1986.

Chapter 13: *Regulation as a Means of Control*

1. E. Shostak, interview July 8, 1985; B. Modan, interview, October 1, 1985.

2. E. Shostak, interview, July 8, 1985.

3. B. Modan, interview, October 1, 1985.

4. B. Modan, interview, October 1, 1985.

5. Ministry of Health Archives, Minister of Health file (correspondence), minutes of meeting on the Project Committee, July 31, 1978.

6. Ministry of Health Archives, Minister of Health file (correspondence), letter announcing the establishment of the Project Committee, March 12, 1978; Ministry of Health Archives, Director General's file, Project Committee: Working Papers, November 2, 1978, January 4, 1979.

7. E. Shostak, interview, July 8, 1985.

8. Details on the working procedures of the committee from in-depth interviews with

J. Epstein, December 25, 1983 and U. Keren, July 26, 1985, July 28, 1985, August 5, 1985, and August 14, 1985.

9. See note 8.

10. A. Ellenzweig, interview, July 11, 1985.

11. B. Modan, interview, October 1, 1985.

12. B. Modan, interview, October 1, 1985.

13. E. Shostak, interview, July 8, 1985.

14. B. Modan, interview, October 1, 1985.

15. E. Shostak, interview July 8, 1985; A. Ellenzweig, interview, July 11, 1985.

16. Laws of the State of Israel, *National Health, Public Health,* Vol. 4, p. 1567. I made the statistical calculations by counting all relevant regulations starting at p. 1567.

17. Laws of the State of Israel, *National Health, Public Health,* p. 1674a: Amendment to the Public Health Order on Hospital Registration.

18. Laws of the State of Israel, *National Health, Public Health,* p. 1711–12: Amendment to the Public Health Order on Medical Equipment.

19. Laws of the State of Israel, *National Health, Public Health,* p. 1720: Amendment to the Public Health Order on Hospitalization.

20. B. Modan, interview, October 1, 1985.

21. Ministry of Health Archives, Minister of Health files (V. Shem Tov), letter dated May 14, 1976.

22. Ministry of Health Archives, Minister of Health files (V. Shem Tov), letter dated May 27, 1976.

23. Ministry of Health Archives, Minister of Health files (V. Shem Tov), letter dated July 22, 1976.

24. Ministry of Health Archives, Minister of Health files (E. Shostak), letters dated April 9, 1978, October 4, 1978.

25. E. Shostak, interview, July 8, 1985.

26. *Ma'ariv,* August 1, 1981.

27. H. Doron, Speech at the opening of the Kupat Holim Physicians Convention (May 30, 1984), *Meida Larofeh (Information for the physician),* No. 37.

28. H. Doron, interview, September 19, 1985; Kupat Holim Archives, File of Kupat Holim Chairman (Haim Doron), speech to the national committee, October 28, 1982; H. Doron speech to the 10th annual convention of Kupat Holim, December 19, 1979.

29. See note 28.

30. See note 28; H. Doron speech to the 10th Annual Convention of Kupat Holim, December 19, 1979, p. 45.

31. Report to the 11th Convention of Kupat Holim, presented by the National Committee, 1984, pp. 9, 36; R. Hareuveni, interview, August 7, 1985.

32. R. Hareuveni, interview, August 7, 1985.

33. See note 32.

34. R. Hareuveni, interview, August 7, 1985; because no written information was available, Hareuveni served as the major source.

35. Report to the 11th Convention of Kupat Holim, presented by the National Committee, 1984, pp. 9, 36; R. Hareuveni, interview, August 7, 1985.

36. R. Hareuveni, interview, August 7, 1985.

37. Report to the 11th Convention of Kupat Holim, presented by the National Committee, 1984, pp. 4–9; Managerial Report to the 11th Convention of Kupat Holim, 1984, pp. 3–4.

38. H. Doron, interview, September 19, 1985; Kupat Holim Archives, File of Kupat Holim Chairman (Haim Doron), speech to the National Committee, October 28, 1982; H. Doron speech to the 10th Convention of Kupat Holim, December 19, 1979.

39. R. Hareuveni, interview, August 7, 1985.

40. B. Modan, interview, October 1, 1985.

41. U. Keren, nterview, August 5, 1985.

42. J. Epstein, interview, December 25, 1983.

43. R. Hareuveni, interview, August 7, 1985.

44. A. Ellenzweig, interview, July 11, 1985.

45. B. Modan, nterview, October 1, 1985.

46. R. Hareuveni, interview, August 7, 1985.

47. H. Doron, interview, September 19, 1985; Kupat Holim Archives, File of Kupat Holim Chairman (Haim Doron), speech to the National Committee, October 28, 1982; H. Doron speech to the 10th Convention of Kupat Holim, December 19, 1979.

48. B. Modan, interview, October 1, 1985. Uzi Keren, the Project Committee secretary, said in a personal interview, July 28, 1985, that, " . . . Kupat Holim wanted to turn Tel Baruch into a hospital, submitted a plan for a clinic. So we cut back on construction footage, but Kupat Holim just put its own footage next to every cut we made."

49. Managerial Report to the 11th Convention of Kupat Holim, 1984, pp. 62–65.

50. See note 49, p. 14.

51. *Davar,* special issue marking Kupat Holim's 70th anniversary, 1982, p. 40.

52. H. Doron, Kol Israel Radio, channel B (2), December 20, 1985.

53. R. Hareuveni, interview, August 7, 1985; Kupat Holim, *Development Budget Proposal for the Fiscal Year,* 1980 –1981.

54. M. Brickman, interview, February 11, 1987; A. Rosengarten, interview, March 5, 1987; Solel Boneh, Public Building Company, *Statistical Journal, 1970–1975.*

55. Y. Meshel, interview, July 25, 1985.

56. A. Rosengarten, interview, March 5, 1987.

57. Y. Meshel, interview, July 25, 1985.

58. Kupat Holim Archives, File of Kupat Holim chairman (H. Doron); Letter to the director general of the Ministry of Health, August 5, 1981.

59. Kupat Holim Archives, File of the chairman, letter from the general director of the Ministry of Health to the chairman of Kupat Holim, May 21, 1982.

60. According to government data, between 1% and 30% of all Kupat Holim patients were sent to government-owned hospitals; according to Kupat Holim data, 24 clinics sent 25% or more of their patients who were in need of hospitalization to hospitals outside their regions.

61. B. Modan, interview, August 25, 1985.

62. *Ha'aretz,* January 27, 1982

63. *Ha'aretz,* January 29, 1982.

64. Kupat Holim Archives, File of Kupat Holim chairman, letter from the chairman to the Histadrut Executive Committee, September 21, 1981.

65. M. Shani, interview, July 22, 1985.

66. *Ma'ariv,* April 13, 1982.

67. Y. Brandeis, interview, October 9, 1984.

68. *Ma'ariv,* April 18, 1984.

69. B. Modan, interview, August 25, 1985; *State Comptroller Report,* 1983, pp. 155 –56.

70. *Ha'aretz,* October 9, 1924 to February 1984.

71. Speech to the delegates of the 11th Convention of Kupat Holim, 1984, pp. 20 –21; Report to the 11th Convention of Kupat Holim, presented by the National Committee, 1984, p. 36.

72. *Ha'aretz,* February 24, 1984.

73. *Ha'aretz,* April 19, 1984.

74. Speech to the delegates of the 11th Convention of Kupat Holim, 1984, pp. 20 –21; Report to the 11th Convention of Kupat Holim, 1984, p. 36.

75. B. Modan, interview, October 1, 1985.

76. B. Modan, interview, August 25, 1985.

Chapter 14: Restructuring: National Health Insurance to Establish Government Authority

1. M. Roemer (1993) provides information and analysis on almost all types of medical service organizations.

2. *Ma'ariv,* February 13, 1981; *Ha'aretz,* June 7, 1983.

3. E. Shostak, interview, July 8, 1985.

4. Likud Platform for the 9th Knesset Elections (1977), Section C, Social Welfare: Health Services, p. 16. The platform can be found in the archives of the daily newspaper, *Ha'aretz.*

5. Y. Meshel, *The Real Test of the Health Services in Israel,* 1978.

6. See note 5, p. 7 –8.

7. See note 5, p. 6; Y. Meshel, interview July 25, 1985.

8. See note 5, pp. 9 –10.

9. See note 5, p. 10.

10. *Davar,* February 5, 1978.

11. H. Doron, "Organizing Health Services—How?" Mimeographed pamphlet, 1978, pp. 2 –9.

12. Kupat Holim Archives, File of Kupat Holim Chairman, Principles for a National Health Insurance Law, April 1978.

13. See note 12.

14. *Davar,* February 5, 1978.

15. Ministry of Health Archives, Minister of Health File (Eliezer Shostak), *Principles of National Health Insurance,* September 1978. Issued by the office of the minister.

16. See note 15.

17. Kupat Holim Archives, File of Kupat Holim Chairman, Memorandum from the Histadrut secretary general (Meshel) to the minister of health (Shostak), Histadrut position on the Ministers' Health Insurance Principles, August 17, 1978.

18. *Davar,* March 4, 1979.

19. Report to the 11th Convention of Kupat Holim, presented by the National Committee, 1984, p. 40.

20. A. Kover, interview, June 16, 1985.

21. *Knesset Minutes,* booklet 18, February 9 –11, 1981, p. 1575.

22. See note 21, p. 1587.

23. *Ma'ariv,* February 9, 1981.

24. *Davar,* February 10, 1981.

25. *Ma'ariv,* February 9, 1981.

26. *Ha'aretz,* February 9, 1981; *Ma'ariv,* February 9, 1981.

27. *Ma'ariv,* February 9, 1981.

28. *Ma'ariv,* February 10, 1981.

29. See note 28.

30. *Ha'aretz,* February 10, 1981.

31. *Ma'ariv,* February 9, 1981.

32. *Ma'ariv,* February 11, 1981.

33. *Ha'aretz,* February 11, 1981.

34. Knesset, National Health Insurance Law of 1981, Proposed Bills, 1981, p. 1510.

35. See A. Becker, *A State Law for Undermining Public Medicine and Liquidating Kupat Holim,* 1981.

36. *Ma'ariv,* February 13, 1981.

37. *Knesset Minutes,* Booklet 18, February 9–11, 1981, p. 1577.

38. See note 37, p. 1569.

39. See note 37, p. 1584.

40. *Ma'ariv,* February 13, 1981.

41. Report to the 11th Convention of Kupat Holim, presented by the National Committee, 1984, p. 42.

42. *Ma'ariv,* February 13, 1981.

43. *Ha'aretz,* February 11, 1981.

44. *Ma'ariv,* February 11, 1981.

45. *Davar,* February 10, 1981; *Ma'ariv,* February 11, 1981; February 13, 1981.

46. Ads in the daily newspapers, *Davar, Ha'aretz, Ma'ariv,* February 11, 1981.

47. *Ha'aretz,* March 26, 1981.

48. *Ha'aretz,* March 26, 1981.

49. *Ha'aretz,* March 26, 1981.

50. *Ha'aretz,* April 2, 1981.

51. Kupat Holim Archives, File of Kupat Holim Chairman, Meeting minutes, August 12, 1981; see especially chaps. 1–3.

52. *Ma'ariv,* February 10, 1981.

53. S. Arbeli-Almozlino, interview, June 14, 1985.

54. E. Shostak, interview, July 8, 1985.

55. *Ha'aretz,* February 3, 1982. Ehod Ulmert, currently the mayor of Jerusalem, is a long-time Likud Party activist who has served as an MP, and minister for several years. Among the portfolios he held is that of the Ministry of Health).

56. A. Nahmias, interview, March 16, 1983.

57. See note 56.

58. Kupat Holim Archives, File of Kupat Holim Chairman, Memorandum to the secretary general of the Labor Party, May 10, 1982.

59. A. Nachmias, interview, March 16, 1983.

60. Kupat Holim Archives, File of Kupat Holim Chairman, Memorandum to the secretary general of the Labor Party, May 10, 1982.

61. See note 60.

62. A. Nachmias, interview, March 16, 1983.

63. S. Haber, interview, December 18, 1983; Ministry of Health, *A Comprehensive Review of the Ministry's Activities Prior to the Knesset Discussion of the Ministry's Budget for the Year 1982–1983,* p. 34.

64. *Davar,* February 10, 1981, November 25, 1982.

65. An impression garnered from A. Ellenzweig, interview, July 11, 1985.

Chapter 15: The Obstructive Veto

1. *Ma'ariv,* January 23, 1987.
2. Report to the 11th Convention of Kupat Holim, p. 32. The poll was conducted by the Israeli pollster Mina Zemach in May 1993.
3. *Ma'ariv,* March 19, 1984; Recommendations of the Committee for the reorganization of Kupat Holim's health services, coordinated by Lehaim Nagan, 1984, p. 27.
4. H. Doron, Speech to the delegates of the 11th Convention of Kupat Holim, 1984, p. 28.
5. Managerial Report to 12th Convention of Kupat Holim, the period from December 1984–May 1988.
6. Y. Meshel, interview, July 25, 1985.
7. *Ma'ariv,* June 3, 1988.

PART IV: THE EROSION OF THE VETO

Chapter 16: Erosion of the Veto

1. Labor Party, Meeting of the party bureau, September 19, 1985; Kfar Saba, Labor Party Archives, Beit Berl.
2. Ministry of Health, *Budget Proposal and Explanatory Notes for the Fiscal Year 1992,* presented to the 12th Knesset, October 1991, p. 75.
3. Ministry of Health, *Budget Proposals and Explanatory Notes for the Fiscal Years 1985, 1987, 1988, 1992.* I made the calculations looking for the percentage of the transfer to public health institutes from the total Ministry of Health's budget in each year.
4. Y. Gadish, *Report on Kupat Holim's Current Situation,* presented to Shimon Peres (the prime minister), March 6, 1986, p. 22; *Ma'ariv,* March 11, 1986.
5. Kupat Holim Position, *Yediot Ahronot,* March 5, 1986.
6. *Yediot Ahronot,* March 27, 1986.
7. Y. Gadish, *Report on Kupat Holim's Financial Situation,* March 6, 1986, presented to the Prime Minister Shimon Peres.
8. Ministry of Finance, Budget Division, Kupat Holim Recovery Plan, submitted to the Knesset Finance Committee Chairman, April 5, 1990.
9. *Yediot Ahronot,* March 5, 1986; *Ma'ariv,* June 29, 1988.
10. Ministry of Finance, *Current Report on Kupat Holim Rehabilitation Program—Progress and Implementation,* Report No. 10, August 29, 1989.
11. Kupat Holim, *Response to the Ministry of Finance Report,* September 5, 1989. See note 10. Kupat Holim, General Administration headquarters.
12. *Yediot Ahronot,* December 28, 1987; *Ma'ariv,* July 8, 1988.
13. *Yediot Ahronot,* May 17, 1988; May 20, 1988.
14. *Ha'aretz,* June 6, 1988.
15. State of Israel, *State Commission of Inquiry into the Operation and Efficiency of the Health Care System in Israel, Vol. 1, The Majority Opinion,* 1990.
16. *Ma'ariv,* May 23, 1988; *Yediot Ahronot,* May 23, 1988.
17. See note 15, pp. 17–31.
18. M. Mautner, 1993; G. Barzilai, E. Yuchtman-Yaar, & Z. Segal, 1994; R. Gabison, 1995.
19. A. Friedberg, B. Geist, N. Mizrahi, I. Sharkansky, 1991. See esp. pp. 74–94.
20. See for example *State Comptroller's Reports* Vols. 37–47 for the years 1986–1997.
21. The sources of information are in-depth interviews with high-ranking officials: M. Lengerman, macro economic coordinator at the Budget Division, Ministry of Finance;

M. Aaharoni, senior civil servants coordinator, Central Office, Civil Service Commission; and S. Vax, former general director, Ministry of Communication.

22. D. Caspi & Y. Limor, 1992; D. Caspi, 1997.

23. R. Freedman, 1982; D. Horowitz, 1977. *Jerusalem Quarterly*.

24. See Y. Zalmanovitch, 1991, Table 13, p. 138.

25. *Ma'ariv*, August 15, 1986.

26. *Yediot Ahronot*, February 27, 1987.

27. Managerial Report to the 12th Convention on Kupat Holim.

28. *Yediot Ahronot*, November 9, 1987, December 13, 1987, April 15, 1988, May 30, 1988; *Ma'ariv*, June 20, 1988.

29. *Ha'aretz*, January 25, 1994, January 27, 1994, January 30, 1994, January 31, 1994, March 8, 1994; *Yediot Ahronot*, January 26, 1994, January 28, 1994, January 31, 1994.

30. *Ha'aretz*, June 16, 1994.

Chapter 17:   Stateness in Health

1. Fogel, interview, February 5, 1986.

2. *Yediot Ahronot*, October 16, 1998; *Ha'aretz*, November 13, 1998.

3. *Ha'aretz*, November 16, 1999.

4. *Ha'aretz*, November 8, 1999.

5. *Yediot Ahronot*, September 19, 1996.

6. *Ha'aretz*, November 22, 1999.

Bibliography

Archival Sources

Archives of the Israeli Labor Party, Beit Berl. Minutes of party bureau meetings, 1970 –
1984, at which subjects relating to the health system in general and Kupat Holim in particular were discussed.

Pinchas Lavon Institute for Labor Party Research, Labor and Hehalutz Archives, Tel Aviv.
Minutes of the Histadrut Executive Committee meetings, 1970 –1984, at which subjects
relating to the reciprocal relations between the Histadrut and Kupat Holim were discussed, and Kupat Holim and Histadrut publications.

Ministry of Health Archives, Jerusalem. General Kupat Holim files, and correspondence of
the Ministers of Health Victor Shem Tov and Eliezer Shostak.

Kupat Holim Archives, Tel Aviv. File of Kupat Holim Chairman Haim Doron, 1974–1984, and
documents and correspondence between the Kupat Holim and Ministry of Health executives.

Daily Newspaper Archives of *Ha'aretz, Davar, Ma'ariv,* and *Yediot Ahronot,* all in Tel Aviv.

State Archives, Jerusalem.

Interviewees by Position, Institutional Affiliation, and Date(s) of Interview(s)

Ministry of Health

Arbeli-Almozlino, Shoshanah, former deputy minister and minister of Health, June 14, 1985.

Brandeis, Yosef, former director of the Rambam Hospital (Haifa), October 9, 1984.

Ellenzweig, Avi-Yakar, former advisor to minister of Health Shostak, July 11, 1985.

Epstein, Josette, representative of the Division for Budgeting, Planning and Medical Economy in the professional subcommittee of the Project Committee, December 25, 1983.

Haber, Shraga, assistant director general and director of the Division for Budgeting, Planning and Medical Economy in the Ministry of Health, December 4, 1983, December 18,
1983, and June 17, 1985.

Modan, Baruch, former director general of the Ministry of Health, August 23, 1985, and
October 1, 1985.

Nevo, Ya'akov, commissioner for financial negotiations with Kupat Holim at the Ministry
of Health, Division for Budgeting, Planning and Medical Economy, February 5, 1984.

Riftin, Uri, assistant director general for special assignments in the Ministry of Health,
June 17, 1985.

Shani, Mordechai, former director general of the Ministry of Health and director of the
Sheba (Tel HaShomer) Medical Center, July 22, 1985.

Shem Tov, Victor, former minister of Health, May 20, 1985, and September 15, 1985.
Shostak, Eliezer, former minister of Health, July 8, 1985.
Keren, Uzi, Project Committee secretary, July 26, 1985, July 28, 1985, August 5, 1985, and August 14, 1985.

Ministry of Finance, Budget Division

Almog, Rivka, former health commissioner ("referent") in the Budget Division, February 5, 1986.
Fogel, Aharon, former commissioner of the Budget Division, December 16, 1985, and February 5, 1986.
Snapiri, Avraham, former deputy commissioner to the Budget Division, August 13, 1985.
Tokatly, Oren, former health commissioner ("referent") of the Budget Division, December 11, 1983, February 15, 1984, and February 26, 1984.

The Histadrut

Brickman, Mordechai, former executive secretary at Solel Boneh, February 11, 1987.
Eini, Giora, coordinator of the Labor Alignment in the Histadrut Executive Committee, June 18, 1985.
Kover, Aharon, former director of the Payments Division in the Central Tax Bureau, June 16, 1985.
Meshel, Yeruham, former secretary general of the Histadrut, July 25, 1985, and July 31, 1985.
Rosengarten, Andy, former director of the Solel Boneh Haifa District, March 5, 1987.

Kupat Holim

Doron, Haim, former chairman of Central Office, September 19, 1985
Hareuveni, Rafi, director of Building Division, August 1, 1985, and August 7, 1985.
Ron, Aviva, former director of the Planning and Information Division, June 24, 1985.
Shapnitz, Eli, treasurer, November 4, 1985.
Shavit, Adi, comptroller, August 14, 1985, and September 3, 1985.

Other Organizations and Institutions

Almogi, Yosef, former minister of Labor, December 11, 1987.
Ben-Ya'akov, Avraham, chairman of Kupat Holim Leumit, August 7, 1985.
Grossman, Haika, former chairperson for the Knesset Public Services Committee, October 2, 1985.
Nahmias, Aharon, former Knesset member and coordinator of the Labor Alignment in the Ulmert Committee, March 16, 1983.
Shalish, Zevulun, head of the Likud faction in the Kupat Holim Executive Committee, July 19, 1985.
Tamir, Yosef, former assistant director general for research and planning in the National Insurance Institute, May 25, 1987.

Primary Sources

Central Bureau of Statistics

Statistical Yearbook of Israel. 1976 (27), 1988 (39).
Misrad Habriut [Ministry of Health].(1977). *Review of health services use,* Special Publications Series, no. 639.

Misrad Habriut [Ministry of Health]. (1981). *Review of health services use,* Special Publications Series, no. 717.

Hahotza'ah Haleumit Lebriut, 1979 –1980 Veomdan mukdam le, 1980 –1981 [National expenditure on health for 1979 –1980 and preliminary estimate for 1980 –1981] (1982). Reprint from *Musaf Leyarhon Hastatisti Leyisrael* [Supplement to the statistical monthly in Israel], no. 2.

Histadrut

Kupat haholim shel poalei eretz yisrael, Prakim mehadin veheshbon [The sick fund of the workers of Palestine, chapters from the report]. (1923). Jerusalem.

Central Committee Decisions. (1972, April 30). Tel Aviv: Pinhas Lavon Institute for Labor Party Research, Labor and Hehalutz Archives: Minutes of Central Committee meeting, April 1972.

Central Committee Meeting. (1986, August 10). Printed minutes. In the General Secretary's Bureau.

Central Tax Bureau. (1962). *Esrim vehamesh shanim lamas ahid 1937–1962* [Twenty-five years of the single tax]. Tel Aviv.

———. 1982, January. *Hevrot umisim bahistadrut (Hahlatot vehoraot) [Histadrut membership and dues (Decisions and provisions)].* Tel Aviv.

———. Accountancy Division. Reports and Budget Proposals, 1970 –1977. Tel Aviv.

Report to the 14th National Convention, 1981. Tel Aviv.

Report to the 15th National Convention, 1985. Tel Aviv.

Report to the 16th National Convention, 1990. Tel Aviv.

Histadrut Comptroller. (1978, 1983). *Report of the central tax bureau.* Comptroller's audit for 1975 –1977 and 1978 –1982. Tel Aviv.

Histadrut. (1985). *Hokat hahistadrut [The Histadrut constitution].* Tel Aviv.

Executive Committee, Social Security Division (1987, December). *Kupat Holim, misparim veuvdot* [Kupat Holim, facts and figures]. Tel Aviv.

Hevrat Haovdim [Hisdatrut Holding Company] (1985). Tel Aviv: Mifalei Tarbut Vehinuch Ba'am.

Solel Boneh (1970 –75). *Hoveret Statistit 1970–1975 [Statistical Journal, 1970 –1975].* Tel Aviv.

Ministry of Health

Report of the Committee on Kupat Holim. July 1950.

The Health System in Israel, 1948 –1968, Jerusalem, 1968.

Lishkat Sar Habriut [Bureau of the Minister of Health]. (September 1978). *Ekronot hok bituah briut mamlahtik* [Principles of national health insurance]. Jerusalem.

Staff for Establishing the Hospitalization Authority. (1983, August). Plan for transferring the government health services to a statutory authority, first stage (prepared by Oren Tokatly). Jerusalem.

Staff for Establishing the Hospitalization Authority (1984). *Reshut Ishpuz* [Plan for transferring the government health services to a statutory authority, second stage (prepared by Oren Tokatly)]. Jerusalem.

Division for Budgeting, Planning and Medical Economy. (1983, August). *Sugiot bahotza'ah lebriut* [Issues in health expenditures]. Mimeographed pamphlet. Jerusalem.

Bureau of the Minister of Health. (1985, June). *Skira klalit al peulot hamisrad likrat hadiun baknesset al peilut hamisrad lishnat hataktziv 1982–1983; 1984–1985* [A comprehensive review of the ministry's activities prior to the Knesset discussion of the ministry's activities for the budget years 1982 –1983; 1984 –1985). Jerusalem.

———. (1973, 1975, 1977–1989, 1991, 1994). Budget proposals and explanatory notes for the fiscal years 1974, 1976, 1978–1990, 1992, 1995. Presented to the eighth, ninth, tenth, eleventh, twelfth Knessets. Jerusalem.

Zohar Committee. (1978, January). *Doch hatzevet lereforma besherutei habriut—Doch vaadat zohar [Report of the Health Services Reform Team—Zohar Committee Report].* Tel Aviv: Tel Hashomer Hospital.

Ministry of Finance

Laor Committee report of 1977. On *Kupat Holim's Budget.*

State of Israel Budget Principles for 1976. Jerusalem.

State of Israel Budget Principles for 1980. Jerusalem.

State of Israel Budget Principles for 1981. Jerusalem.

———. Budget proposal for 1983: and explanatory notes presented to the tenth Knesset (Booklet D). Jerusalem.

Budget Division (1990, April 5). Kupat Holim Recovery Plan. Document submitted (by David Boaz, Head of the Budget Division) to the Knesset Finance Committee chairman (Avraham Shochat).

Sick Funds

KUPAT HOLIM OF THE HISTADRUT

(1912–1913). *Contrass takanot vehahlatot Kupat Holim shel Poalei Yehudah* [A collection of regulations and decisions of the Judea Kupat Holim]: Sivan (July) 1912–13, a collection of printed pages, kept in the Pinchas Lavon Archive.

(1926). Activities and development in the four years 1923–1926. Report to the third Histadrut convention, p. 6.

(1930). Activities and development from 1929–1930. Tel Aviv: Hahistadrut Haklalit shel Haovdim Haivriim Be'eretz Yisrael.

(1943). Ten years of Kupat Holim, 1933–1942 (facts and figures), chapter of a report to the Kupat Holim Convention. Tel Aviv.

(1957). Kupat Holim in the state, Reports to the 6th Convention.

(1984). Kupat Holim regulations—1983. Tel Aviv. Central Administration of Kupat Holim.

(1987). Kupat Holim regulations (2d edition). Tel Aviv.

(1981). Development budget proposal for the fiscal year 1980–1981. Tel Aviv.

(1974). Managerial report to the 9th convention, March 26–28, 1974, Tel Aviv.

(1979). Managerial report to the 10th convention, March 1974–December 1979. Tel Aviv.

(1979). Managerial report to the 10th convention, March 1974–December 1979. Tel Aviv.

(1984). Managerial report to the 11th convention, December 1979–December 1984. Tel Aviv.

(1984, December 24–25). Report to the 11th convention of Kupat Holim, presented by the National Committee. Tel Aviv.

(1988). Managerial report to the 12th convention, December 1984–May 1988. Tel Aviv.

(1990, April). Major improvements in Kupat Holim services—Facts and figures. Tel Aviv.

(1992, September). Activity Report for the years 1988–1992. Tel Aviv.

(1973). Recommendations of the Committee to Examine the Organizational-Managerial System of Kupat Holim. Tel Aviv.

(1984). Recommendations of the Committee for the Reorganization of Kupat Holim's Health Services.

Doron, H. (1978, June). *Irgun sherutei habriut—Keytzad?* [Organizing the health services—How?]. Mimeographed pamphlet. Tel Aviv.

———. (1979, December 19). *Kupat Holim, yesodotea, darkeha vesheruteha bein veida leveida—Pituham shel Anfei Briut Nosafim [Kupat Holim, foundations, course of action and services between conventions—the development of additional health services]*. Speech to the delegates of the 10th annual Kupat Holim convention. Tel Aviv.

———. (1984, July). Speech at the opening of the Kupat Holim physicians convention, *Meida Larofeh [Information for the physician]*, No. 37. Tel Aviv: Kupat Holim Publications.

———. (1984, December 12). *Hesegeha ubayoteha shel Kupat Holim [Kupat Holim's achievements and problems]*. Speech to the delegates of the 11th convention of Kupat Holim. Bound pamphlet. Tel Aviv: Kupat Holim Publications.

———. (1988, May). Conversation with Professor H. Doron, outgoing chairman of Kupat Holim. *Meida Larofeh [Information for the physician]*, No. 49 –50. Tel Aviv: Kupat Holim Publications.

Doron, H., & Ron, A. (1978). *Kupat Holim's Hospitalization Plan*. Reprint from Kupat Holim's *Medical Annual*, Vol. 7 7 –20. Tel Aviv: Kupat Holim Publications.

MACCABI, UNITED, LEUMIT SICK FUNDS

Maccabi Sick Fund, Research and Statistics Department. (1975). *Kupat Holim Maccabi besherut briut ha'am, tzmiha vehitpathut [The Maccabi Sick Fund in the service of national health, growth and development]*. Tel Aviv: Merkaz Kupat Holim Maccabi.

United Sick Fund, *Haveida hartzit harishona (June 1976)* [*The 1st national convention (June 1976)]*. Tel Aviv: Merkaz United Kupat Holim.

Meuhede Sick Fund, *Haveida Hartzit Hashnia (May 1981)* [*The 2nd national convention (May 1981)]*. Tel Aviv: Merkaz United Kupat Holim.

Leevai and Leevai Accounting Firm. *Din veheshbon al hadohot hakaspiim shel kupat holim leovdim leumiim shel Histadrut Haovdim Haleumit Be'eretz Yisrael [Report on the financial reports of the Leumit Sick Fund of the National Federation of Labor in Israel]*. Tel Aviv. Reports for December 31, 1972, March 31, 1975, and March 31, 1977.

Kost Lev-Ari and Furer Accounting Firm. (1977, March). *Sikum hahahnasot behistadrut "Maccabi" Yisrael, Kupat Holim Maccabi Kolelet Kupat Holim Asaf, Aguda Le'ezra Refuit [Balance sheet of Kupat Holim Maccabi]*.

State Comptroller Reports, Jerusalem

GENERAL REPORTS

(1969). *19th annual report for 1968 and for accounts of the fiscal year 1967–1968*.

(1972). *22nd annual report for 1971 and for accounts of the fiscal year 1970–1971*.

(1973). *23rd annual report for the year of 1972 and for accounts of the fiscal year 1971–1972*.

(1975). *25th annual report for the year of 1974 and for accounts of the fiscal year 1973*.

(1976). *26th annual report for the year of 1975 and for accounts of the fiscal year 1974*.

(1977). *27th annual report for the year of 1976 and for accounts of the fiscal year 1975*.

(1979). *29th annual report for the year of 1978 and for accounts of the fiscal year 1977*.

(1983). *33rd annual report for the year of 1981 and for accounts of the fiscal year 1981*.

(1986). *36th annual report for the year of 1985 and for accounts of the fiscal year 1984*.

(1987). *37th annual report for the year of 1986 and for accounts of the fiscal year 1985*.

(1988). *38th annual report for the year of 1987 and for accounts of the fiscal year 1986*.

SPECIAL REPORTS

(1979). *Report on the audit of the Leumit Sick Fund of the National Worker's Federation of Labor in Israel.*

(1979). *Report on the audit of Kupat Holim of the general Federation of Labor in Israel.*

(1985). *Report on the audit of Kupat Holim of the general Federation of Labor in Israel.*

(1982). *Report on the audit of the United Sick Fund.*

(1982). *Report on the audit of the Maccabi Israel Sick Fund, including the Assaf Sick Fund, The Association for Medical Aid.*

Other Organizations and Institutions

Atias, M. (Ed.). (1963). *Sefer hateudot shel Havaad Heleumi leknesset Yisrael Be'eretz Yisrael 1918–1948 [The book of documents of the National Committee of the* yishuv *in Palestine 1918–1948].* Jerusalem. National Archives, Jerusalem.

Havad Haleumi Leknesset Yisrael Be'eretz Yisrael. (1942). *Din veheshbon lamoshav ha'asiri shel asefat hanivharim [The National Committee for the* yishuv *in Palestine. Report to the 10th session of the delegate's meeting].* Jerusalem: The State Archives.

———. (1946). Report for November 1944–January 1946. Jerusalem: State Archives.

National Insurance Institute, Finance Division. (1984, August 29). *Financial Report for 1983.* Presented to the Employer Participation Tax Board, Jerusalem.

———. (1993). *Annual Survey 1992–1993.* (Ch. 6- Shteiner, R., Twenty Years of Parallel Tax Implementation). Jerusalem: National Insurance Institute.

———. (1995). *Annual Survey 1994–1995.* (Ch. 6- Cohen, S., and Shteiner, R., National Health Insurance Law-Background, Principles and Implementation). Jerusalem: National Insurance Institute.

Knesset Minutes. (1972) Vol. 65.

———. (1972). Vols. 66, 68.

———. (1973). *The National Health Insurance Law, 1973. Proposed Bills, 1077.*

———. (1980). Vol. 88.

———. (1981). *The National Health Insurance Law, 1981. Proposed Bills, 1510.*

———. (1993). *The National Health Insurance Law, 1993. Proposed Bills, 2189.*

———. (1994). *The National Health Insurance Law, 1994. Proposed Bills, 2249.*

Laws of the State of Israel. *National health, public health.* Tel Aviv: Dr. R. Gidon Publishing House. (Second ed., Public Health Regulations, 1959). Revisions to the laws published periodically.

———. *Employer Participation Tax Law.* (2nd ed.) Tel Aviv: Dr. R. Gidon Publishing House. Revisions to the tax laws published periodically.

State of Israel. (1990). *The State Commission of Inquiry into the operation and efficiency of health care system in Israel: Vol. 1, The majority opinion.* Jerusalem: State of Israel. (The Netanyahu Report).

Labor Party. (1985). Meeting of the Party Bureau, September 19, 1985 and December 12, 1985. Kfar Saba, Labor Party Archives, Beit Berl. (File 25/ 85).

Gadish, Y. (Ed.). (1986, March 6). *Doch bedikat matzav Kupat Holim Klalit shel Hahistadrut [Report on Kupat Holim's Financial Situation],* presented to Prime Minister Shimon Peres.

Tamir, Y. (1987). *Tazkir lamenahel haklali shel Hamosad Lebituach Leumi bidvar halukat hamas hamakbil, meta'arich shevi'i beyanuar 1987 [Memorandum to the managing director of the National Insurance Institute concerning the division of the employer participation tax, January 7, 1987].* Office of the Assistant Director General for Research, National Insurance Institute.

Secondary Sources

Sources in Hebrew

Aharoni, Y. (1979). *Hevrot memshaltiot beyisrael ubaolam [State-owned companies in Israel and abroad]*. Tel Aviv: Cherikover-Gomeh.

———. (1991). *The political economy of Israel*. Tel Aviv: Am Oved.

Arieli, A. (1986). *Misrad haotzar: Tafkidim, mivneh vetahalichei avoda [The Ministry of Finance: Functions, structure and work procedures]*. Jerusalem: Van Leer Institute.

———. (1988). *Haheybet hamishki shel ma'arechet habriut hatziburit [The economic aspect of the public health system]*, Jerusalem: Van Leer Institute.

Aveni, A. (1976). *Sapir.* Givaataim: Peleg Publishing House.

Baron, A. (1978). *Tesumot meida lekovei hahlatot politiim bemediniut sotizliat tziburit: Hamikre shel hatza'at hok bituach briut 1973, Beve'adat Hashrutim Hatziburiim shel Haknesset. [Information input for political decision-makers in public social policy: The case of the Health Insurance Bill, 1973, in the Knesset Public Services Committee]*. Unpublished master's thesis, Hebrew University of Jerusalem, Israel.

Bartal, G. (1989). *Hahistadrut: mivneh v'tafkidin. [Histadrut—structure and activities]*. Tel Aviv: Histadrut Executive Committee.

Baruch, N. (1973). *Hairgun hamosdi shel sherutei habriut beyisrael [The institutional structure of the health services in Israel]*. Jerusalem: Center for Policy Research.

Barzilai, A. (1996). *Ramon.* Tel Aviv: Shokan.

Barzilai, G., Yuchtman-Yaar, & E., Segal, Z. (1994). *Beit hamishpat haelion v'hatsibur b'yisrael [The Israeli Supreme Court and the Israeli public]*. Tel Aviv: Papiros, Tel Aviv University Press.

Becker, A. (1981). *Hok mamlahti leirur harefuah hatziburit ulehisul Kupat Holim [A state law to undermine public medicine and liquidate Kupat Holim]*. Tel Aviv: Hahistadrut Haklalit, Havad Hapoel, Ha'agaf Lebitahon Sotziali [Histadrut, Executive Committee, Social Security Division].

———. (1982). *Im hazman ubnei hador [With the time and its generation]*. Tel Aviv: Am Oved.

Ben Gurion, D. (1951–1957). *Hazon vederekh [Vision and objectives]* (Vols. 1–5). Tel Aviv: Mapai Political Party.

———. (1964). *Nezech israel [Israel forever]*. Tel Aviv: Ayanot.

———. (1964). *Hapoal haeyivri vhistadrutu [The Hebrew worker and his Histadrut]*. Tel Aviv: Mifaley Tarbut Wechinuch.

Ben Meir, D. (1978). *Hahistadrut [The Histadrut]*. Jerusalem: Carta.

Ben-Non, G., & Ben-Uri, D. (1996). *International comparison—Israel and the OECD countries*. Jerusalem: State of Israel, Ministry of Health.

Ben Porat, Y. (1982). Hamahapach shelo hayah: Haideologia vemediniut kalkalit 1977–1981 [The change that wasn't: Ideology and economic policy, 1977–1981]. *Rivon Lekalkala [Economic Quarterly]*, 29, 325–33.

Bondi, R. (1981). *Sheba rofeh lehol adam [Sheba, every man's physician]*. Tel Aviv: Zmora, Bitan, Modan.

Bracha, B. (1986). *Mishpat minhali [Administrative law]*. Jerusalem: Shokan.

Caspi, D. (Ed.). (1997). *Tikshoret v'democratia b'yisrael [Communication and democracy in Israel]* Tel Aviv: Hakibbutz Hammeuchad.

Caspi, D., & Limor, Y. (1992). *Hametavhim: Tikshoret hamonim b'yisrael. 1948–1990. [The mediators: The mass media in Israel 1948–1990]*. Tel Aviv: Am Oved.

Doron, A. (1975). *Hama'avak al habituach haleumi beyisrael, 1948–1953 [The struggle for national jnsurance in Israel, 1948–1953].* Jerusalem: Hebrew University of Jerusalem, School of Social Work.

Doron, A., Ninio, D., & Fishoff, Y. (Eds.). (1969). *Mediniut revaha beyisrael* [W*elfare policy in Israel*]. Jerusalem: Academon.

Eliav, B. (Ed.). (1976). *Heyeshuv beyemei habayit haleumi [The Jewish community at the time of the national home].* Jerusalem: Keter.

Ellenzwieg, A. Y., De-Freis, A., Halevi, H. S., & Chernichovsky, D. (1983). *Behinah hashva'atit shel hatohniot lehanhagat bituach briut beyisrael [A comparative study of the programs for health insurance in Israel],* Jerusalem: Center for Social Policy Research in Israel.

Friedberg, A. (1985). *Bikoret tziburit beshulei ma'arehet haminhal vtziburi beyisrael [Public audit of the margins of the public administrative system in Israel].* Unpublished doctoral dissertation, Hebrew University of Jerusalem, Israel.

Gabison, R. (1995). The court and its involvement in social policy. In Kopp, J. (Ed.). *Resource allocation for social services 1995–1995.* Jerusalem: Center for Social Policy Research in Israel, pp. 215–25.

Goldberg, G. (1992). *Miflagot politiot b'yisrael: m'miflagot hamon l'miflagot electoraliot [Political Parties in Israel—From Mass Parties to Electoral Parties].* Tel Aviv: Ramot.

———. (1994). *Haboher hayisraeli [The Israeli voter 1992].* Jerusalem: Magnes Press.

Gross, R., Greenstein, M., Greenberg, S., Tabenkin, H., & Harison, M. (1999) *Rofim Rishonim b'yisrael, 1997: Mafianim v'tmurot b'edan shel reforma [Primary care physicians in Israel 1997: Characteristics and changes in an era of reform].* Bitahon Sotziali [Social Security], 54, pp. 169–90.

Halevi, H. S. (1979). Hairgun hapluralisti shel sherutei habriut beyisrael [The pluralistic organization of health services in Israel], *Bitahon Sotziali [Social Security],* 17, 5–50.

Horowitz, D. (1983). Hayeshuv vehahevrah hayisrelit—hemshehiut veshinui [The yishuv and Israeli society—continuation and change] *Medinah, Memshal Veyahasim Beinleumiim [State, Government, and International Relations],* 21, 31–68.

———. (1977). More than a change in government. *Jerusalem Quarterly,* 5, 3–20.

Hareuveni, Y. (1974). *Haminhal Hatziburi Beyisrael [Public administration in Israel].* Ramat Gan: Masada.

Ishay, R. (1986). *Shvitat Harofeim [Doctors' Strike].* Tel Aviv: Zmora Bitan.

Jabotinsky, Z. V. (n.d.). Geula Socialit-Sicha [Social salvation—A talk]. In *Reshimot [Notes].* Tel Aviv: Amichai and Ari Jabotinsky.

Kanivsky, Y. (1944–1945). *Tohnitenu Bebituah Hasotiziali [Our plan for social insurance].* Tel Aviv: Sefer. (Reprinted from Ahdut Ha'avoda.)

———. (1948), *Tohnit Lebituah Sotziali Bemedinat Yisrael [A plan for social insurance in the State of Israel].* Tel Aviv: Social Research Institute.

Kopp, J. (Ed.). (1995). *Hakzaat Mashabim L' Sherotim Hevrateim 1994–1995 [Resource allocation for Social Services 1994–1995].* Jerusalem: Center for Social Policy Research in Israel.

———. (Ed.). (1997). *Hakzaat Mashabim L'Sherotim Hevrateim 1996 [Resources allocation for Social Services 1996].* Jerusalem: Center for Social Policy Research in Israel.

Korn, D. (1994). *Time in gray, National Unity Governments 1984–1990.* Tel Aviv: Zmora-Bitan.

Korn, D., & Shapira, B. (1997). *Coalition politics in Israel.* Tel Aviv: Zmora-Bitan.

Makover, R. (1988). *Shilton Uminhal Be'eretz Yisrael, 1917–1925 [Government and administration in Palestine, 1917–1925].* Jerusalem: Yad Yitzhak Ben Zvi.

Manor, A. (1965). *Yitzchak Kaneb—Hametachnen Hasosiali [Yitzchak Keneb—The social planner].* Tel Aviv: Mekorot.

Margalit, E. (1994). *Trade unions in Israel: Past and present—their role in the Histadrut and in society*. Tel Aviv: Ramot.

Mautner, M. (1993). *The decline of formalism and the rise of values in Israeli law*. Tel Aviv: Ma'agalay Da'at.

Meshel, Y. (1978). *Mivhan ha'emet shel sherutei habriut beyisrael [The real test of the health services in Israel]*. Printout by the Histadrut Executive Committee.

———. (1980), *Shlihut vederech [Mission and way]*. Tel Aviv: Am Oved.

Milstein, A. (1972). Mashbir hahistadrut bemedinat Yisrael [The Histadrut crisis in the State of Israel]. *Hauma [The Nation]*, 4, 430–39.

Modan, B. (1985). *Refuah bematzor [Medicine under siege]*. Tel Aviv: Adam.

———. (1986). Ma'arehet habriut beyisrael—shoresh haholi, tmunat matzv venekudot lepitaron [The health system in Israel—the source of the disease, current situation and proposals for solution]. *Skira Hodshit [Monthly Review]*, 12, 13–19.

Naor, N. (1987). *Tsmichato shel manhig: Pinhas Sapir 1930–1949 [Emergence of a leader: Pinhas Sapir 1930–1949]*. Tel Aviv: Papyrus.

Nederland, D. (1983). Hashpa'at harofim haolim megermania al hitpathut harefuah be'eretz Yisrael (1933–1948). [The influence of the immigrant German doctors on the development of medicine in Palestine (1933–1948)]. *Katedra, 30*, 111–60.

Ofir, Y. (1982). *Sefer haoved haleumi [The book of the national worker]*. (Vol. 1–2). Tel Aviv: Histadrut Haovdim Haleumit [The Union of National Workers].

Pilowsky, W. (Ed.). (1990). *Hama'avar meyishuv lemedinah 1947–1949: Retzifut Vetmurot [The transition from yishuv to State, 1947–1949: continuity and change]*. Haifa: Haifa University.

Rabin, L. (1997). *Oulecet b'edarko [Following his footsteps]*. Tel Aviv: Yediot Ahronot.

Reshef, Y. (1984). Hamemshala vehahistadrut bashanim 1973–1982: Anatomia shel shituf peula umahloket [The government and the Histadrut, 1973–1982: Anatomy of cooperation and conflict] *Medina, Memshal Veyahasim Beinleumiim [State, Government and International Relations]*, 22, 75–90.

Rubinstein, A. (1974). *Hamishpat haconstituzioni shel medinat Yisrael [Constitutional law in the State of Israel]*. Tel Aviv: Schoken.

Rubenstein, A. (1976). Meyishuv lemedina: Mosdot umiflagot [From *Yishuv* to state: Institutions and parties]. In: B. Eliav (ed.), *Hayishuv beyemei habayit haleumi [The yishuv in the days of the national home]*. Jerusalem: Keter.

Rosenthal, A. (1988). *Ma'amad Hasochnut Hayehudit bemedinat Yisrael bashanim 1948–1960 bepersectiva shel yahasei "merkaz-shulaim" [The status of the Jewish Agency in the state of Israel between 1948–1960 from the perspective of "core-margin" relations]*. Unpublished master's thesis, Haifa University, Israel.

Shapiro, Y. (1977). *Demokratia bisrael [Democracy in Israel]*. Ramat Gan: Massada.

———. (1989). *Lashilton behartano [Elected to Govern]*. Tel Aviv: Am Oved.

Sharkansky, I., & Radian, A. (1981). Hamahapach vehashinui bemediniut hapnim (1981) [Change in government and change in domestic policy (1981)]. *Netivei Irgun Uminhal [Paths in Organization and Administration]*, 136, 24–29.

Shenhar A., & Yarkoni, A. (Eds.). (1993). *Tarbot hanihol byisrael* [Israeli management culture]. Tel Aviv: Cherikover.

Sorocca, M. (1970, January). *Kupat Holim le'et tmura [Kupat Holim at a time of change]*. Mimeographed memorandum. Tel Aviv: Kupat Holim.

Slutzky, Y. (1973). *Mavo letoldot tnuat ha'avoda ha'yisre'elit [Introduction to the history of the Israeli labor movement]*. Tel Aviv: Am Oved.

Steinberg, J. M. (1989). Mihsholim baderech leshinui ma'arehet habriut beyisrael [Obstacles to change in the structure of the health system in Israel]. *Bitahon Sotziali [Social Security]*, 34, 61–78.

Tevet, S. (1980). *Kinaat David [David's fanaticism]*. (Vols. 1–3). Tel Aviv: Shokan.

Vilan, Y. (1980). *Bitahon sotziali, ye'adim veuvdot [Social security, objectives and facts]*. Tel Aviv: Histadrut Executive Committee.

Yadlin, A. (1980). *Edut [Testimony]*. Jerusalem: Idanim.

Yishai, Y. (1986). *Kvutzot interes beyisrael [Interest groups in Israel]*. Tel Aviv: Am Oved.

Zalmanovitch, Y. (1981). *Histadrut, Kupat Holim, memshalah: Gishot halifin heskemi vesihsuhii kehesber politii [The Histadrut, Kupat Holim, government: Consensual and conflictual exchange approaches as a political explanation]*. Unpublished master's thesis: Haifa University, Israel.

———. (1990). Hama'avak lehahalat marut hamerkaz: harefuah hatziburit beyisrael [The struggle to impose core authority: Public medicine in Israel]. In V. Pilovsky (Ed.), *Hama'avar meyishuv lemedinah 1947–1949: Retzipfut vetmurot [The transition from yishuv to state 1947–1949: Continuity and change]*. Haifa: Haifa University.

———. (1991). *Kviat mediniut stiborit beshulei hamimshal v'haminhal hastibori beyisrael— Hamekrei shel mediniut habriut b'Yisrael ben hashanim 1970–1984 [Public policy making at the margins of government and administration in Israel: The case of health policy making in Israel, 1970–1984]*. Ph.D. Dissertation: The Hebrew University of Jerusalem.

Zartal, A. (1975). *Yamim vema'asim: Sipur hayav shel Moshe Soroka [Days and deeds: The life story of Moshe Sorocca]*. Tel Aviv: Mahbarot Lesifrut.

Zohar, E. (1974). Betzvat hamishtar o madua af ehad lo kam *[In the grip of the regime or why no one stands up]*. Jerusalem: Shikmona.

———(1987). *Sdom O Helem [Sodom or Chelm]*. Tel Aviv: Dvir.

Sources in English

Aharoni, Y. (1986). *The evolution and management of state owned enterprises*. Cambridge, Mass.: Ballinger.

Abel-Smith, B. (1994). *An introduction to health: Policy, planning and financing*. London: Longman.

Abel-Smith, B., Figueras, J., Holland, W., McKee, M., & Mossialos, E. (1995). *Choices in health policy—An agenda for the European union*. Dartmouth, U.K.: Aldershot.

Allsop, J. (1995). *Health policy and the NHS towards 2000* (2nd ed.). London: Longman.

Anderson, J. E. (1975). *Public policy making*. London: Nelson.

Arian, A. (1981). Health care in Israel: Political and administrative aspects. *International Political Science Review*, 1, 43–56.

———. (Ed.) (1983). *The elections in Israel—1981*. Tel Aviv: Ramot.

———. (1985). *Politics in Israel, the second generation*. Chatham, N.J.: Chatham House.

Arian, A., & Barnes, S. H. (1974). The dominant party system: A neglected model of democratic stability. *Journal of Politics, 3*, 592–614.

Aronoff, M. J. (1989). *Israeli visions and divisions, cultural change and political conflict*. New Brunswick, N.J.: Transaction.

Asher, K. (1987). *The politics of privatization: Contracting out public services*. London: Macmillan.

Ashford, D. E. (Ed.). (1992). *History and context in comparative public policy*. Pittsburgh, Penn.: Pittsburgh University Press.

Bardrach, E. (1977). *The implementation game: What happens after a bill becomes a law*. Cambridge, Mass.: MIT Press.

Barker, A. (Ed.). (1982). *Quangos in Britain—government and the networks of public policy making*. London: Macmillan.

Baumgartner, F. R. (1993). *Agendas and instability in American politics*. Chicago: University of Chicago Press.

Baumgartner, F. R., & Jones, B. D. (1991). Agenda dynamics and policy subsystems. *Journal of Politics, 53*, 1044–74.

Beilin, Y. (1992). *Israel—A concise political history*. New York: St. Martin's Press.

Bell, D. (1976). *The cultural contradictions of capitalism*, New York: Basic Books.

Ben-Ner, A. (1994) Who benefits from the nonprofit sector? Reforming law and public policy towards nonprofit organizations. *Yale Law Journal, 104*, 731–62.

Berg, A., Rosen, B., Gross, R., & Chinitz, D. (1996). Public perception of the health system following implementation of the National Health Insurance Law: Selected preliminary findings from a survey of the general population. Jerusalem: JDC–Brookdale Institute, ES-12-96.

Blau, P. (1964). *Exchange and power in social life*. New York: Wiley.

Caiden, G. E. (1970). *Israel's administrative culture*. Berkeley: University of California Press.

Cambell, A. K. (1986). Private delivery of public services: Sorting out the policy and management issues. *Public Management, 68*, 5.

Chernichovsky, D., & Chinitz, D. (1995). The political economy of health system reform in Israel. *Health Economics, 4*, 127–41.

Chinitz, P. D. (1994). Reforming the Israeli health care market. *Social Science and Medicine, 39*, 1447–57.

———. (1995). Israel's health policy breakthrough: The politics of reform and the reform of politics. *Journal of Health Politics, Policy and Law, 20*, 909–32.

Curry, R., & Wade L. (1968). *A theory of political exchange*. Englewood Cliffs, N.J.: Prentice Hall.

Danish Council of Ethics. (1997). *Priority-setting in the health services*. Copenhagen: Danish Council of Ethics.

Dash, J. (1979). *Summoned to Jerusalem—The life of Henrietta Sold*. New York: Harper and Row.

Davidson, M. (1976). *The Golda Meir story*. New York: Scribner's.

Day, P., & Klein, R. (1992). Constitutional and distributional conflict in British medical politics: The case of general practice, 1911–1991. *Political Studies, 11*, 462–78.

Doron, A. (1980). The ailing health services. *Jerusalem Quarterly, 14*, 82–93.

Dowty, A. (1988, July). Expressions of the Jewish political tradition in contemporary Israel politics. Paper presented at 1988 workshops on University Teaching of Jewish Civilization, Center for Public Affairs, Jerusalem, Israel.

Dunning, A. (1992). *Choices in health care: A report by the government Committee on Choices in Health Care*. Rijswijk: Ministry of Welfare, Health and Culture.

Duverger, M. (1967). *Political parties*. New York: Wiley.

Dye, T. R. (1978). *Understanding public policy*. Englewood Cliffs, N. J.: Prentice Hall.

Eisenstadt, S. N. (1985). *The transformation of Israeli society*. London: Weidenfeld and Nicolson.

Elazar, D. J., & Dortort, A. M. (1985). *Understanding the Jewish agency*. Jerusalem: Center for Public Affairs.

Ellenzweig, A. Y. (1983). The new Israeli health care reform: An analysis of a national need. *Journal of Health Politics, Policy and Law, 8*, 366–86.

Elon, A. (1972). *The Israelis: Founders and sons*. New York: Bantam.

Etzioni, A. (1973). The third sector and domestic missions. *Public Administration Review, 33*, 315.

Fesler, J. W., & Kettl, D. F. (1991). *The politics of the administrative process.* Chatham, N.J.: Chatham House.

Freedman, R. (Ed.). (1982). *Israel in the Begin era.* New York: Prager.

Friedberg, A., Geist, B., Mizrahi, N., & Sharkansky, I. (Eds.). (1991). *State audit and accountability—A book of reading.* Jerusalem: State Comptroller's Office.

Friedman, W., & Garner, J. F. (Eds.). (1970). *Governmental enterprise: A comparative study.* London: Stevens.

Galbraith, J. K. (1956). American capitalism: *The concept of countervailing power.* Boston: Houghton, Mifflin.

———. (1985). *The anatomy of power.* London: Corgi Books.

Galnoor, I. (1982). Steering the polity: Communication and politics in Israel. Beverly Hills Calif.: Sage.

George, A. L. (1979). Case studies and theory development: The method of structured, focused comparison. In P. G. Lauren (Ed.), *Diplomacy—New approaches in history, theory and policy.* New York: Free Press.

———. (1979). The causal nexus between cognitive beliefs and decision-making behavior: "The operational code." In Lawrence S. Falkowsky (Ed.), *Psychological models in international politics* (pp. 113–19). Boulder, Colo.: Westview Press.

Greve, C., Flinders, M. & Van Thiel, S. (1999). Quangos—What's in a name? Defining quangos from a comparative perspective, *Governance, 12,* 129–46.

Hadassah Medical Organization. (1939). *Twenty years of medical services to Palestine, 1918–1938.* Jerusalem: Author.

Halevi, H. S. (1980). *The bumpy road to national health insurance: The case of Israel.* Jerusalem: JDC-Brookdale Institute.

Hall, M. H., & Reed, P. B. (1998). Shifting the burden: How much can government download to the non-profit sector? *Canadian Public Administration, 41,* 1–20.

Horowitz, D., & Lissak, M. (1978). *Origins of the Israeli polity: Palestine under the Mandate.* Chicago: University of Chicago Press.

———. (1989). *Trouble in Utopia, the overburdened polity of Israel.* Albany, N.Y.: State University of New York Press.

Hood, C. (1983). *The hidden public sector: The quangocratization of the world?* Glasgow: University of Glasgow Press.

Hsiano, C, W. (1992). Comparing health care systems: What nations can learn from one another. *Journal of Health Policy, Politics and Law, 17,* 613–36.

Hurst, J. W. (1991). Reforming health care in seven European nations. *Health Affairs, 10,* 7–21.

Ilchman, W. F., & Uphoff. T. (1969). *The political economy of change.* Berkeley: University of California Press.

Immergut, M. E. (1992). *Health politics interests and institutions in Western Europe.* New York: Cambridge University Press.

———. (1998). The theoretical core of the new institutionalism. *Politics and Society, 26,* 5–34.

Israel Yearbook and Almanac (1996). Vol. 50. Jerusalem: IBRT Translation.

Kaufman, H. (1971). *The limits of organizational change.* Tuscaloosa, Ala.: Universtity of Alabama Press.

Keren, M. (1995). *Professionals against populism—The Peres government and democracy.* Albany, N.Y.: State University of New York Press.

Kettl, D. F. (1988). *Government by proxy: (Mis?) managing federal programs.* Washington, D.C.: Congressional Quarterly Press.

――――. (1993). *Sharing power: Public governance and private markets*. Washington, D.C.: Brookings Institution.

Kingdon, J. W. (1984). *Agendas, alternatives, and public policies*, Boston: Little Brown.

Kickert, W. J. M. (1997). *Public management and administrative reform in Western Europe*. Cheltenham, U.K.: Edward Elgar.

Kornhauser, W. (1962). Power elite or veto power. In S. M. Lipset & L. Lowenthal (Eds.), *Culture and social character—The work of David Riesman reviewed*. New York: Free Press.

Krasner, S. D. (1978). *Defending the national interest: Raw materials investment and U.S. foreign policy*. Princeton, N.J.: Princeton University Press.

LaPalombara, J. (1974). *Politics within nations*. Englewood Cliffs, N.J.: Prentice Hall.

Lehman-Wilzig, N. S. (1991). Loyalty, voice, and quasi-exit: Israel as a case study of proliferating alternative politics, *Comparative Politics, 24*, 97–108.

――――. (1992). *Wildfire grassroots revolts in Israel in the post-socialist era*. Albany, N.Y.: State University of New York Press.

Lijphart, A. (1977). *Democracy in plural societies*. New Haven, Conn.: Yale University Press.

Mahler, G. (1990). *Israel government and politics in a maturing state*. San Diego, Calif.: Harcourt, Brace, Jovanovich.

Marmor, T. R. (1994). *Understanding health care reform*. New Haven, Conn.: Yale University Press.

Medding, P. Y. (1972). *Mapai in Israel, political organization and government in a new society*. Cambridge: Cambridge University Press.

――――. (1990). *The founding of Israeli democracy*. New York: Oxford University Press.

Meir, G. (1975). *My Life*. Jerusalem: Steimatzky.

Milward, H. B., Else, B. A., & Raskob, J. T. (1991, August 29 –September 19). *Managing the hollow state*. Paper presented at the meeting of the American Political Science Association Meeting, Washington, D.C.

Milward, H. B., Provan, K. G., & Else, B. (1993). What does the hollow state look like? In B. Bozeman (Ed.), *Public management theory: The state of the art*. San Francisco: Jossey-Bass.

――――. (1994). Nonprofit contracting and the hollow state, *Public Administration Review, 54*, 73–83.

Nachmias, D., & Rosenbloom, D. H. (1978). *Bureaucratic culture—Citizens and administration in Israel*. New York: St. Martin's Press.

Nadel, M. V. (1975. The hidden dimension of public policy: Private governments and the policy-making process. *The Journal of Politics, 37*, 5–14.

Nordlinger, E. A. (1981). *On the autonomy of the democratic state*. Cambridge, Mass.: Harvard University Press.

Organization for Economic Cooperation and Development. (1992) *Health reform in seven European nations*. Paris: Author.

Peres, Y., & Yuchtman Yaar, E. (1992). *Trends in Israeli democracy, the public view*. Boulder, Colo.: Lynne Rienner.

Peters, G. B. (1979). Bureaucracy, politics, and public policy (review article), *Comparative Politics, 11*, 339–58.

Peters, G. B., & Savoie, D. J. (Eds.). (1995). *Governance in a changing environment*. Montreal: McGill-Queen's University Press.

――――. (1996). *American public policy—promise and performance* (4th ed.). Chatham, N.J.: Chatham House.

Peters, G. B., & Van Nispen, F. K. M. (Eds.). (1998). *Comparative politics—theory and methods.* New York: New York University Press.

———. (1998). *Public policy instruments.* Cheltenham, U.K.: Edward Elgar.

———. (1999). *Institutional theory in political science—The new institutionalism.* London: Pinter.

Peterson, M. A. (1993). Political influence in the 1990s: From iron triangles to policy networks, *Journal of Health Politics, Policy and Law, 18,* 395–438.

Powell, W. W. (Ed.). (1987). *The nonprofit sector: A research handbook.* New Haven, Conn.: Yale University Press.

Rabin, Y. (1996). *The Rabin memoirs* (rev. ed.). Berkeley: University of California Press.

Rehfuss, J. (1989). *Contracting out in government.* San Francisco: Jossey-Bass.

Riesman, D. (1968). *The lonely crowd.* New Haven: Yale University. Press.

Rhodes, R. A. (1994). The hollowing out of the state: The changing nature of the public service in Britain. *The Political Quarterly, 65,* 138–51.

———. (1996). The new governance: Governing without government. *Political Studies, 44,* 652–67.

Roemer, M. I. (1993). National health systems throughout the world. *American Behavioral Scientist, 36,* 694–708.

Rosen, B. (1998). *Price competition and the 1998 "Budget Arrangements Law."* JDC–Brookdale Institute Web site: www. Jdc. org. il/ brookdale/bkd. html.

Rosen, B., & Shamai, N. (1998). *Financing and resource allocation in Israeli health care.* JDC–Brookdale Institute Web site: www. Jdc. org. il/ brookdale/bkd. html.

Rosen, B., & Steiner R. (1996). *Recent trends in sick fund market shares* (research report: 275–96). Jerusalem: JDC–Brookdale Institute.

Rothstein, B. (1996). Political institutions: An overview. In R. E. Goodin & D. H. Klingemann (Eds.). *A new handbook of political science.* Oxford: Oxford University Press.

———. (1996). *The social democratic state—The Swedish model and the bureaucratic problem of social reforms.* Pittsburgh, Penna.: Pittsburgh University Press.

———. (1998). *Just institutions matter—The moral and political logic of the universal welfare state.* Cambridge: Cambridge University Press.

Sabatier, P., & Mazmanian, D. (1980). The implementation of public policy—a framework of analysis. In B. H. Roven (Ed.). *Policy Studies Review Annual:* Vol. 4 (pp. 181–203). London: Sage.

Sabatier, P. (1983). *Implementation and public policy.* Glenview, Ill: Scott, Foresman.

———. (1986). Top-down and bottom-up approaches to implementation research: A critical analysis and suggested synthesis. *Journal of Public Policy, 6,* 21–48.

Salamon, L. M. (1981). Rethinking public management: Third party government and the changing forms of government action. *Public Policy, 29,* 255–75.

———. (1995). *Partners in public Service—Government nonprofit relations in modern welfare state.* Baltimore: Johns Hopkins University Press.

Saltman, R. B., & Figueras, J. (1997). *European health care reform analysis of current strategies.* Copenhagen: World Health Organization Regional Office for Europe.

Saltman, R. B., & Von Otter, C. (1992). *Planned markets and public competition—Strategic reform in Northern European health systems.* Buckingham: Open University Press.

Sartori, G. (1997). *Comparative constitutional engineering—an inquiry into structures incentives and outcomes* (2nd ed.). New York: New York University Press.

Savas, E. S. (1987). *Privatization: The key to better government.* Chatham, N.J.: Chatham House.

Savoie, D. J. (1994) *Thatcher, Reagan, Mulroney: In search of a new bureaucracy.* Pittsburgh, Penn.: Pittsburgh University Press.

Schlozman, L. K., & Tierney, J. T. (1986). *Organized interests and American democracy.* New York: Harper and Row.

Schut, F. T. (1995). Health care reform in the Netherlands: Balancing corporatism, etatism, and market mechanisms. *Journal of Health Politics, Policy and Law, 20,* 615–52.

Shalev, M. (1992). *Labor and the political economy of Israel.* Oxford: Oxford University Press.

Shalev, M., & Grinberg, L. L. (1989). *Histadrut–Government relations and the transition from a Likud to a National Unity Government.* Tel Aviv: Pinhas Sapir Center for Development, Tel Aviv University.

Sharkansky, I. (1970). *The routines of politics.* New York: Van Nostrand Reinhold.

———. (1979) *Wither the state.* Chatham, N.J.: Chatham House.

———. (1980). Policy making and service delivery on the margins of government: The case of contractors. *Public Administration Review, 40,* 116–23.

———. (1982), *Public administration—Agencies, policies, and politics.* San Francisco: W. H. Freeman.

———. (1983, June). *The environmental dependence of public enterprise.* Paper presented at the Public Enterprises Conference, Caracas, Venezuela.

———. (1985). *What makes Israel tick.* Chicago: Nelson-Hall.

———. (1987). *The political economy of Israel.* New Brunswick, N.J.: Transaction.

Sharkansky, I., and Zalmanovitch, Y. (2000). Improvisation public administration and policy making in Israel. *Public Administration Review, 60,* 311–19.

Shimshoni, D. (1982). *Israeli democracy—the middle of the journey.* New York: Free Press.

Skocpol, T. (1994). *Social policy in the United States—future possibilities in historical perspective.* Princeton, N.J.: Princeton University Press.

Smith, B. L. R. (Ed.). (1975). *The new political economy: The public use of the private sector.* New York: Wiley.

Smith, M. J. (1993). *Pressure, power and policy—state autonomy and policy networks in Britain and the United States.* New York: Harvester.

Smith, S. R., & Lipsky, M. (1994). *Non-profit for hire: The welfare state in the age of contracting.* Cambridge, Mass.: Harvard University Press.

Spitzer, R. J. (1988). *The presidential veto.* Albany, N.Y.: State University of New York Press.

Steinberg, G. M., & Bick, E. (1992). *Resisting reform—a policy analysis of Israeli health care delivery system.* Lanham, Md.: University Press of America.

Steinmo, S., Thelen, K., & Longstreth, F. (Eds.). (1992). *Structuring politics—historical institutionalism in comparative analysis.* Cambridge: Cambridge University Press.

Suleiman, E. N. (1987). State structures and clientelism: The French state versus the 'nataires.' *British Journal of Political Science, 17,* 257–79.

Swedish Parliamentary Priorities Commission. (1995). *Priorities in health care.* Stockholm: Ministry of Health and Social Affairs.

Tilly, C. (Ed.). (1975). *The formation of national states in Western Europe.* Princeton, N.J.: Princeton University Press.

Waldman, S. (1977). *Foundation of political action: An exchange theory of politics.* Boston: Little Brown.

Wilsford, D. (1995). States facing interests: Struggles over health care policy in advanced, industrial democracies. *Journal of Health Politics, Policy and Law, 20,* 571–613.

World Bank. (1996). *World development report 1996, from plan to market.* New York: Oxford University Press.

World Health Organization. (1996). *Global health-for-all, indicators database.* Geneva: Author.

Wootton, G. (1985). *Interest groups—policy and politics in America.* Englewood Cliffs, N.J.: Prentice Hall.

Yishai, Y. (1982). Politics and medicine: The case of Israeli national health insurance. *Social Science and Medicine, 16,* 285–91.

———. (1991). *Land of paradoxes: Interest politics in Israel.* Albany, N.Y.: State University of New York Press.

Zalmanovitch, Y. (1997). Some antecedents to health care reform: Israel and the United States. *Policy and politics, 25,* 251–68.

———. (1998). Transitions in Israel's policymaking network, *The Annals of the American Academy of Political and Social Science, 555,* 193–208.

Index